CHEVY NOVA
HOW TO BUILD AND MODIFY
1968–1974

Wayne Scraba

CarTech®

CarTech®

CarTech®, Inc.
838 Lake Street South
Forest Lake, MN 55025
Phone: 651-277-1200 or 800-551-4754
Fax: 651-277-1203
www.cartechbooks.com

© 2017 by Wayne Scraba

All rights reserved. No part of this publication may be reproduced or utilized in any form or by any means, electronic or mechanical, including photocopying, recording, or by any information storage and retrieval system, without prior permission from the Publisher. All text, photographs, and artwork are the property of the Author unless otherwise noted or credited.

The information in this work is true and complete to the best of our knowledge. However, all information is presented without any guarantee on the part of the Author or Publisher, who also disclaim any liability incurred in connection with the use of the information and any implied warranties of merchantability or fitness for a particular purpose. Readers are responsible for taking suitable and appropriate safety measures when performing any of the operations or activities described in this work.

All trademarks, trade names, model names and numbers, and other product designations referred to herein are the property of their respective owners and are used solely for identification purposes. This work is a publication of CarTech, Inc., and has not been licensed, approved, sponsored, or endorsed by any other person or entity. The Publisher is not associated with any product, service, or vendor mentioned in this book, and does not endorse the products or services of any vendor mentioned in this book.

Edit by Bob Wilson
Layout by Monica Seiberlich

ISBN 978-1-61325-696-1
Item No. SA392P

Library of Congress Cataloging-in-Publication Data Available

Edited printed and designed in the U.S.A.

Title Page:
Whether building for the strip or the street, the Nova is an excellent and attractive platform.

Back Cover Photos

Top:
This is where four-link tuning gets interesting! As you can see, there are several ways to come up with the same instant center (or at least instant centers that are close). One tends to wheelstand and/or rattle the tires. The other does not. (Illustration Courtesy Jerry Bickel Race Cars)

Middle Left:
The spring might look "bowed" in this photo, but it's not. What worked for this Nova was a stock small-block spring for a car with power steering and a few other options. The car will eventually receive a big-block.

Middle Right:
The RobbMC -8 AN pickup for a Nova measures 1/2 inch in diameter. Note there is no problematic sock filter. This means an inline filter of some sort is mandatory.

Bottom:
Cores for a Davis radiator are of proprietary design. They're Nocolok furnace brazed and, whereas most companies offer one fin count, Ron Davis Racing Radiators sizes the fin count and thickness to the application. Davis incorporates quality Spal fans in the package. Note the way the fans are completely sealed to the radiator by way of the aluminum shroud.

CONTENTS

Introduction 4

Chapter 1: Starting from Scratch 6
- Reference Material 6
- Stripped Ease 9

Chapter 2: Getting Framed 17
- Bare Bones 17
- Mounting Points 21
- A-Arms 22
- Installing the Rest 28
- Frame Connectors 29

Chapter 3: Rear Axle 31
- 12-Bolt 31
- Ford 9-Inch 34
- Dana 60 40
- Gear Sets 41
- Axles 42

Chapter 4: Rear Suspension 50
- Bolt-On Bars 50
- Tuning CalTracs 52
- Four-Links and Ladder Bars 54
- Chassis Instant Center 55
- Pinion Angle 57
- Laterally Linked 59
- Controlling the Roll 60
- Torque Rotation 61
- Solutions 62
- Rod Ends 63

Chapter 5: Springs and Shock Absorbers ... 67
- Springs 67
- Shock Absorbers 70
- Shackles and Bushings 75

Chapter 6: Brakes 77
- How to Build Drum Brakes 82
- Master Cylinder and Proportioning Valves 86
- Roll Control 87
- Brake Flex Hoses 89
- Brake Hard Lines 91

Chapter 7: Engine Swaps 94
- Frame Mounts 94
- Motor Mounts 96
- Transmission Crossmembers 96
- Transmission Mount 96
- Flywheels, Flexplates and Starters 97
- Clutch Linkage 98
- Alternators, Water Pumps and Pulleys 102
- LSD rives 102
- Throttle Linkage 103
- Heater 104
- Ignition Controls 104
- Headers 104

Chapter 8: Wheels and Tires 107
- Critical Parts of a Wheel 107
- Stuffing Fenders 110
- Wheel Studs 113
- Drag Radials 115

Chapter 9: Fuel System 119
- Gas Tanks and Fuel Cells 119
- High-Flow Pickups for Stock Nova Tanks 126
- Mechanical Fuel Pumps 127
- Electric Fuel Pumps 129
- Fuel Pressure Regulators 130
- Fuel Filters 132

Chapter 10: Radiators and Electric Fans 134
- Radiator 134
- Cooling Fans and Shrouds 137

Source Guide 143

INTRODUCTION

Over the past 40 years or so, I've had four Novas in my shop(s) along with five of their close cousins, the first-gen Camaro. I like these cars a lot (and you probably do too, considering you're reading this!). There's a good reason: They're simple and easy to work on. They have massive aftermarket support (both from a high-performance and restoration point of view). They're light. They have a huge engine compartment (which means they can pretty much swallow any performance engine Chevrolet ever built). They accept almost any gearbox Chevrolet built. Choices for rear ends are similar: You have a ton of options. Compared to the Camaro, they have a smaller rear wheelwell, but for drag duty, they make up for it with rear overhang (rear weight bias). The cars are narrow too. That doesn't make them great for burning corners, but light, narrow, and a good rear overhang is the right recipe for street/strip or dragstrip duty. They also make for an "okay" Pro Touring combination, but honestly, a Camaro is likely a far better choice.

The biggest issue with a Nova is the room for rear rubber; they're tire limited. Sure, you can mini-tub the car to make room for big tires, but when you do that, you must move the rear shocks inboard. You must replace the shocks with Camaro models too. The springs must be moved. That means you need to weld new perches on the rear end. And finally, you need to either section the gas tank or install a narrow job. That's a lot of fab work. Certainly there's the odd kernel of knowledge in here for someone building a Pro Touring car, but this book is geared toward street and street/strip Novas. Finally, 1968–1974 Novas are still somewhat affordable. Do your homework and you can find one to fit almost any budget.

The way a car feels isn't mentioned much when discussing car builds. To me, the Nova feels just right. Aside from occasionally knocking your head as you enter, a 1968–1974 Nova has a great seating position. With something such as a stick shift combination, the pedal and shifter relationship is great. And your view of the road is, well, commanding; just like in a pickup truck! But the real bottom line here is, these cars were made for banging gears. I love 'em!

Every one of my Novas was built in my own shop. That shop has, over the years, changed considerably. It grew to accommodate some of my old racing endeavors and then shrunk when I decided the time was right to downsize. Today that shop is a two-car garage attached to my house. I don't think it exceeds 500 square feet. There's no lift (the ceiling is too low) and, honestly, no fancy tools either. Just a collection of tools that fit inside an old Snap-on rollaway cabinet and chest along with a larger Mac rollaway cabinet. And my guess is that's pretty close to what many of you have. It might not be fancy, but the truth is, it's sufficient to build a nice Nova. I'll get to that in a bit.

Fair enough. I've probably mentioned a lot of things you already know! But what can this book do for you? Remember those Novas and Camaros I worked on over the years? Well that trail of Chevys taught me a lot about car building in general and Novas in particular. I made mistakes along the way (the truth be told, a lot of them!). But at the same time, I also came up with a good number of solutions. It's all about education, and it's my plan to share that learning with you.

What kind of projects can benefit from this book? Is it limited to restorations? Heck no. I've built race cars, hot rods, restorations, and street machines over the years. And I've learned that they have one thing in common. They all take the same path during preliminary construction: Strip it. Clean it. Catalog it. Inventory it. Refurbish it. Store it. Reinstall it. It really doesn't matter what kind of project you have; this book provides insight into how and where to begin.

You'll find an abundance of do-it-yourself paint and body books out there. Some good (S-A Design has some really, really good ones; I dig Pat Ganahl's *Paint Your Car on a Budget*). Some decidedly crappy. What really bugs me is that most of them forget that you must somehow get to either the paint and body or the chassis shop. The car didn't fall apart by itself and say "Paint Me" or "Tub

INTRODUCTION

Me"! A huge amount of work comes first. And if you haul the beater directly to the body or chassis shop, guess who's going to pay for the labor? Besides, I think there's a good amount of satisfaction involved in doing this stuff yourself and simultaneously, you'll be certain the work is done right. After all, there's no one else to blame, right?

The issue of cost is something everyone must address sooner or later in a car project. Sure, with a full-tilt frame-off build you can amortize the costs over several years, but for most folks (me included), paying as much as $100 per hour to peel apart a car and then put it together is simply gut wrenching. I can appreciate paying skilled labor to paint a car, but gee whiz, coughing up that kind of dough to pay a kid to do the work for the shop makes me, well, anxious! And especially so if that same kid has a regular job of sweeping the floor in the shop and he's called in to strip cars on occasion. One of the primary ideas behind this book is to show you how to save money. Trust me, by doing the dirty work yourself you can save a ton. You also save plenty of frustration in the end.

Speaking of saving (cash), one itsy-bitsy detail plenty of folks overlook is the value of their junk. You might be pleasantly surprised at how much value there is in the used, unwanted hardware you peel off a project car. Case in point: I once sold a Nova (I had moved on to other things and this deuce was excess baggage) to a buyer who didn't want the rubber floor mat that originally came with the car. On a lark, I placed it on eBay with what I thought was a ridiculously high reserve. Yeow! Two, ughm, well-heeled collectors went after the floor mat. Yes, it was mint, but I didn't think it was $1,500 mint. To a little guy like me, that was a considerable bonus. And it just goes to show how much value there might be in your Nova junk.

Notice that I have left out engines and transmissions in the book. What's up with that? It's very simple. The good folks from S-A Design have given me 144 or so pages to write about building Novas. If I include engines and transmissions in the book, I take away from the total. You and I both lose valuable room for valuable information. And to be honest, I can't tell you how to build an engine in a chapter. Nor can I show you how to go through any number of transmissions (automatic and stick) in a chapter. Instead, you should pick up one of S-A Designs engine books for that info. There's no shortage of good Chevrolet engine books in the CarTech catalog!

When everything is said and done, you have to consider the difficulty of actually doing this stuff. Just how difficult is it? Not very. The truth is, there's probably more to the actual organization than there is to turning wrenches. Certainly you must be a wee bit more advanced than the righty-tighty, lefty-loosey crowd, but I think anyone with the desire can perform the mechanical work. Sure, I've been involved with car construction for probably too long (more than 45 years and counting—Yikes!), so some of the tasks have become second-hand, but I'm quite confident someone just starting out can get the job done by reading and following this book. It's not a blow-by-blow how-to publication though (there's not enough room in a 144-page book to accomplish that). Be sure to couple this book with a good shop manual (Chevy's OEM Service and Overhaul manuals along with an OEM Fisher Body Manual are good examples, and so is a reproduction Chevrolet Assembly Instruction Manual). Those manuals certainly help you get the job done. There's more too: This is a hobby. That means it is supposed to be enjoyable. Don't sweat it if you come across a stumbling block. Remember, nothing involved in building a Nova is insurmountable. In fact, I'm pretty sure all of you will come away with a smile on your face when you're working on your project. I do.

In a nutshell, that's the entire premise of this book: how to build a high-performance Nova and have fun and save money doing it. I know what follows is something you can use. And I trust both of us will have a good time as we go through the various chapters. Check it out. You won't regret it.

CHAPTER 1

STARTING FROM SCRATCH

Okay. You have the project Nova. Now what? It's obvious you can start tearing it apart to begin your build, but first things first: You should gather reference material for your project.

Reference Material

When it comes to information, you never get enough. The reality is, if you're armed with information on basic mechanics and high performance the work will proceed in a much smoother fashion. But what information should you get?

You need to come up with a selection of resource books, factory service publications, and just as important, catalogs from the various aftermarket companies. Knowledge of your particular Nova is one thing, but when it comes time to disassemble a specific component, restore or rebuild it, and then reassemble it, you often require more than a knack with hand tools. Before one screw or bolt is loosened on your car, do yourself a favor and purchase (or scrounge where necessary) the publications noted below.

Factory Service Manual

Chevrolet printed factory service manuals for each model year of the Chevrolet passenger car(s), Novas included. They're not easy or light reading, but they do deal with minor service procedures, vehicle maintenance, and component adjustment. In addition, they also show the correct way to remove and replace various components and subassemblies. The service manuals cover all Chevrolet passenger cars as well as Corvettes.

Factory Overhaul Manual

In GM Land, the Overhaul Manual takes over where the Service Manual ends. It details the repair and replacement of major components.

Building a car such as a Nova doesn't necessarily mean that you need a huge-by-large shop. With a little bit of planning you can get by with a workspace that measures less than 600 square feet.

Don't be fooled into thinking the World Wide Web can provide you with all of the technical details you need to build and rework a vintage Nova. What you see here is a good collection of "must have" books and manuals.

Nothing can replace a Chevrolet factory Service Manual. The original equipment Service Manuals handle minor service, adjustment, tune up, and other repairs.

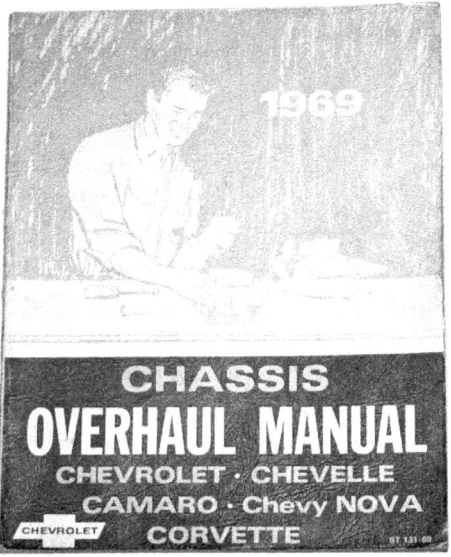

For more comprehensive repairs, Chevrolet issued an Overhaul Manual. It is a supplement to the Service Manual. As you might have guessed, it looks at how to completely rebuild major components.

GM's Fisher Body Division also printed repair manuals for various automobiles, including Novas. If you're befuddled about how to remove a piece of trim or adjust a window (or any number of body-related topics), you need this.

While the Service Manual deals with minor repairs, this book examines the down and dirty hard jobs. This manual is designed for use in conjunction with the Service Manual. And like the other publication, it covers all passenger cars and Corvettes.

Body Service Manual

General Motors had a special manual that examined topics that were not covered in either the service or overhaul publications. If you're left scratching your head about how to fix something, the Fisher body service manual might solve it. For example, the General may have included one type of molding clip on all vehicles. This manual tells you how to remove and replace that clip. It might be generic, but it shows how the task is done. Fisher Body Service Manuals for a given year cover all passenger cars (Chevrolet, Pontiac, Olds, Buick, and Cadillac).

Assembly Instruction Manual

Reprinted Assembly Instruction Manuals, or "AIMs," are available for almost all older Chevys. These are the manuals used on the assembly line during vehicle construction. Examples are printed in a loose-leaf format and feature large, sometimes-exploded, drawings of all components and subassemblies that are pieced together during the manufacturing process. These drawings show where the parts go and how they go together.

Part numbers are included, but these are production numbers, not service (replacement or dealership parts department) numbers. The AIM also shows you where and how components are glued together, correct fastener installation, proper clamp location and orientation, the correct location of pierced holes, and ride height specifics. Production options are included along with location mounting points and special torque specifications for almost all parts of the Nova.

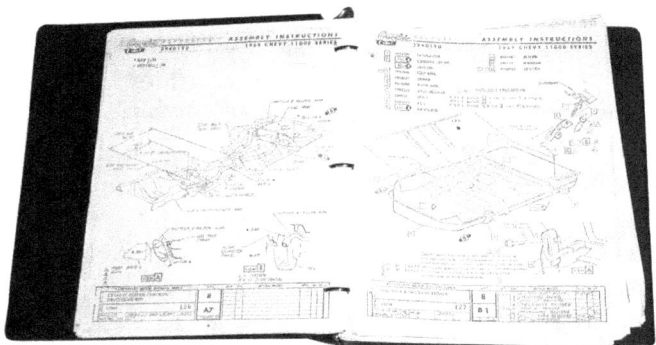

Most Nova enthusiasts know what an "AIM" is. It's the Assembly Instruction Manual that Chevrolet used on the assembly line to build a Nova. The factory AIM is loaded with assembly drawings, descriptions of options, and more.

CHAPTER 1

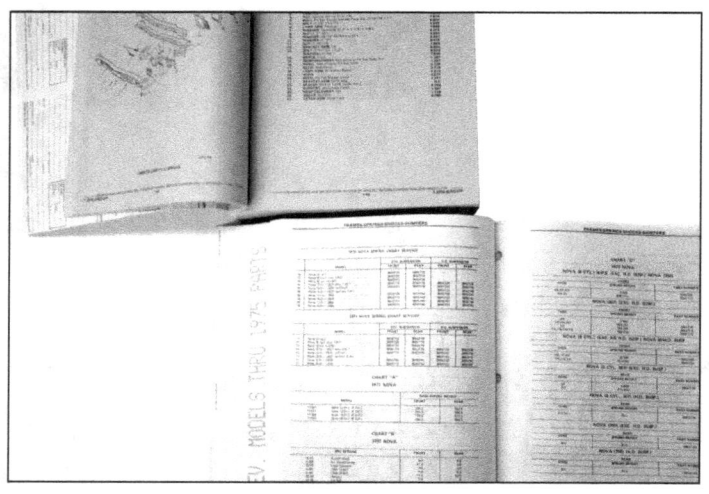

Chevrolet Parts Catalogs are important. They're usually made up of an illustration catalog (or section) along with a parts book. You need them both. If you dig around, you can find reprints or lightly used originals.

Wrecking yards originally used this old monster book to identify parts and show interchanges. Hollander publishes them. The company still prints manuals and it even has smaller examples dedicated specifically to one line of car (for example, 1968–1979 Novas). Honestly, this is the go-to book when scrounging for parts.

The AIM is broken down into two parts. The first part covers approximately one dozen basic assembly areas that range from labels to stickers to complete electrical installation. This portion of the Assembly Instruction Manual is called the "Uniform Parts Classification." Following the UPC section is the RPO, or "Regular Production Option," portion of the book.

Factory (OEM) Parts Catalog

Reprints of vintage Chevrolet parts catalogs (or originals) are readily available if you do a bit of digging. These catalogs not only list the part numbers for various components, they also feature blow-up illustrations of many parts. If you're dealing with, say, a 1970 Nova, among the best bets for a parts catalog is the reprinted 1971 versions (if your Nova is a 1971 or older model). They cover all years of Chevrolets through 1971. Obviously, almost all the part numbers have been discontinued and the few remaining have been changed in the past decades.

Hollander Interchange Manual

Scrounging parts for your car can sometimes feel like an impossible dream. Fortunately, many pieces are direct interchanges with similar (or not so similar) "corporate" offerings. As an example, a Nova four-door sedan or even something such as a Buick Apollo can supply a host of goodies for your SS396 project. Items such as suspension pieces, electrical components, some transmission components, and even certain trim parts and myriad accessory or RPO components are virtually identical.

So how in the world do you know which parts interchange and which don't? The big parts are by far the easiest. A company called Hollander provides massive manuals to wrecking yards that outline the various interchanges between respective marques. Hollander manuals are typically 4 inches thick and include information on all "hard" parts, including identification of those components. Small items, such as trim pieces, are not included.

For a Nova, consider Volumes 1 and 2 of the 1964–1974 issue. This is an expensive package, but the dollars saved during the restoration will be well worth the expense.

If the high price scares you off, try searching for a used "41st Auto-Truck Interchange Edition" (such as the one shown in the accompanying photos). It covers domestic vehicles from 1965 to 1975 and, as a result, encompasses all Chevrolets of that era. Where do you find used Hollanders? Your local wrecking yards are good bets. The Hollander Interchange Manual is considered the "bible" of the dismantling business. Any reputable wrecker knows what you're talking about. Wreckers don't have much need for an old Hollander if no older cars are left in their yard. You can also try online sources such as eBay.

Aftermarket Support

Some cars have great aftermarket support. Our old Novas are among these. Before you begin the build (and long before you buy a car), you contemplate things including reproduction parts, NOS parts, and aftermarket parts availability. With good resources such as these, it's a whole bunch easier to piece together a good

8   CHEVY NOVA 1968–1974: HOW TO BUILD AND MODIFY

STARTING FROM SCRATCH

Sooner or later you'll need help from the restoration or high-performance aftermarket. These are just a few catalog examples. A Camaro parts catalog is a good idea for your Nova too, because there's a lot of interchange between Novas and Camaros. Sometimes a Nova reproduction isn't available but a Camaro piece is. Keep that in mind.

Should you decide to remove all the front sheet metal on a Nova, options are limited. The hood must come off before the fenders. To warm up to the idea (and the job), remove the trim first. Besides, the anodized aluminum is rather fragile, so it's best to get it out of the way first.

car. The bottom line here is, gather up as many pertinent catalogs from various vendors as possible. Some of the vendors offer decent discounts to regular customers too. When it comes to aftermarket vendors, some are good, some are great, and some are not so good.

Stripped Ease

Conventional wisdom states you should drain the fluids, peel out the engine, the radiator, and the rest of the power train, and start from there. That works, but there's another way that might be better: Consider removing the sheet-metal parts and other bits that you know need replacing well before stripping out the mechanicals. Here's why: If you have a small shop, space is always at a premium. When you take out heavy, messy stuff such as the engine and transmission, you'll be tripping over it. The option of moving the car (driving it) while removing bulky (and sometimes delicate) sheet-metal pieces can be advantageous. Honestly, it works very well in a crowded garage.

Remove the Hood

Nova hoods are usually a pain in the you-know-where to remove. They're heavy and bulky, and if you're not careful, they can slide backward and take out the windshield. Here's a system you can use to do most of the heavy lifting by yourself (although for a big hood you have to enlist your wife, girlfriend, kid, or the guy next door for a few minutes):

Place a couple of 2 x 4s (1½ to 2 feet long) between the hood, front fenders, and the windshield. Depending upon the car and the state of the paint you might want to wrap each board with a heavy terry towel. When you remove one side of the hood, it can slide down to the 2 x 4 without contacting the windshield. You can slowly remove the other side using a ratchet and appropriate socket (it is difficult with a regular combination wrench). With a Nova, you need help for the second side. The only thing that your helper has to do is to hold

This placement of lumber (2 x 4s) is very useful when removing the hood. Softwood doesn't damage the paint if you're careful, but if you think you'll lose sleep over the process, wrap the lumber with heavy terry towels. With a bit of care, the 2 x 4s will help you remove the hood without any damage to the car.

A car can be stripped using a variety of methods. Some just happen to be better than others. If it's coming down to a full-bore restoration, the car must be stripped completely, as with this example.

CHEVY NOVA 1968–1974: HOW TO BUILD AND MODIFY

CHAPTER 1

> ## Frozen Fasteners
>
> On some cars, you soon discover that the odd fastener (or maybe the majority) is frozen solid. The cure is simple; plenty of folks use PB Blaster as a penetrating oil. Give the stubborn nut/bolt/washer a blast with the goop and let it soak. In most cases it should loosen. If the penetrating oil doesn't work, it's time for more aggressive tactics. Use a good old-fashioned propane torch and heat the fastener. If it's been thoroughly coated with penetrating oil, you know it because it smokes and stinks! As soon as it's hot, try turning out the fastener. By the way, this works perfectly for super-stubborn Phillips-head screws (such as the type General Motors used for door latches). They can be problematic to remove, but if you use the above process and whack the fastener with an impact screwdriver, it will loosen.
>
>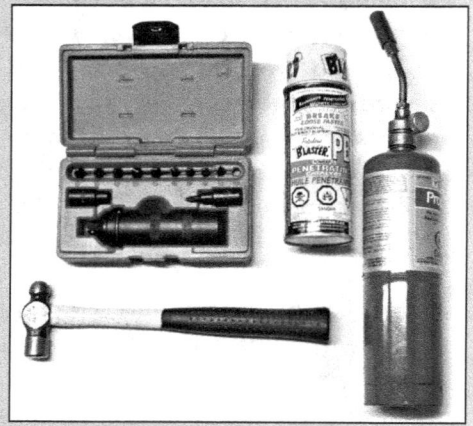
>
> *One thing is certain when you're working on any old car: Sooner or later you run into a frozen fastener. These are the tools of the trade when it comes to removing stubborn bolts and screws. Sometimes penetrating oil works. And sometimes you have to resort to heat.*
>
>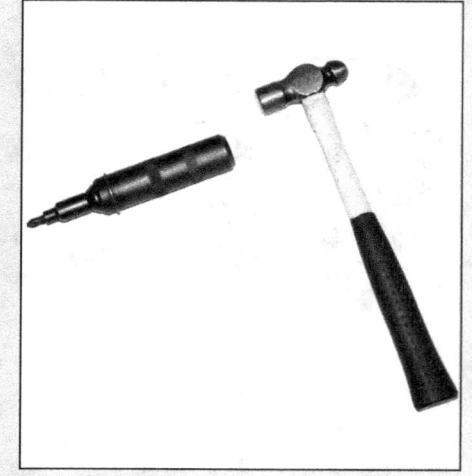
>
> *Up close are two tools you can't do without on a Nova rebuild: an impact driver and the hammer you need to run it. The impact driver can be set up to both tighten and loosen, and that's something some folks overlook. If you have a frozen screw or other small fastener, this thing works wonders.*

the hood upright on the hinges while you loosen and remove the fasteners. After the bolts are removed, you can slide the hood backward toward the windshield where it can contact the 2 x 4s. At this point you can safely lift it off the car and set it aside. By the way, it's a good idea to remove the hood from the hinges, and then remove the hinges separately. It's easier that way.

Peel Out the Powertrain

Right about now, your project car should be staged and ready for engine and transmission removal. What you need here is a cherry picker (engine hoist), a floor jack, a couple of axle stands, a small collection of hand tools, and a good-sized drain pan. Depending upon how you chose to remove the engine (with the front sheet metal removed or with it on the car) you might need a set of ramps.

You need a helper to balance the hood while you remove the two bolts per side. Remove one side, set the hood down on the 2 x 4, and then go to the other side of the car. It works and you never damage a windshield or cowl vent panel with this process.

Now you're getting somewhere in the disassembly process. If you leave a Nova in a running (or a least rolling) mode as long as possible, it makes life easier (and less cluttered) in the shop. Right about now, though, it's time to change that. Check it out.

Drain the Fluids

The subtitle of this section should probably read, "Drain the Appropriate Fluids." Truth be known, you don't need to drain everything. The rear axle doesn't need to be emptied, especially if you're swapping in another. Ditto with the engine oil. The engine oil isn't going anywhere unless you manage to turn the whole thing upside down, and that sure isn't likely (fingers crossed). That leaves three things to drain: the cooling system, the fuel system, and the transmission fluid. You don't necessarily have to drain the transmission if it's a stick, but if it's an automatic, fluid goes everywhere, no matter what you do.

When it comes to gasoline, ensure the car didn't have much in the tank to begin with. The reason is that 15 or so gallons of fuel are difficult to deal with. You'd rather deal with 1 gallon. Aside from the question of where to keep the extra gas, you also must concern yourself with weight. A U.S. gallon of gas weighs roughly 6.2 pounds; therefore, 15 of them tip the scales at 93 pounds. If you drop the tank with an extra 93 pounds of fuel in it, you appreciate why it's a good idea to work with a nearly empty tank! Of course, the hazard of slopping around with a lot of raw gas in the general vicinity is something that should be avoided too.

If there's a bit more gas in the tank than you care to have, it's a good idea to push the car outside the shop door to drain it. It's safer, and you don't have to worry about raw gas flowing all over the shop floor. It also saves on making a stink.

To drain the gas tank, it's likely easiest to remove the lines. All Novas have a "soft" (rubber) flex connection on the frame rail rear of the passenger-side rear tire, and that's as good a spot as any to initiate the draining process. Use a clean drain pan and pour the collected fuel into a sealed (clean) fuel jug. It's now gasoline for your lawn mower.

With the tank close to empty, you can unhook the tank straps and lower the gas tank to the ground. At this point, you can completely unhook any fuel lines (return or feed lines) if you haven't already done so. The tank should come out easily, provided nothing is caught. At this stage, you can just tip it over and drain the works into the "lawn mower" fuel jug.

The next big mess (no kidding) is the coolant. First things first: Chase your dog and/or your cat out of the shop. Keep the shop off limits to them until you're done. Most of you know the reason: Antifreeze (coolant; call it what you will) can kill animals if ingested.

It's best to drain the radiator first, and then follow up by draining the cylinder block. Be sure the engine is dead cold. Being scalded by hot coolant is never fun. Slide a big drain container under the radiator and open the petcock. It starts as a trickle. Loosen the radiator cap. Now a torrent of coolant should come out. Keep in mind that coolant is slippery, foul-smelling stuff. If there's an appreciable spill, you have an equally big cleanup. For that, you need plenty of floor dry absorbent.

When the radiator has stopped dripping, you can drain the block. Chevy drains are near the oil pan rails (sometimes they're hard to see because they can be obscured by the exhaust manifolds). Usually these drains have a hex head that you can

What to Do with Old Fluids

You now probably have more old waste fluid than you ever dreamed possible. What do you do with this stuff? First and foremost, don't toss it in the ditch, over the fence, or in the neighbor's back yard.

The environment is important. That's a no-brainer because it's the only one we have. So what's the best way to get rid of waste oil and coolant? In some jurisdictions, the folks who sell oil and coolant are obliged to accept it as waste at no charge. Collect a couple of older race fuel jugs (5 gallons each). Designate them for used oil and used coolant (don't mix them up). When you fill them, simply transfer the contents to the drop-off facility tank. Check it out. It's most often free. And the bonus is, it's usually pretty clean.

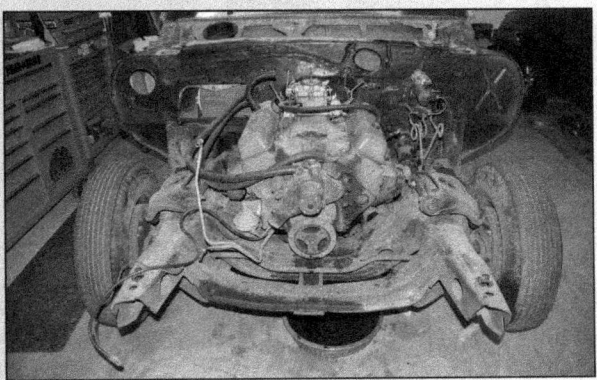

No matter what you're doing with a project Nova, sooner or later you'll be faced with getting rid of stuff such as used oil, antifreeze (coolant), transmission fluid, and rear-end lube. It is your social responsibility to get rid of this mess the proper way. Recycle it.

Keeping Track of Your Stuff

When you're slaving over a big project such as a complete Nova build, it's easy to lose track of parts. A lot of them can go missing, and it becomes particularly painful when the time comes to reassemble the car. The best solution is to get organized. To keep things under control consider using temporary folding tables to store parts. These are particularly useful for large and perhaps fragile pieces. FYI: You can buy inexpensive folding tables from Costco.

Rubbermaid Totes are perfect for small-parts storage. For most Nova projects, the 21 x 15.5 x 9–inch size (shown) work well and happen to be the most manageable (bigger bins get pretty heavy when filled with parts).

As bits and pieces are removed from the car, tag and bag them. For smaller parts, sandwich bags are best. Bigger parts can be stored in freezer bags. If the part is too big, simply tag it using a parts tag. Include the fasteners that go with the part in the bag. If the part is too big to bag, fasten the accompanying hardware bag right to it and tag it.

Save almost all parts, even if they will be replaced eventually. A good example is a set of fasteners you know you never will use. Mark them as "replace" on the tag. Then add the respective fasteners to your "want list." This way, you can keep track of what needs replacing instead of searching for new hardware and pieces at the last minute. Keep the originals for reference in the event the replacements are not the same.

Mark "for sale" the parts you're confident you can sell and where you're positive the replacement is a perfect fit (for example, marker lamp assemblies). Eventually, you can start a dedicated Rubbermaid bin with "for sale" stuff.

Finally, a little luxury most of us can afford today is an inexpensive digital camera or a cell phone that has a decent built-in camera. Even a cheap job such as this old Nikon Coolpix is adequate. Basically, if you shoot photos along the way, it makes reassembly much easier (and in some "scratch-your-head" instances, a whole lot easier). ∎

With any major project, you're going to end up with a bunch of loose parts. Keeping track of them is incredibly important. And that's what this sidebar is all about. This is a metal storage rack used just for that purpose. This is where the loose parts stay until they're needed.

A few big Rubbermaid bins go a long way toward keeping things tidy. Keep parts separated: those that are restored or rebuilt, those that need to be rebuilt, and those that you plan to sell.

Bag, tag, and ID everything. As time wears on with the project, you might not remember where every part goes on a car. You'd be surprised how much easier it is to reassemble a car when the parts are all identified.

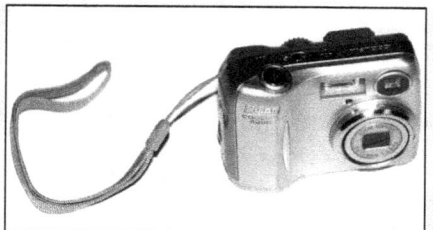

When you take something apart, it's easy to forget exactly how it went back together. An inexpensive digital camera takes great photos (better than a cell phone) and it's equally easy to download those images to your computer.

get an open-end wrench onto. Place a pan under the block drain and allow gravity to do its thing. Repeat with the drain on the opposite side of the block. You might be surprised at how much coolant remains in the block after the radiator is drained.

Last on the list of stuff to drain is the transmission (as pointed out above, there's little need to drain a stick). Some automatics have a drain plug (lucky you). Others don't. Typically, the drain plug is located on the transmission pan. If there is no drain plug, the only way to drain the automatic is to remove the pan. Try to drop one corner (obviously the lower) to drain it. There could be more oil than you would expect. If there is no drain plug, expect a (big) mess.

Peel Out Pieces

You should be ready to start peeling out pieces. First things first: Remove the radiator. Remove the fan too, simply because slicing yourself with sharp objects while you're toiling away isn't fun. Pulling this stuff off also provides you with a load of elbowroom. You should also remove accessory connections at the engine. You're probably saying, "Like what?" There's more hardware here than you might think. Here's a thumbnail of what must be unhooked and/or removed, and this is just for a basic Nova (in no particular order).

Radiator and heater hoses: Usually a wire Corbin clamp or a good old-fashioned screwdriver hose clamp. If the hoses are stubborn (frozen on the fittings) you might have to cut them off.

Fuel line connections: The best place to unhook it is at the fuel pump. Unhook the line from the frame rail to the pump. This means that the pump can come out with the engine. FYI, you should use a flare wrench on the fitting.

Automatic transmission cooler lines: Such as the fuel line, you should use a flare wrench here. Years of use, heat cycles, and corrosion can make the flare nuts difficult to crack. If you've tried everything and you're finding the hex on the nut is getting rounded, try Vise-Grips. The flare nut (and, most likely, the line) will be finished, but you should be able to remove the lines. It is possible to remove the fittings at the radiator and take the lines off the trans when it's out of the car, but this only works if the engine and transmission are removed in one piece.

Power brake vacuum hose: This frequently amounts to a hose clamp on an intake manifold fitting.

Throttle linkage: Another easy job that often is either a single nut or a little clip that has to be unfastened or released. In the odd case, there's also a bracket that can be attached to the intake or carb that supports the linkage. That might have to be removed too. When it's unhooked, tie up the cable or hard linkage so that it doesn't get hung up when pulling the engine.

Transmission and kick-down linkage: Depending upon the car, you either have a column shift or floor shift linkage to remove. It doesn't matter if it's a stick or an automatic; the linkage must be removed. Some cars have a back drive/interlock setup that maintains the transmission in park or neutral for starting. That must be removed too (it's attached to the steering column). On floorshift-stick cars, you can simply remove the shifter handle, but on others where clearance is tight, the entire shifter mechanism must come out.

Here's the objective: an empty engine compartment. For this Nova project the fenders and front sheet metal remained, but after pulling the engine the subframe looked far too crusty. Everything eventually came out.

After the fluids are drained, you can remove the various hoses. Most of the time, they're relatively easy to remove. Don't concern yourself with saving hoses or hose clamps (unless you're a matching-numbers type). You can simply cut off a hose if it's stubborn.

CHAPTER 1

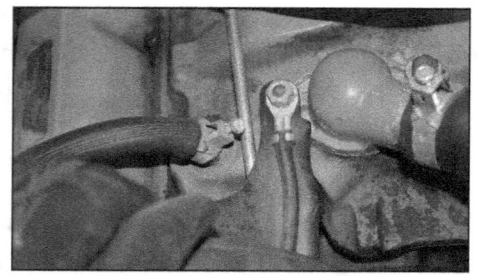

Before peeling out the engine, don't forget about the ground straps; a few more than just the battery cable ground are shown here. Depending upon the options, the Nova can have from almost none to three or four engine grounds.

Old, sometimes frozen hard lines (fuel line, trans cooler, etc.) are often a royal pain. If a flare wrench slips during disassembly, try clocking it another direction. If that fails, the best suggestion is to get out the Vise-Grips! Otherwise you'll have to cut off the hard line.

Speedometer cable: The cable unhooks at the transmission tailshaft. When free from the tailshaft, pull the entire thing out, or tie it out of the way.

Clutch linkage: This is pretty much a basic unbolt situation. The cross shaft hooked between the frame and the engine must be removed. Attachment clips are similar to those found on shifter rods.

Ground straps: More than one ground strap has caused an engine to hang up during removal. The straps often go from the engine to the body and/or the frame. Sometimes they're hidden between the engine and the firewall.

Battery cables: Two heavy cables run to the engine, a positive cable to the starter and a negative cable going somewhere to ground on the engine. In addition, you may find smaller wires going directly from the positive battery cable to one or more power blocks.

Starter and ignition wiring: A few wires must be removed at the ignition (coil) as well as the starter. These aren't difficult to find, but Novas usually incorporate a clamp at the back of the engine to retain the wiring harness. Remove it.

Alternator or generator wiring: A plug at the back of the alternator requires removal. These are simple clip-on devices that can be unfastened with a flat-blade screwdriver.

Sending unit wiring or hard lines: The oil pressure sender has an electrical connection that requires unhooking. Ditto with an electric water temperature gauge or idiot-light connection. For the most part, these are simple clip-on jobs that remove with a flat-blade screwdriver. If the car has mechanical gauges, you must remove the fittings on the engine. Be careful (and gentle) with mechanical water-temperature gauge fittings. They regularly bind, and during the removal process you can damage (or destroy) the gauge line. Most often, there is no easy fix and the entire gauge must be replaced.

Power steering pump: Some folks remove the hoses now, but it's often more convenient to simply remove

Unhooking the exhaust usually follows the same path as dealing with frozen hard lines. Soak the respective fasteners with PB Blast before leaving the shop at night. The next day, the bolts should be ready to cooperate. If not, an impact wrench does wonders.

the pump from the engine and tie it aside (on the frame). With this approach, you can remove the hoses later. If you choose to remove the hoses right now, keep in mind that a flare wrench makes life a bit easier. Sometimes it takes quite a bit of force to crack open the flares.

Exhaust manifolds/headers: You must unhook the exhaust whether it's header- or manifold-equipped. With manifolds, the connections to the exhaust pipes can regularly be a pain to break free. Penetrating oil is a good idea. Allow the fasteners to soak overnight. An air-powered impact wrench is your best friend in this situation. As far as headers are concerned, you must look at your car. In some cases, after you remove the headers from the engine (at the cylinder heads), they can remain in the engine compartment (tied away so that the engine can come out). In other cases, you must remove the headers (or the bigger parts of them) before the engine can come out.

Driveshaft: The driveshaft must be removed before the engine and transmission can come out. Typically, it is mounted with four nuts on U-bolts fitted over the rear universal joint. Remove the bolts and drop the shaft downward. Tape the U-joint caps so they don't fall off. Why? If the caps fall off, you'll be chasing more than a few needle bearings across your shop floor. After it's taped, pull the shaft (front yoke and all) away from the transmission.

Transmission crossmember/mount cushion: When removing the engine and transmission in one piece, you can remove the entire transmission crossmember at this stage of the game. Some folks just remove the transmission mount cushion and pull the engine forward, but it's far easier to pull the engine and transmission with the crossmember out of the way. You need to support the transmission (a floor jack under it works). Then remove the cushion bolts along with the crossmember fasteners. Next, slide the crossmember out of the way. You can leave the floor jack in place under the transmission for the time being.

Distributor and/or cap: Remove the cap or the complete distributor before pulling the engine. Why? The cap is inevitably crunched against the firewall sometime during the engine removal process.

Motor mount bolts: Take the nuts off the motor mount bolts (this is the lone bolt that joins the rubber mount to the steel mount). You can't remove the bolt completely until you take weight off it.

Break Out the Cherry Picker

The engine can be removed either with or without the transmission attached. If the nose of the Nova is still covered with sheet metal, you can get the engine and transmission out in one piece, but you must lift the entire car quite a bit to allow for clearance between the transmission tailshaft and the floor. Figure it this way: To clear something such as the radiator support, the engine and trans must come out at a big angle. If you don't have the front of the car high enough off the ground, the trans tailshaft will hit the floor and you will be stuck. The solution is to place a set of wheel ramps under the front wheels. In most cases, you have enough room to pull the engine with the transmission attached. Keep in mind that this also means the cherry picker has a much higher lift.

The other option is to pull the transmission and engine separately. Remember that a transmission can be heavy. That's why shops use transmission jacks. If you choose this

This is a major step in the disassembly process. The old lump is coming out! No real tricks are needed for this job, and as you can see; you don't even need a fancy engine leveler. The engine can come up and out. The process is the same with or without the front sheet metal installed.

route, you must lift the Nova quite a bit to allow the transmission and the jack to roll out from underneath. This certainly isn't insurmountable. In most cases, a set of axle stands set on "high" get the job done. It should go without saying, but no matter what, always give the car a good shake when it's on axle stands before climbing underneath. If it's going to fall off it may as well do it when you're not under the car.

To pull the transmission separately, you must support it and the back of the engine. A floor jack with an adapter works for the transmission. For the engine, use a bottle jack with a piece of 2 x 4 board sandwiched between the oil pan and the jack for support. The jack also allows you to drop the rear of the engine down a bit for extra bellhousing bolt access. With an automatic, remove the torque converter dust shield to gain access to the bolts that hold the torque converter to the flex plate. Remove those and then remove the transmission bellhousing–to–engine mount bolts. You should be able to roll the jack backward with the transmission attached, although it might take bit of persuasion (with a big flat screwdriver) to break it free. No matter how careful you are when draining an automatic, you still get fluid on the floor because there is ATF inside the torque converter that can't drain. Expect it to leak and have floor dry on hand.

For a stick-shift Nova, you don't have to remove the bellhousing. You still must support the back of the engine and the transmission. In this case, you simply remove the transmission-to-bellhousing bolts and then slide the gearbox backward. A straight pull backward is required to clear the pilot bushing and clutch assembly.

In either case (stick or automatic) you can now lower the floor jack and pull the transmission out the side of the car. You see why you need the car lifted high on axle stands to get the works out.

Pulling the engine is pretty easy after all (or most of the above) is completed. If the sheet metal is removed from the nose, it's even easier. Basically, hook up your engine hoist.

Back to the lift. After you have the chain attached, lift the engine slightly to get the weight off the motor mount bolts. Then it should be a simple matter to pull out the fasteners. With that out of the way, you can pull the engine up and forward. You need some room to get the engine out of the engine compartment. It's not uncommon to roll the car backward a bit as the engine (and transmission) comes out. When it's clear of the car, you can maneuver the engine along with the transmission easily with a cherry picker.

Give yourself a big pat on the back. You've pretty much mechanically stripped the car.

The Nova engine came out with the Powerglide attached. Because the front sheet metal (including the rad support) was already out of the way, pulling the engine and trans in one piece wasn't difficult.

Right about now is a good time to give yourself some credit. Your Nova project is getting a lot closer to being completely stripped and ready to rebuild and rework. This car was stripped clean, ready for new paint. You don't always need to go this far in the disassembly process.

CHAPTER 2

GETTING FRAMED

Getting down the road or getting down the dragstrip isn't just a matter of building power, bolting it in, and pointing the car in the right direction. The rear-suspension setup and balance of the power train are certainly critical, but the part of the Nova that seldom gets respect is the front end. Sure, you can go with a standard setup procedure, but with the technology available, you can bolt together a pretty trick front end (no fabrication necessary) to make your Chevy quicker, faster, and able to handle and stop better (on the street or the strip). Follow along to see how to set up a Nova front end for street and strip duty.

Bare Bones

You have to start somewhere. Unless you're lucky, the subframe in your Nova is the usual crusty mess. It's a good idea to strip everything out of the subframe: A-arms, motor mounts, steering linkage, sway bar, springs, shocks, steering box, etc., and then drop it out of the car. It's a matter of removing six bolts: four subframe-to-body bolts and two subframe-to-radiator support bolts.

With the subframe naked and out of the car, drag it outside, coat it in degreaser, and then pressure wash it. Scrape off any undercoating. Here, a propane torch, a putty scraper, and a brace of wire brushes (in varying sizes) work wonders. After the grease, grime, and undercoating are gone, consider grinding the factory welds and weld splatter. FYI: this is a dirty job, but the only way to get it done is to grind it with an angle grinder and a die grinder, and then finish it

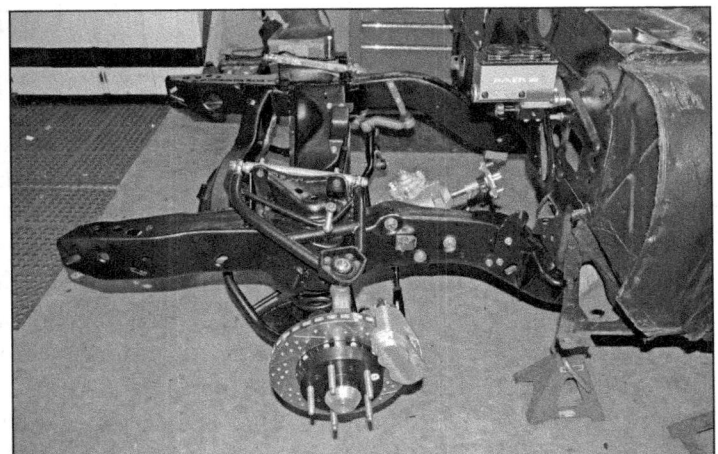

It's no secret the subframe on a 1968–1974 Nova is fundamentally the same as the subframe on a 1967–1969 Camaro. That means huge aftermarket support: A-arms, springs, shocks, steering, brakes, and so on.

You don't have to completely remove the front sheet metal on your Nova to get at the subframe, but it sure does make it easier to work on. The condition you see here is typical. This car sat unused for decades.

The back four body mount bolts are easy to access. Note that the OEM body mounts are still intact in this photo. The other two body mount bolts (total of six) are actually radiator support mounts.

Stripped! The subframe can be totally stripped by using hand tools, but access to a good air compressor and impact gun makes disassembly super easy.

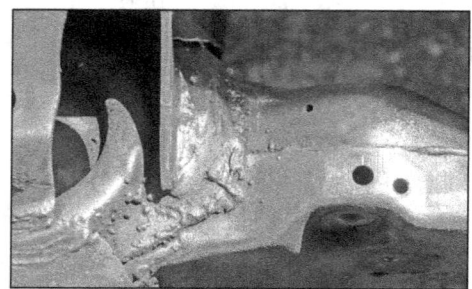

This welding mess is typical of these cars. The robot welders used back then weren't exactly sophisticated, and, as a result, welding splatter is everywhere.

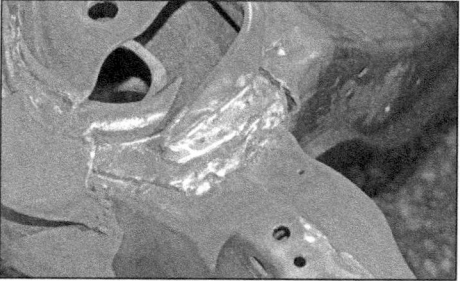

This is the same area on the subframe from a slightly different angle. The welding splatter is removed with a combination of a 4½-inch angle grinder and a small air-powered die grinder. Sharp edges should be taken into consideration too.

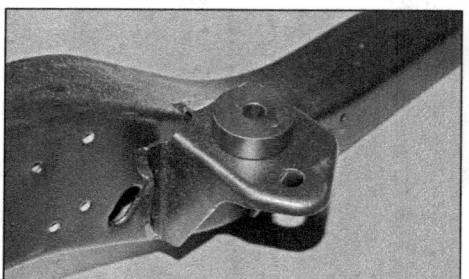

This subframe is back from the powder coating shop and fit with the top half of a Detroit Speed solid body mount set. As you can see from this close-up, time spent prepping the subframe with a grinding wheel is well worth it. Copy this. Your hands will appreciate the lack of sharp edges!

off with a wire wheel. It works, but it takes time. You can also grind down sharp edges on these subframes (there are a lot of them). Why bother? To minimize the chance of tearing up your skin while working on the car. When that is complete, it's ready to be sandblasted. From there, it can go to your favorite powder coater, or you can paint it.

Speaking of powder coating, its reputation is that of a remarkable coating. Although accurate for the most part, it's not enchanted and it's certainly not without faults.

After you paint or powder coat the subframe, you can reunite it with the body. You can use OEM-style rubber cushion mounts or solid mounts. Solid body mounts eliminate flex between the body and subframe connection. The overall performance of the car improves with this extra chassis stiffness.

The accompanying photos show the use of Detroit Speed mounts. They're CNC-machined from billet aluminum and hard-coated (not bright anodized). Hard coating resists corrosion that occurs between steel and aluminum surfaces. CNC-machined stainless-steel bevel washers are included. They're also available in 1/2-inch-height sizes. Half-height mounts lower the car (obviously), but they also bring their own issues (dimensions for things such as the rag joint stack up). Nova applications have two cowl area bolts that are 1/2 inch longer than a Camaro's, and they also include a special spacer that fits above the first body mount at the cowl. The kits are complete with a similar set of solid radiator core support mounts, and the optional stainless-steel ARP bolt kits are available. Solid mounts

Detail Plating and Coating

When you're building your Nova, quite a few parts lend themselves to chrome plating, cad plating, zinc dichromate plating, and powder coating. When it comes to chrome (and its close cousin, nickel plate), the respective processes are much the same.

Chrome Plating

Almost any metal can be chrome plated, including "pot metal," common carbon steel, and even aluminum. Prior to plating, the metal must be completely cleaned, most often in a hot alkaline immersion. Previously plated parts (such as bumpers) must be "un-plated," which involves immersion in a tank containing sulfuric acid. Direct current is applied and the old plate is drawn into a lead cathode. Rusty pieces are placed in a tank containing hydrochloric acid (sometimes referred to as the "acid pickling" tank). Unfortunately, the extensive use of corrosive and caustic chemicals can have a drastic effect on die-cast components. If handled without care, they simply disappear into the acid bath.

After stripping, the component is buffed. The buffing procedure smooths the surface, removing high and low spots, and gives the surface a high luster, or sheen. This is the key to good chrome plating.

After buffing, the component is copper electro-plated. The part is centered in a tank containing a mixture of cuprous cyanide, sodium cyanide, and sodium thiosulfate. Heated to 104 degrees F, the tank is charged with DC current. Depending upon the construction or condition of the part, it must remain in this environment approximately 20 minutes (longer if it is heavily pitted or previously corroded).

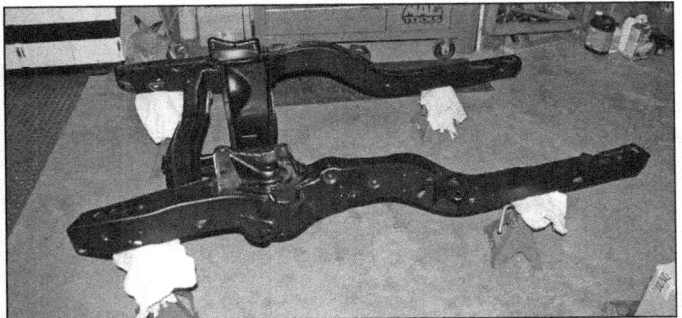

Powder coating something such as a subframe makes for a neat, clean finish. This coating method provides protection for the inside of the component as well as the outside. Just keep in mind that while powder coating is durable, it's not "bulletproof"!

The part is removed from the tank, completely rinsed, and re-polished. The buffing or polishing stage is again critical.

The next stop is the nickel tank. The most common "bath" is called the Watts Composition, which is a mixture of nickel chloride, nickel sulfate, and boric acid, as well as other small composites. Approximately 30 minutes later, the part emerges from the nickel tank. Re-polishing is not necessary, and for the most part, not possible at this stage because the nickel plate is very thin (on the order of .001 inch thick). The part is rinsed and readied for a final bath in the chrome tank.

The part looks perfect after leaving the nickel tank. The use of chrome is for protection; it prevents the nickel from tarnishing. The chemical solution in the chrome tank includes sulfuric acid and chromic acid. The final chrome plate is extremely thin (approximately 40 millionths of an inch).

Cad and Zinc Plating

What about cad plating or zinc dichromate plating? Cad plating provides a dull gold or silver color to your parts and slightly better protection from corrosion than zinc plate. It was much more common in the past, but due to the toxicity of the process (and, consequently, the environmental issues), it isn't used much. It's easy to confuse cad with zinc plate.

Zinc dichromate plating is composed of a thin coat of zinc applied mechanically or by way of electroplating. A chemical chromate conversion is used in the process, which can either be a clear with a blue tinge, or iridescent yellow. The yellow or "gold" on cadmium-plated parts is solid, while zinc plate has a sort of rainbow effect.

Decorative Plating

Not all is bliss with plated parts (and this is particularly important when it comes to high-performance applications). Decorative plating creates a byproduct called "hydrogen

Although this 1969 Nova front bumper has been detailed and assembled with park lamps and bumper brackets, it has also been re-plated. In the process, the bumper is pickled in a sulfuric acid bath. Plenty of corrosive chemicals are used in the plating process, and, as a result, costs for chrome plating have escalated over the years.

Detail Plating and Coating CONTINUED

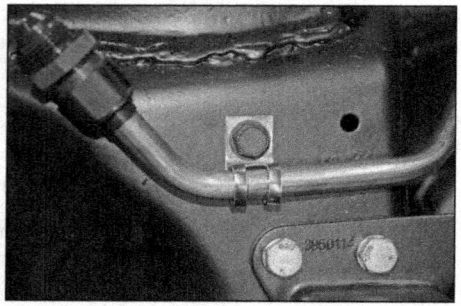

The AN (aircraft) bolts at the bottom of the photo (on the motor mount) are factory zinc-plated. The clamps have been re-plated in zinc. Zinc plating differs from cadmium plating in that the finish has a sort of rainbow effect.

embrittlement." Fasteners above SAE Grade 5 are susceptible to hydrogen embrittlement in the cleaning and coating processes (particularly the electroplating aspect). Because of the various forms of acid involved in the prep stages of chrome plating, a hydrogen byproduct is released into the tank; it is absorbed by the metal part being cleaned. When a current is applied to a parent metal, it too can create brittleness. As the name implies, hydrogen embrittlement causes the parent metal to become brittle, and eventually it can crack under stress.

Certain methods of heat-treating can lessen the chance of hydrogen embrittlement. The most common involves baking the chrome-plated part in a special oven at approximately 375 to 400 degrees F for a predetermined length of time. Theory is that the heat pulls the free hydrogen atoms from the metal pores, reducing the chance of embrittlement. It is clear that decorative plating of load bearing members isn't desirable. Springs, stressed suspension components, steering parts, and so on should never be chrome plated.

Powder Coating

Fair enough, but what if you need some form of tough external protection for various pieces on your Nova? Consider powder coating. Powder coating involves the use of special plastic or epoxy powders sprayed onto a subject component with a special spray gun. The component is given a negative charge (grounded). As the powder is discharged through the spray gun, it receives a positive electrical charge. Next, the component is baked in a proprietary oven (set at 300 to 400 degrees F) for approximately 25 minutes so that the powder solidifies. By the way, stripping (as in Redi-Strip), sandblasting, or glass beading a component produces a squeaky clean surface for the powder to adhere.

The real beauty of powder coating is its inherent durability. Powder coatings are almost impervious to automotive chemical spills, except for brake fluid. Powder coating has gained a reputation as a remarkable coating, but it's not infallible. We've all heard the sales pitch claiming you can smack a coated part with a hammer and it doesn't chip. Fascinating, but not exactly true. Powder coating is durable, but not invincible! It also has drawbacks. For example, it cannot be used on a part that cannot withstand the baking process. The baking process can distort certain critical machined surfaces (in the same way a heat treatment can). In addition, some items may have to be re-machined after powder coating. ■

What's up here? This is an "inventory" photo. If you send out a bunch of parts for powder coating or chroming, it's an extremely good idea to take a photo of all the pieces. This way, if something goes missing (and it seems like it always does), you can identify it.

Almost every major component has been powder coated on this Nova subframe. You find that it's often better not to have some items powder coated. Spindles are a good example. They get beat up during the assembly process and chip easily. Sometimes, good old-fashioned rattle-can paint is hard to beat!

GETTING FRAMED

install the same as cushion jobs, but you must use anti-seize on all stainless bolt threads. You'll be cursing yourself if you don't.

When the subframe is installed, do not torque to specs. The subframe

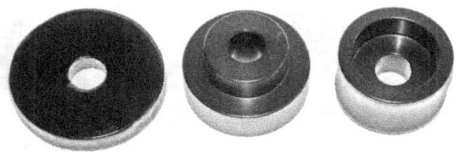

The Detroit Speed body mount package includes an upper and a lower mount manufactured from aluminum. The spacer on the left is a factory Chevrolet piece that has been powder coated. It mounts above the top "biscuit," next to the body mount bracket. Detroit Speed includes a thick, hard-anodized aluminum spacer with its Nova body mount kits. This is the primary difference between a Camaro and a Nova from a subframe mount perspective. Camaros don't use the spacer.

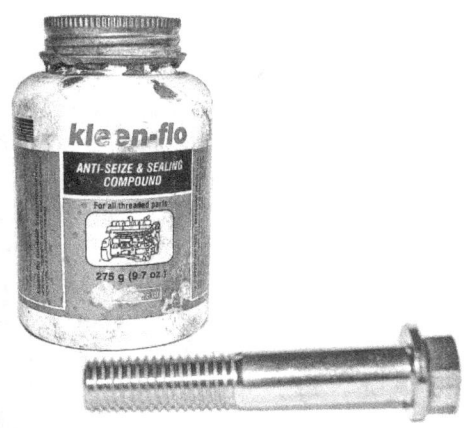

Anytime you use a stainless-steel fastener, you must use anti-seize; otherwise, the dissimilar materials will gaul. If they do gaul, the fastener will freeze up. You might be surprised at how difficult they are to remove after they have seized.

must be squared in the car. Here's a quick way to do it at home: At the rear of the body (ahead of the front spring eye) is a body crossmember with two trammel alignment holes. They're easy to spot: They measure

This hole next to the body mount opening in the subframe is for a factory alignment pin that was used during assembly to mate the body to the subframe. A large punch (or the jack handle from the car) can be used to replicate the initial body-subframe alignment process. It's also a good point to measure from when squaring the subframe.

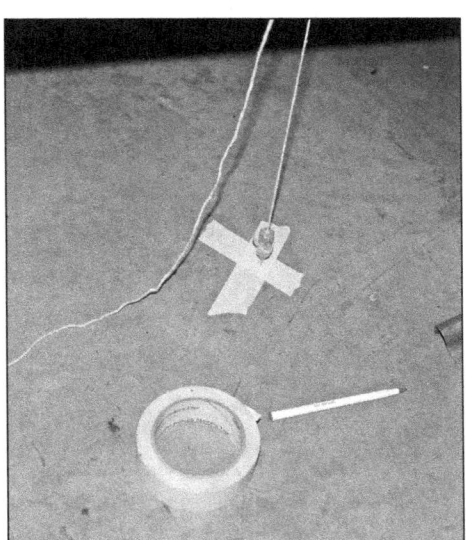

What's with the "X" on the floor? The plumb line has been dropped from a rear body trammel point. It's a point from which to measure diagonally to the opposite side of the car when squaring the subframe to the body.

approximately 5/16 inch in diameter and they're near the rocker panel. With the car level to the floor, drop a plumb line down from the center of each of these trammel holes. Mark that point with a piece of tape on the floor. Beside the forward body mount point on the subframe is an extra hole (see the photos). Drop a plumb line down from the center of this hole. Mark that location on the floor with another piece of tape. Measure front to back on both sides. Then measure diagonally from the passenger-side rear trammel hole to the driver-side plumb line mark. Do the same from the driver-side rear trammel hole to the passenger-side subframe plumb line. What you need to do is get the front-to-back and diagonal measurements as close to the same as possible. That will mean that the subframe is square in the car. Keep in mind these are old production line cars and might be out 1/8 inch or so over 6 feet. When done, you can torque to specs (typically 90 ft-lbs) and move forward on the build.

Mounting Points

The upper A-arms are held in place with a set of studs. They have knurls near the head, like those on a wheel stud. Most used jobs are well past their "best before" date. New examples are the way to go. Classic Industries and others sell them, and they're easy enough to install: Slip them in from the back and lightly tap the head with a hammer and punch to seat them. When you install the upper A-arm, the nuts pull the studs into place as you tighten them.

It's a good time to install the engine frame mounts. On a Nova, the hardware for the mounts proves to be far easier to install before the

CHAPTER 2

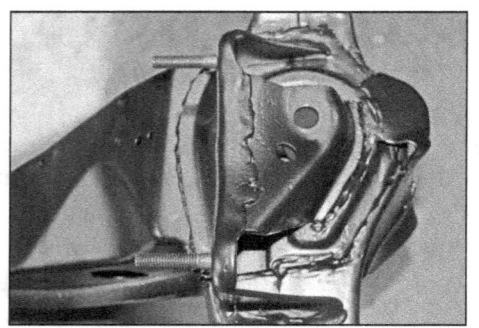

With the subframe apart, it's a good time (and a very good idea) to replace the A-arm studs on your Nova. These studs resemble wheel studs: hex head on one end with a knurl under the head. These examples are from Classic Industries.

Another tip is to install the engine frame mounts before the lower A-arms are installed on your Nova subframe. This is because the nuts on the backside are more difficult to reach with the lower A-arms installed. FYI: Those are AN (aircraft) bolts you see here.

Three bolts are used to install the stock Nova steering box. The box is actually threaded. Note the thick washers used under the bolt heads. They're required because of the fastener torque. This car includes a new Delphi manual steering box from Classic Industries.

A-arms go on. To learn more about the mounts, go to Chapter 7, Engine Swaps, Mounts and Hardware. You'll be glad you did.

Consider how you'd like to steer your car. Sure, you can swap to a rack and pinion arrangement. It offers a lot of advantages, but a rack swap isn't exactly a bolt-in. Plenty of Novas were factory-fit with power steering. If you don't want or need the heft or complexity, consider replacing it with a manual box. Classic Industries offers brand-new Delphi steering boxes with a simple bolt-in arrangement. Remove three bolts from the frame, drop out the old steering box, and reinstall the new box. Unfortunately, manual steering box pitman arms aren't exactly wrecking yard parts anymore. You need a good reproduction. Before you install it, center the steering box (basically, mark the shaft, count the turns lock to lock, and turn it back halfway). Point the wheels straight ahead, and only then should you install the pitman. It needs big torque to tighten to specs (140 ft-lbs according to a Chevy service manual). It's a good idea to use a new lock washer here.

Next up is the idler arm. It's a good time to replace it. Note in the photos, the idler was installed with 6AN fasteners (lock nuts, bolts, washers). The bolts are "backward," heads to the engine compartment side. This adds clearance for headers (and hands) within the engine compartment.

A-Arms

It should be no secret that bolt-in A-arms for the nose of a purpose-built car are readily available from plenty of sources. Why the need for aftermarket upper and lower control arms? Simple: The stock front suspension components bolted to the nose of your Nova as it rolled down the Detroit assembly line were never optimized for quarter-mile use or for burning corners. Vehicle manufacturers were typically conservative when it came to built-in caster. Chevrolet was certainly no exception.

Let's stop right here for a minute. What's caster? Caster is the backward

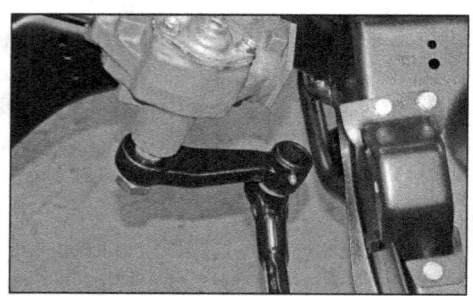

The steering should be centered, and then you can install the pitman arm. The pitman arm and the pitman arm shaft are splined, and they can only mate one way. A lock washer is between the pinion nut and the pinion arm. Torque for the nut is honking at 140 ft-lbs.

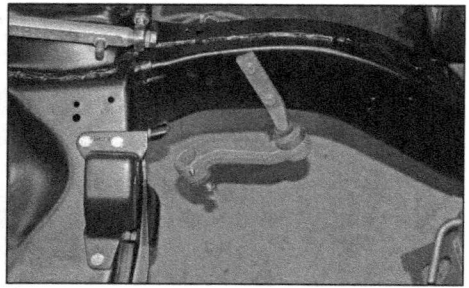

Nova idler arms are easy to install via two large access holes on the outside of the frame for the fasteners. Here, two more AN bolts have been used and, as pointed out in the text, they're actually installed backward. See the text for more information (there's a good reason for doing it this way).

GETTING FRAMED

The selection of A-arms out there is absolutely massive, ranging from reproduction factory-style pieces to road components to drag race hardware. These A-arms are TRZ Motorsports components from the drag racing end of the equation. They offer much improved geometry when compared to the stock A-arms.

Obviously, this is not a Nova, but look at the wheel camber! You can well imagine how the landing feels through the steering wheel on this Chevelle. Camber change on a vintage Nova is very similar. And it's not a good feature.

or forward tilt of the spindle as you view it from the side of the wheel and tire. When caster is positive, the spindle tilts backward, which places weight behind the tire contact patch. If the caster is negative, the top of the spindle is tilted forward, which places weight in front of the tire contact patch. Caster is expressed in degrees and measures the amount the centerline of the spindle is tilted from true vertical. For the most part, OEM caster figures seldom go beyond –3/4 degree (negative), but in almost all drag race applications, positive caster is required. Why? Consider positive caster a way to "self-center" the steering. Ponder bicycles for a minute. A comfy long-distance touring bike has a fork that's kicked out. This fork "kick out" provides a big chunk of positive caster. In turn, the bicycle experiences a significant amount of directional stability. Then look at a mountain bike. Here the fork is much closer to vertical. The benefit of the mountain bike is that it can turn very quickly; however, it definitely lacks directional stability. The bottom line is, you can easily ride a touring bicycle with your hands off the handlebars. It's not that easy with a mountain bike.

Camber is the tilt of the wheel at the top (tilting in or tilting out). Camber is expressed and measured in degrees and looks at the tilt of the wheel from true vertical. If the wheel and tire package tilt out at the top, it means that the camber is positive. If the top of the wheel and tire package tilt in, camber is negative. The idea behind camber is to keep the tire planted squarely on the pavement. This creates maximum front tire grip. In theory, zero degrees of camber seems like a good idea, but that isn't always the case for Novas that were originally production-line cars (not purpose-built as in a tube frame car). Most production line cars require different camber figures (while at rest) so that good grip and tire wear are maintained as the car travels down the road. Typically, a car with a small amount of negative camber exhibits better dragstrip handling characteristics without killing the tire.

A typical stock 1968–1972 Nova has a factory caster specification of ± 1/2 degree. To adjust the caster in a stock Nova, transfer shims front to rear or rear to front. If you transfer one shim (1/32 inch) from the rear bolt to the front it decreases positive caster by approximately 1/2 degree. The opposite (transferring one shim from the front bolt to the rear bolt) increases positive caster by approximately 1/2 degree. That same vintage Nova has a camber specification of 1/4 degree, ± 1/2 degree. To set camber you must add or subtract an equal number of shims from the front and the rear bolts on the A-arm cross shaft. One shim (again, 1/32 inch) at each location changes the camber by approximately 1/5 degree. Adding a shim at each end decreases positive camber.

Camber and caster are usually set together. In a high-performance application, you will probably run out of room to properly adjust the caster and camber on a car with stock A-arms. This becomes very apparent when you try to get a reasonable (for

Camber and caster are set by way of shims on the top A-arm cross shaft. More positive caster leads to better tracking at speed. You add and subtract shims to get to the desired settings. You can only do so much with the stock setup or with an offset cross shaft (as shown here). In the end though, you usually end up with a compromise in the settings.

Aftermarket A-arms such as these uppers from TRZ offer a big benefit with improved caster built in. These examples allow for 5 to 7 degrees (depending upon the setup). Similar A-arms from Detroit Speed and a few others also offer improved caster.

drag racing) caster number in a 1968–1974 Nova. To get something such as 5 or 6 (or even 7) degrees of caster is difficult, if not impossible. That's one big reason why an aftermarket A-arm package is a serious problem solver for drag race applications. When TRZ Motorsports engineered the control arms shown in the photos, they built in 5 to 7 degrees of positive caster. TRZ points out, "Caster varies on cars that have different ride heights. If the rear of the car is higher than the front, it then has less caster. In some cases people can only get 5 degrees or so due to variances in the frames, prior accident damage, front frame damage, or the rear of the car sitting too high." It all means it's possible to come up with way more positive caster than stock. With a lot of caster your car won't like backing up so much, but it sure will track well at speed.

The 1968–1974 Nova has considerable camber change as the front end goes through its travel. In an all-out drag car, you can really see the change as the car dangles the front end in a wheelstand. But the situation worsens when the car drops back down to the tarmac. The take-off and flight part of a wheelstand is easy. Landing isn't. The result is often a series of hairline cracks on factory A-arms. That's a big reason quality materials are important when it comes to front suspension hardware. The same applies to the welds and component finishing. A-arms are no place for lousy material choices. Or for backyard welding.

Speaking of welding and materials, the TRZ upper and lower control arms shown in the accompanying photos are manufactured from 4130 chrome moly tubing and they're TIG welded. Depending upon the model of car you have, they can reduce the weight of the control arm package (upper and lower) by 15 pounds per side; that's a total diet plan of 30 pounds if you're keeping track. And half of it is unsprung.

Another (huge) part of the front-end equation involves the front bushing choice. You find some A-arms out there that make use of bushings that just don't work for drag racing or other forms of motorsports. If you've been around the block with race car suspension, you've discovered that the road-style urethane bushings have a tendency to seize or stick (or as Penske and other big-time suspension folks refer to it, "stiction"). When the suspension system in a race or performance car has this stiction, it means the shock can't do its job effectively.

A-arms that make use of a bearing (rod end) or use some form of Delrin bushing (Delrin, by the way, is a form of very hard "plastic" material) are far better suited to high-performance applications. Delrin does not have

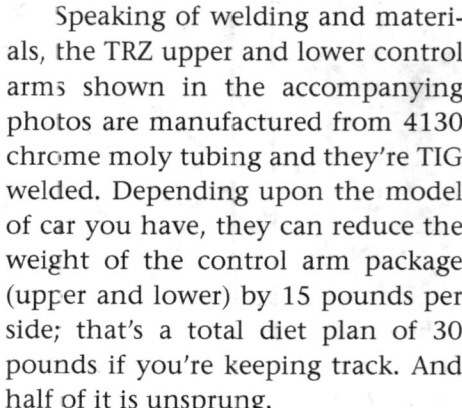

Aside from geometry, what do you look for in aftermarket A-arms? Material choice is important, as is material thickness. Weld quality is critical (check out the high-quality welds on these TRZ A-arms). Bushing and ball joint selection is equally important.

Dialing in Caster, Camber and Toe for Drag Duty

If you decide to drag race your Nova, try adding more caster. Keep an eye on the car's toe-change through its travel while the car is jacked. Toe-in change must be kept to a minimum. The very last thing you need is toe-out as the front end travels. Before you do a wheel alignment, place weight in the driver's seat that is equal to the driver's weight. Shot bags or weight-lifting equipment work. Be sure to top the fuel tank with the appropriate level of gasoline. Set the tire pressures to the level you normally race with (i.e., high pressure on the nose, and lower pressures at the rear). With the car on the alignment rack, jack the nose up to duplicate a normal race "attitude" (an inch or two seems to be about right). Jack and block the back of the car to compensate for the height of the front-wheel-alignment turn tables. The car is ready for the alignment.

Remember that every car is slightly different, but here are the OEM alignment figures.

Because every car in competition is different, use the following basic guidelines for your Nova wheel alignment.

- Camber should be set at zero; you should try to keep the front wheels straight up and down.
- Toe-in should be as close to zero as possible on a production line chassis. Watch for toe-out while the nose is in the air.
- Caster should be between 3 and 6 degrees. As the speed of the car increases, the need for more caster also increases. This stabilizes your car at speed. You likely need aftermarket A-arms to gain this much caster. ■

Stock Production Line Wheel Alignment Specs

	Typical	Nova
Caster (degree)	1/2	± 1/2
Camber (degree)	1/4	± 1/2
Total Toe (inch)	1/8	± 1/4

This is a Delrin bushing insert. Delrin is a hard plastic type of material that is naturally self-lubricating. Note that a steel sleeve is pressed inside the bushing, and that's where the lower attachment bolt passes through.

cold flow tendencies, and, as a result, maintains alignment over time. It is also oil-impregnated. When it encounters friction, it releases its own lubricant. That's what makes it a good choice for high-performance applications. In construction, quality Delrin bushings are multi-piece affairs. For example, the bushing layout found in the TRZ lower A-arms (shown in the accompanying photos) consists of a chrome-moly housing. Inside is a Delrin insert, and inside that (where the bolts pass through) is another metal sleeve. The way it's designed, the Delrin also acts as a thrust washer, which controls the fore and aft movement of the A-arm without binding.

The TRZ upper A-arms are engineered with 1/2-inch rod ends that mount on the respective cross shafts (instead of bushings). There is (obviously) no stiction with a rod end, and in terms of strength, a typical 1/2 x 1/2–inch rod end has a radial static load rating of more than 6,500 pounds (each!). You never experience those sorts of forces in any high-performance application. There is zero deflection without any sort of suspension bind. Some of the pieces aren't really dedicated drag-race components. Some are road-race inspired. A few of them can pack plenty of sophistication.

A big issue with any A-arm (stock or aftermarket) is controlling suspension travel. It's no secret that, for quarter-mile applications, huge suspension travel can be a good thing on low-powered cars or on greasy tracks, but if the horsepower wick is turned up and/or there's some bite in the track surface, adjustability in the A-arms becomes rather important. In those cases, a means to control the travel so that you can limit a wheel-stand is important.

Most early GM production-line cars (including Novas) feature a system of limiting the downward movement of the front control arms. In a race car (especially a low-horsepower race car), you need as much front-end travel as possible. Front-end travel in these vehicles can be increased without the addition of ball joint extensions (which in most sanctioning body rule books are illegal). Chevrolet used a rubber snubber mounted to the upper control arm to limit A-arm travel. If the snubber is trimmed, the front end of the car has more travel. Keep trimming the snubber until the car slows down (of course, in some cases, you must remove the snubber altogether). If you trim too much of the snubber away, swap the snubber for a common traction-bar component. When trimming snubbers, watch the brake flex line. You can go too far!

Certain limitations come into play as well. If you need to reduce the travel, you have no choice but to re-install a new snubber. Moreover, at the best of times, that stock snubber is too short for a high-power car running on a track with "teeth." The aftermarket provides fixes for this (some involve cables attached to the chassis; some are based upon steel snubbers), but with some of the drag race–inspired A-arms (such the TRZ jobs in the photos), it's not an issue. They already come assembled with adjustable travel limiters (basically, a Grade-8 bolt). The bolts thread into a boss on the upper A-arm and you adjust the travel you need for your car on the track you're running from the topside. It's a simple nut/jam nut operation. And you can do the tuning with a couple of common 3/4-inch wrenches.

Virtually all aftermarket road race/Pro Touring–style A-arms for Novas come equipped with mounting tabs for front sway bars. In drag racing, corners don't count. The front bars restrict control arm movement, effectively linking both sides of the front suspension. Disconnecting or removing the sway bar allows the suspension to rise and fall rapidly; that, in turn, translates to better launch capabilities. The solution is simple for Novas that see dragstrip duty: Dump the sway bar.

When contemplating aftermarket A-arms, consider a couple of other factors: one, the cross shaft found on the upper A-arm. The many manufacturers of A-arms don't rely upon the stock (heavy) steel shaft. Instead, they use a cross shaft that is milled from billet aluminum. It shouldn't be an issue because the loads experienced in a street/strip car aren't sufficient to compromise the structure, even when you take regular wheelstands and, particularly, landings into consideration.

Another consideration when buying aftermarket A-arms (drag race or otherwise), is the respective

The upper cross shaft found on many aftermarket A-arms is machined from billet aluminum. Aluminum can be used here, because the loads experienced aren't that great. Note too the use of aircraft-style (three-piece) rod ends rather than bushings. They eliminate stiction and make large geometry adjustments rather simple (although you can still use conventional shims for minor adjustments).

ball joints. Extended ball joints are available today for stock A-arms, but they're not required in aftermarket A-arms simply because they already incorporate geometry that has been "fixed." You should be able to service a good aftermarket A-arm easily (without going out of your way to find replacement parts). It's a good idea to use aftermarket A-arms built to accept replacement ball joints for the given car (for example, 1970

In this photo, you can see the large Grade 8 bolt protruding through the upper A-arm. This is a suspension travel limiter. The idea here is to have control over how much the suspension travels at the dragstrip. Cars with big power don't need as much suspension travel as low-horsepower cars, and this bolt provides the necessary adjustment.

Don't overlook the obvious when shopping for aftermarket A-arms. Service items such as easily replaceable ball joints are important. Here, the upper joint is a conventional bolt-in and it installs with four simple fasteners.

GETTING FRAMED

> ### Longer Ball Joints and Taller Spindles
>
> Some ball joints are available with a longer-than-stock pin length to correct roll centers. These longer-pin ball joints feature hardened pins in stock-type housings; they are not rebuildable. Fair enough. What is the advantage?
>
> The Nova (along with its Camaro brethren) suffers from a too-short spindle. This prevents the tire from cambering properly when powering through a corner (the top of the tire cambers out too long before it starts pulling in). In turn, this causes the tire to scrub on the outside instead of running on the complete tire contact patch.
>
> Tall ball joints add spindle height by increasing the distance between the two pivot points. Essentially, they're a quick way to get 1/2 inch or so additional spindle height.
>
> Taller upper ball joints have no effect upon the ride height of the car because the upper arms are not weight bearing.
>
> On the other hand, a taller spindle has a higher overall height than the factory spindle. This is designed to relocate the upper ball joint pickup points to achieve better front-end geometry. The taller spindle height improves handling by modifying the camber curve. The result is a negative camber gain during suspension compression (when carving a corner). Some aftermarket spindles (for example, a Belltech) are simply lowered; they're not taller. You can find taller-than-stock spindles without any drop or you can get spindles that are both dropped and tall (for example, certain spindles from Detroit Speed).
>
> *It is possible to purchase longer-than-stock upper ball joints for vintage Novas. The purpose is to fix the camber curve. You don't gain much spindle height with the swap (perhaps 1/2 inch total), but for these cars, every little bit helps.*

Nova A-arms use replacement ball joints for a 1970 Nova). Service parts are available just about anywhere.

What about spring types? I look at springs in Chapter 5, but you can source A-arms in two configurations: one with a stock lower-spring pocket and another for coil-over shock applications. For Novas, you need to make a modification to the shock mount on the upper frame for most coil-overs. TRZ offers a kit just for that application. If you're using a stock-style spring, the A-arms are a simple bolt-in.

Before leaving A-arms, the final thing you should think about (particularly when it comes to aftermarket A-arms) is the lower shock absorber mount. The problem here is the size of some aftermarket shock absorber bodies, particularly the adjusters. Plenty of these aftermarket shocks have big adjusters on either side of the shock, and they don't fit inside stock A-arms. Many aftermarket A-arms have a shock opening in the lower A-arm that needs to be ground away so that you can fit the shock body. That's not the end of it, either. In many cases, after you get the shock in, you cannot access the shock adjuster (which is a wee bit counterproductive). Look for A-arms with the largest possible opening for the adjusters to pass through, and where the inner pocket that surrounds the shock has been relieved to free space for the adjuster knobs. Finally, look for lower shock mounts that are designed with built-in weld-nuts. This will eliminate the need to stick a wrench inside the control arm to fasten the shock.

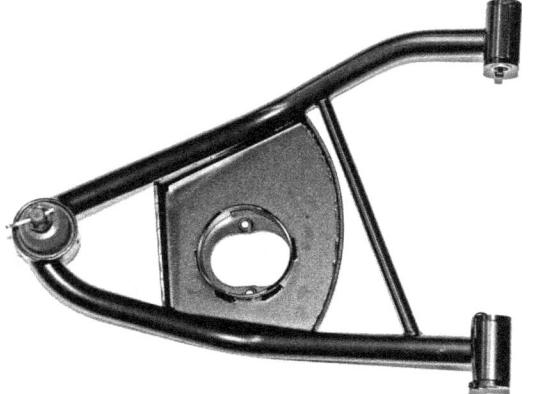

Downstairs, this A-arm from TRZ is engineered to work with a factory coil spring. You can specify coil-over shocks for many A-arms, but keep in mind that coil-overs do not store as much spring energy as a stock spring (which is important for a relatively heavy car such as a Nova when traversing the quarter-mile). Note too, the shock opening is large enough to accept an aftermarket shock with external adjuster knobs.

Installing the Rest

Aftermarket A-arms install just like factory parts; they bolt right in. You need a spring compressor for the coil springs (more on spring selection in Chapter 5). Always watch where the spring is pointed when you're compressing it. Always heavily lube the threads on the spring compressor too, and always make it a practice to heavily lube the threads during the tightening process. Finally, watch the spring compressor to make sure it's centered in the spring. They can dance around and move off-center while tightening. In most cases, the rod of the spring compressor must protrude through the upper shock stud hole in the subframe during installation. If it's off-center in the spring, it won't fit and you'll have to start all over again (it can also slip when compressing the spring).

Inspect the spindle carefully. Over time they can develop fractures, and of course, they can wear, particularly on bearing surfaces. For tie rod ends, source new inners and outers. To join them, consider using solid tie-rod sleeves. The setup from Hotchkiss includes machined hex bodies (so you can easily turn them

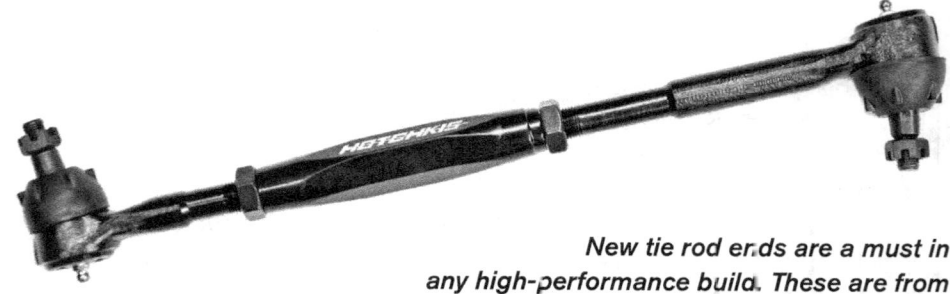

New tie rod ends are a must in any high-performance build. These are from Classic Industries. Another important (but seemingly minor) piece is the tie rod sleeve. The factory pieces are flimsy. Period. These billet jobs from Hotchkiss make toe adjustment easy; they're also beefy.

This is an overall look at a finished built-for-performance Nova subframe. Almost every critical fastener was replaced with either a new reproduction or a new AN component. It's not difficult to copy this plan, but it does take time to complete.

In this example, the spindle is a stock Chevrolet piece. Be doubly cautious when it comes to OEM spindles. Some can fatigue to the point that they develop stress cracks. It's not a bad idea to have them Magnafluxed.

In this side view of the same finished subframe you see that several fasteners and brackets were either zinc plated or powder coated. Those treatments might not make your Nova quicker or faster, but they sure make it easier to work on.

GETTING FRAMED

Eliminate the Back Drive

Every Nova 1969–on was fitted with a steering-mounted ignition switch along with a steering column/ignition key interlock/back drive (of some sort) for the transmission. What this did was ensure the car was in park or reverse before it was started. In turn, the linkage insured a moveable collar on the steering column was positioned fully counterclockwise. Only then could the ignition key be installed or removed. When you moved the shifter, the collar on the steering column moved. It meant that you couldn't remove the ignition key while the car was being driven.

Fair enough, but the maze of mechanical links also fouls up a header installation in a big way and, for the most part, doesn't allow for the install of any headers. The same applies to the install of an aftermarket floor shifter. That's the conundrum. So how do you make it all work together? It's not that difficult. What has been done since the beginning of time is to disable the interlock. Simply remove the back drive completely and then wire up the remaining interlock rod(s) on the base of the steering column so that the collar on the column can't move from the counterclockwise position.

Drill a small hole in the column jacket (as shown in the accompanying photo), and then wire the column back-drive lever in one spot. The wire used in the example is stainless-steel aircraft safety wire. Double up the wire and twist it as shown. This ensures the collar on the column doesn't move. The only catch is that you can start the car without it being in the appropriate gear. Just remember that.

Vintage Novas (and most vintage Chevys, for that matter) use a back drive system that links the steering column to the transmission linkage. The trouble is, it fouls up a header installation. The obvious cure is to eliminate it. The key is to secure the column so that the steering column collar (at the ignition key switch) doesn't flop around without the back drive. This photo shows a good way to wire it in one place.

to adjust toe with a basic open-end wrench) and matching jam nuts. They're powder-coated gloss black and install the same as stock.

Frame Connectors

The Chevy Novas we love were built as simple machines. Carving corners or traversing the quarter-mile with the performance seen today wasn't even a twinkle in the engineer's eye when these things came off the assembly line. The truth is, these old cars, with their big honking bolt-on front subframe mated to a unit construction body were pretty much flexi-fliers. After all, that big front subframe was simply bolted to the body in only four spots. Making it worse was the fact that the four bushings attached by those four bolts deteriorated with age and use. When you pounded on the cars, the bodies moved around. Sometimes they moved around a lot! So much so that door and trunk gaps could permanently change. Doors often didn't close correctly. You might even have seen some with a heavily cracked and buckled floor pan. It's not good.

Here's a look at a set of Competition Engineering bolt-in frame connectors installed in a 1970 Nova. They're a relatively straightforward bolt-in.

The front of the connector slides into the OEM subframe, as shown here. To install it, you must loosen the rear subframe bolts. When that's done, you can slide the front of the connector in place.

Detroit Speed's Hydroformed Subframe

As Nova enthusiasts, we're lucky because the subframe on our favorite car is pretty much identical to the one used by the incredibly popular first-gen Camaro. For all intents and purposes, the subframes are a direct interchange. That means a lot of high-quality, high-tech aftermarket components are out there. If you're set to burn corners, a great choice is the subframe from Detroit Speed. What sets the Detroit Speed subframe apart from the others is the fact the rails are hydroformed. Hydroforming is a process that uses fluid to help form the metal. First, a blank section of tubing is cut to length and then bent to the approximate shape of the subframe rail. The blank is placed into the lower half of a die situated in a huge-by-large hydraulic press. The blank is pressurized with a mix of water, lubricant, and corrosion inhibitor. The press closes the upper half of the die. A mix of external pressure (from the press) and internal pressure (the water mix inside the blank) forms the rail. No heat is added. This creates a subframe rail that has constant wall thickness, is free of wrinkles, and is not compromised by added heat.

After it is hydroformed, Detroit Speed welds in custom-stamped front crossmember assemblies and adds the respective mounts for the front suspension system, along with provisions for the rack-and-pinion steering. Those mounts allow for the installation of their TIG-welded upper and lower A-arms that work in concert with their own forged front spindle. The upper and lower control arms are fitted with Delrin bushings and, as you can see, they're heavily gusseted. The overall geometry allows for more positive camber than stock.

Springs are of the coil-over variety while the accompanying shocks can be single adjustable, double adjustable, or remote canister types. Spring rates are worked out for you depending upon the engine combination you select. The steering is a specifically tuned power rack package, while the sway bar is a splined NASCAR-style job. Sway bar bushings are formed of custom composite Delrin. The package accepts any stock or aftermarket C6 Corvette brake package. It mandates 17-inch-or-larger front wheels (minimum inside diameter of 16.250 inches).

Detroit Speed has thought of everything that a corner-carving Nova enthusiast wants in a high-tech subframe. It's not inexpensive, but the quality is outstanding. If you take that complete, preassembled route, you have only four body mounts and two radiator support mounts to remove and replace to install the subframe. It can't get much simpler.

The back of the connector sandwiches in between the rear subframe and the forward leaf spring perch. You must trim the connector slightly to clear the perch.

This is a good look at how the connector fits the Nova. It's unobtrusive; you really have to look to see it (or know what you're looking at).

What can you do about it? The fix is not difficult. Add frame connectors to stiffen the car, and replace the body mount bushings. These pieces add rigidity to the Nova, eliminate the buckling and cracking, and allow the door gap and panel gaps to remain consistent. In addition, they make the car quicker and faster. You don't lose forward energy that would otherwise be spent twisting the car. As a bonus, that old Nova might just prove to be more fun to drive.

Connectors are available in weld-in, bolt-in, square-, rectangular-, and round-tube configurations. You have a lot of choices, and the truth is, the bolt-in jobs aren't as bad as you might think. The reason is, you can do the work at home and you don't need to cut the car up. Better still, a bolt-in connector is reversible. If you (or someone else) want to return the car to stock, or very close to stock, it's possible.

If you examine the accompanying photos, you can see a set of bolt-in Competition Engineering frame connectors installed in a Nova. They fit nicely, but it is necessary to trim the connector bracket at the spring perch. It's not a big job, but it does take some time.

CHAPTER 3

REAR AXLE

You'd think that selecting a rear end for your Nova would be easy. It's not. There are almost too many choices! From the factory, 1968–1974 Novas were fitted with 8.20-inch-diameter ring-gear 10-bolts, 8.50-inch-diameter ring-gear 10-bolts, and 8.875-inch-diameter ring-gear 12-bolts. On the aftermarket side, custom 12-bolts are available along with Dana 60 models and, of course, 9-inch Fords. Options are many.

While it is possible to make the pair of 10-bolts live in a high-performance Nova application, you're far better off with a 12-bolt, a Dana, or a 9-inch. The reasons are manifold and they range from outright strength to parts availability. Equally important, the aftermarket now has you covered when it comes to the "Big Three" of rear axle assemblies. You don't have to scrounge junkyards for any of them. And you don't have to mess with worn-out 40-year-old components either. In no particular order, here's the inside scoop on the three best choices.

12-Bolt

Quite possibly, the strongest iron-case 12-bolts on the planet come from Mark Williams Enterprises. Mark Williams starts with a custom case. This setup (which is basically like starting from scratch in the design) fixes all the shortcomings of the 12-bolt and then mixes in the right mounting system for any number of new or vintage General Motors (or other manufacturer) vehicles, including Novas. As you see in the accompanying photos, the housing looks pretty much like a conventional 12-bolt. But looks can be deceiving. For example, the area behind the rear caps in a stock GM 12-bolt casting is heavily scalloped (basically hollow). This compromises strength. In the Mark Williams housing, the area surrounding the caps is solid. The actual caps are much larger than those found in a stock GM casting. Why go to all this trouble? Simple. The hypoid action of the rear end tries to force the carrier backward, out of the housing. By increasing the beef in the housing, the fore and aft movement is stopped cold with no need for a billet cap (a common fix for 12-bolts and Dana 60 rear ends).

Mark Williams can build the iron case for a conventional 30-spline (or 33-spline) axle. If you need brute strength, it can be manufactured to accommodate a honking 35-spline axle. The bore size of the case determines the axles you can use. Keep in mind that when an axle spline is increased, the diameter of the axle

This 12-bolt looks tame sitting up inside the Nova, but in reality, this is one trick piece with many improvements over stock.

CHAPTER 3

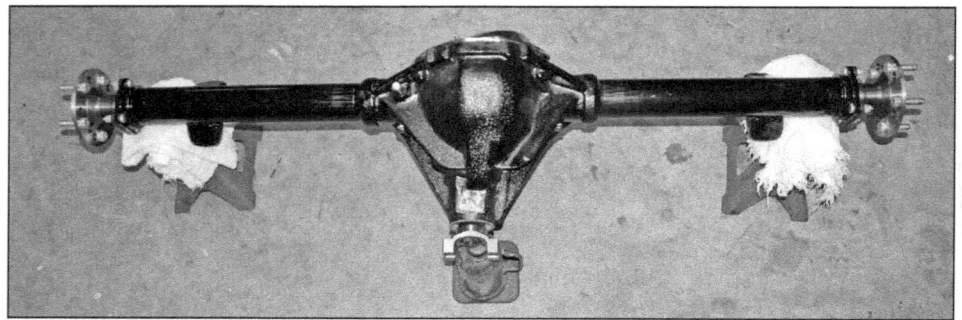

What you're looking at is quite possibly the ultimate iron-case 12-bolt for street/strip applications. Mark Williams custom builds these rear-end assemblies to order.

This 12-bolt from Mark Williams is built with light, strong chrome-moly (4130) axle tubes. The housing ends are engineered to accept an extremely large 45-mm axle bearing. The axle incorporates an external bearing retainer and therefore does not rely upon a C-clip for axle retention.

shaft increases (which in turn dictates the need for a special large-bore case). The 35-spline axle is massive. How massive? Think Dana 60.

Mark Williams can supply the housing with either mild steel or chrome-moly steel tubes. For the housing shown in the accompanying photos, Mark Williams included chrome-moly tubes. Mark Williams fully welds the axle tubes to the center section. In a stock 12-bolt, the tubes are only held in place by way of plug welds. When looking at vintage 12-bolts, you find that in many cases the factory GM welds were not sound, and under close examination, pinholes in the respective welds become evident. This isn't of much consequence in the strength department on a housing such as this (since the tubes have been totally welded to the center section), but there is one small problem: The factory spot-weld system often leaks or "weeps" lubricant. Because of this problem, many a 12-bolt has had seals replaced, gaskets replaced, and drain plugs swapped, only to find that the leak was at a factory spot weld. The solution is rather simple in nature, but is time consuming to accomplish. Each of the tube spot weld locations is filled with a plug weld or "rosette" weld process. The result is a clean, leak-free housing.

One other area you should take note of is the entry point for the axle tubes in the center section. In a stock 12-bolt, this spot is rather fragile. It has been seriously beefed up in the Mark Williams casting to handle much larger loads than a stock GM 12-bolt.

When it comes to dimensions, Mark Williams can pretty much build the housing for any width you require. Several types of housing ends are available from Mark Williams. The featured housing incorporates 45-mm housing ends that accept a sealed bearing and do not use "C-clips" (in fact, none of the Mark Williams housings are constructed for troublesome C-clips). In this example, the car was constructed with drum brakes on the back half,

This 12-bolt was built from the beginning to work with CalTracs bars. The preferred spring perch with CalTracs is this Mopar-style setup. Look closely and you can see how Mark Williams boxed the perch for additional strength.

This photo gives you a good idea how the custom perch built by Mark Williams works with a CalTracs bar. It's a clean and simple arrangement.

REAR AXLE

and this system is a direct bolt-on for early-style Nova four-bolt brake backing plates.

Subtle differences exist in axle perch layout between these housings and an OEM piece. The brackets are usually fully welded (which isn't the case with the factory arrangement), and the housing shown in the photos uses a Chrysler (or Ford) style of spring perch. What's up with that? Simple. The Nova that it's going under is set up with CalTracs bars. Those bars are best suited to a Chrysler perch (rather than a GM perch). Equally important, Mark Williams can install the perches to your pinion angle specs.

In case you're wondering, I double-checked the dimensions between the custom Mark Williams leaf spring housing in the photos and a stock OEM housing. The locations for all brackets are exactly the same as stock. This means the piece will physically bolt into a specific car with zero modifications.

On the nose of their complete 12-bolt setup, Mark Williams incorporates a forged 4340 steel pinion yoke. The pinion yoke is often a potential weak link in the rear-end chain. Most OEM and replacement yokes for the 12-bolt are fragile cast-iron pieces, and for the most part, they can't accept a large-diameter, 1350 Spicer universal joint. That's why Mark Williams includes a 4340 forged steel yoke on its extreme-duty custom 12-bolt. Following forging, the yokes are CNC-machined to exact tolerances; in addition, they're heat-treated to 200,000 psi. Each yoke is symmetrical for balance and alignment. Special snap ring grooves also allow for easy U-joint installation. As mentioned above, they're designed to accept a massive, almost indestructible Spicer 1350 universal joint.

On the outside, the axle flange includes dual patterns. In the case of the 12-bolt in our photos, both patterns are GM 5 on 4¾, but one is drilled to accept a conventional 1/2-inch stud while the other pattern is drilled to accept a set of Mark Williams' huge drive studs. The wheel studs shown in the photos are short 1/2-inch jobs, which the Williams crew designed to fit under a stock Chevy dog dish hubcap (think "sleeper"). I dig deeper into axles later in this chapter.

All sorts of details are inside; some you can't see and some you

A close look shows the double-drilled axles. Both are for a Chevy 5-on-4-3/4 pattern. One set of holes is for a 1/2-inch stud (shown) while the second set is for a 5/8-inch Mark Williams drive stud.

On the backside of the housing bearing flange you can see how Mark Williams trims the bearing retainer studs so that they clear the huge bearing. The retainer is horseshoe shaped to allow for easy axle removal.

Believe it or not, this is a weak spot on all original 12-bolt housings. General Motors used plug welds to attach the axle tube to the housing. Mark Williams welds the axle tubes directly to the (much stronger) custom iron case.

The bearing retainer looks like this when it's off the housing. To use this setup (large 45-mm bearing), minor machining is required on the brake backing plate.

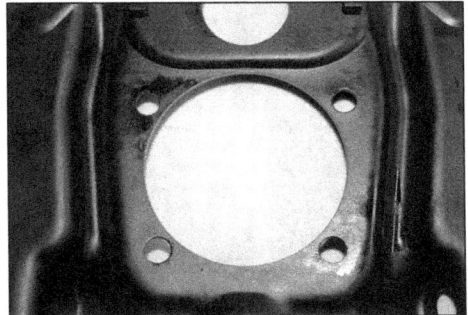

This view shows the modified backing plate. Here, the center bore size on the backing place has been increased to 3.152/3.155 inches to go over the 3.150-inch OD bearing and seal from Mark Williams.

CHEVY NOVA 1968–1974: HOW TO BUILD AND MODIFY

Mark Williams' custom case has a lot more meat in it than a production line Chevrolet piece. The area behind the main caps is solid (instead of hollow) and the caps are massive. A billet cap or a rear cover girdle is not needed.

This is another view of the cap. It's massive, and note how the pair of caps are held in place by way of strong internal socket cap screws.

can. If you check out the photos, you see that each ring gear bolt is safety wired. Each of those bolts is a high-quality piece from ARP. In fact, many of the fasteners used during the build are either ARP or high-strength socket head Allen jobs. The same applies to bearings. You might think it's easy to nail down bearings for a 12-bolt. But you'd be wrong. Today, many offshore parts are available, and it's often difficult to locate quality pieces. That's why Williams makes use of Timken bearings in its rear-end assemblies, and that includes the custom 12-bolt in this series.

On the outside, all the little details (which often go forgotten) are taken care of: The housing includes a correct vent. The rear cover is chrome steel, and it's even fitted with Allen-head fasteners. The studs for the axle bearing retainers (and the brake backing plates) are milled on the backside to clear the huge wheel bearings, and each stud is zinc dichromate plated. The CNC-machined bearing retainers are horseshoe shaped, which allows installation or removal from the axle without having to remove the axle bearings. Timken manufactures the actual axle bearings. In the end, a 12-bolt such as this could very well be the best street/strip rear end available for a Nova, and that includes the two setups that follow.

Ford 9-Inch

Ford's 9-inch rear end is the darling of both drag racing and hot rodding. And for good reason. The rear end allows for easy center section changes (you can remove the pumpkin and service it on your workbench, which sure beats lying under a car getting drenched in rear axle lube). It also offers considerable choice when it comes to gear ratios and hardware. To be quite honest, it's incredibly strong in modified form (likely the strongest by far of any passenger car– and light truck–based rear-end assemblies used in drag racing).

But in stock form, the Ford isn't so hot. The newest junkyard housing you come across is at least 20 years old, so finding a used one isn't easy. Aside from age, the 9-inch is hampered by three major drawbacks from the high-performance perspective: First, the housing axle tubes are not round; they taper from 3½ to 3 inches. Second, all the tubes have

On the nose, the custom Mark Williams 12-bolt makes use of a forged 4340 steel pinion yoke. The CNC-machined yoke is designed to accept a large Spicer 1350 universal joint. This is the same size universal joint found in medium-duty truck applications.

Note how each of the ring gear bolts is safety wired following installation. ARP builds the fasteners especially for Mark Williams.

REAR AXLE

Here's a basic 9-inch Ford housing. This one on the bench is for a GM G-Body, but leaf spring examples are quite similar.

Ford housings usually mandate some sort of brace when you mix them with big power and sticky tires. The reason for bracing a Ford housing is to curb its tendency to move fore and aft (flex on the ends).

Box braces are common in drag racing, but a simple tubular brace such as this works equally well and it's a bit cleaner. Here you can see how the center section is tied to the tube structure.

On the outboard sides, the back brace ties directly to the axle tubes. Here, they're adjacent to the suspension mount points.

"flats" that are somewhat squashed onto the tubes. These two factors force a chassis builder to custom build every bracket, because they aren't symmetrical. There's more, too: The factory Ford housing face is approximately 24 inches wide. Because of this, you must weld brackets to the face in some cars. This means you lose adjustment holes for items such as the four-link.

Much of the detail work that goes into a good 9-inch is hidden; therefore, many of these housings look more stock than they actually are. Even many of the new aftermarket 9-inch housings mandate a ton of work. Case in point: The 9-inch Ford housing shown in the accompanying photos took the better part of a week to rework, but on the outside, it doesn't look much different from other setups. While space precludes a full-blown step-by-step investigation of the methods used to fortify a Ford, I can give you a bit of insight into some of the techniques.

For high-powered cars, it's standard practice to add a brace to the rear of a Ford 9-inch. This brace essentially ties the ends of the axle tubes to one another, and at the same time, anchors the back of the housing. This addition greatly increases the strength of the housing, eliminating the trend for the housing to physically move forward and aft. Fair enough, but there's a catch to the back-brace scenario, one that some chassis builders forget, ignore, or simply don't know about: When the back brace is added, the housing does not deflect forward and back. Instead, it deflects downward under power. The solution? A tube affixed between the four-link brackets (see the accompanying photos for a closer look). Of course, most

CHEVY NOVA 1968–1974: HOW TO BUILD AND MODIFY

This is a custom sheet-metal 9-inch housing I had built for another project. As you can see, it incorporates a similar tubular back brace along with a bottom brace that serves to keep the housing from bending downward.

This is another look at the bottom brace. This type of brace is typically used on cars with four-link. The bar ties the lower four-link brackets together.

builders use custom-built 360-degree four-link brackets (that wrap completely around the respective axle tubes), but there's still more to the 9-inch prep.

Almost all 9-inch housing "banjos" are formed by stamping. When loaded by way of sticky tires, extra weight, and a strong engine, the construction really doesn't work. What ends up happening is the housing flexes at the carrier. In turn, the life cycle of the ring and pinion is shortened. A big issue is the rear "cover" found on the housing. The back of a 9-inch isn't one piece; it consists of a stamped cover pressed into the housing. The hypoid action of the third member attempts to force the carrier out the back of the housing. Welding the cover to the back of the housing doesn't fix the problem.

The fix is to weld the stamped pieces of the housing together and then add an internal housing "cage." This cage is, in essence, a series of tubes that tie the front face of the housing to the rear. What it does is improve ring gear life.

Ford Center Section

What about the center section? Ford center sections were typically manufactured with a separate bolt-in support for the pinion. Cars with nodular center sections were regularly fitted with what was called a "Daytona" pinion support. These supports make use of the same size outer bearing as the more pedestrian supports; however, the inner bearing is much larger, and the inner webbing is much more robust. Most nodular-iron 31-spline muscle-Fords came with Ford's clutch pack–equipped Traction Lok differential (which is a conventional limited-slip arrangement). Then, with the dawn of the 1970 model year, a positive locking (gear-driven) differential manufactured by a company called Detroit Automotive Products

The hypoid action of the ring gear causes a tendency for the Ford to flex fore and aft at the center section. To stop this, the inside of the housing is "caged." Two of the cage braces can be seen at the bottom of the housing.

If you need the ultimate in 9-inch Ford center sections for a street/strip Nova, this is it. It's a Mark Williams through-bolt-configuration aluminum center section, complete with a pinion support, billet carrier adjusters, 1350 universal joint yoke, billet 35-spline Detroit Locker, and in this case, a 3.89:1 ring and pinion.

Detroit Locker

The muscle-car era was filled with interesting and often memorable hardware. The Detroit Locker, found under big-power Fords with a Drag Pack, was one of them. As it turns out, the Detroit Locker was likely the toughest, meanest, gnarliest differential that ever turned a tire on the street. But what does this have to do with Novas? In all honesty, the Detroit Locker is still the most durable and dependable locking differential available. It is certainly not limited to 9-inch Ford applications either. Way back when, the Locker had some decidedly naughty manners (which didn't hurt the bad-boy reputation one bit). The Detroit Locker functions as an automatic locking differential designed to lock both wheels of the axle together automatically with power input when forward or reverse torque is applied. This means that both driving wheels deliver 100 percent of the power to the ground. When "locked," it's like a spool that solidly connects both axles (and consequently connects both wheels). When torque isn't applied, the Detroit Locker "unlocks." The locking and unlocking wasn't exactly invisible (you could hear and feel clunking and banging). Sure, it was a bit naughty, but the Locker also had a reputation for brute strength.

Today, Eaton owns Detroit Locker and most of the bad manners have been banished. The latest "soft lockers" still let you know when they lock and unlock, but not quite with the same ferocity of the older models. They're rather civilized.

Born as a "Thornton Drive" the Locker was first manufactured by Detroit Automotive Product Corporation. Through the 1940s and into the 1950s and 1960s, the Thornton Drive became available as original equipment under all sorts of light- and medium-duty trucks. Over time, Detroit Automotive Product Corporation transformed into Tractech (the name changed in 1979). By the 1960s, the Thornton Drive came to be known as the Detroit Locker.

In 2005, Eaton Corporation purchased Tractech Holdings, Inc. With the purchase came the Detroit Locker. Eaton Corporation offers Detroit Lockers for a wide array of rear-end applications, including Dana 60, Ford 9-inch, Dana 44, Chrysler 8¾, GM 10 (various configurations), and 12-bolts (standard and aftermarket 33- or 35-spline) and others.

The bottom line here is, the Detroit Locker was and still is the toughest limited-slip setup available anywhere. If you need brute strength from the differential in your Nova, your first stop should be a Detroit Locker.

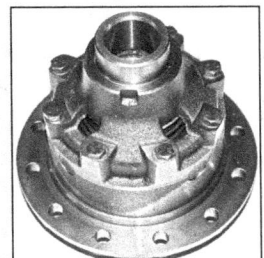

Because Detroit Lockers have "backlash" or "slack" between the drive and driven teeth, they are audible in everyday use going through corners and when going from drive mode to coast mode. Eaton notes that with the Nova on the ground and the transmission in neutral you have 1/4 to 1/3 turn of lash in the driveshaft; this is completely normal.

The case found on a Detroit Locker is extremely beefy. No special setup is required with this limited slip. In many examples, you can use stock replacement bearings. In the unlikely event you break a Locker, it is possible to repair it. Eaton offers a full range of replacement pieces and service parts.

You can see the carrier splines from this angle. This example is engineered for use with 35-spline axles. As far as lubricant for the Locker is concerned, you can use any quality petroleum/mineral-based rear axle lube. Friction additives/modifiers are not required. Eaton does not recommend synthetic lube for the Locker.

Detroit Lockers are available for 3- and 4-series gear sets. The Locker locks up 100 percent when operating in a straight line or if the Nova is spinning, which means power is transmitted to both wheels. In a turn, the unit unlocks for the wheel turning the fastest.

Corporation was made available in high-horsepower cars with gear ratios of 4.30:1. These are the legendary "Detroit Lockers."

Ford did something good with the design and layout of the 9-inch. No secret. It's pretty much the standard go-to rear end for drag racing. If you're so inclined, it is possible to track down most of the stock hardware to piece together a factory-style nodular-iron 31-spline 9-inch, complete with a Daytona pinion support and even a Detroit Locker. However, the truth is that what you find is old, used-up hardware. You should be prepared to drop some serious coin to whip the old stuff into shape. Not good. And not race effective either. What is good is the selection out there (in the racing aftermarket) for updated, brute force Ford center sections. The setups I show you are head and shoulders above the original parts.

Ford 9-Inch Case

Several companies manufacture and sell nodular-iron cases. Nodular iron is a type of cast iron that first saw the light of day in 1943. While most varieties of cast iron prove to be brittle, nodular iron is much more ductile because of its "nodular graphite" inclusions. When you consider aftermarket products, think about the availability of upgrades. Mark Williams has a reinforced nodular-iron case that is stronger than stock but comparable in weight to a stock Ford assembly. These 9-inch cases come complete with billet steel rear-end caps that have been precision alignment bored. They also include special billet-steel adjusters and studs to secure the pinion assembly. They're available with 3.062- or 3.250-inch bore sizes (the larger the bore, the

This is a through-bolt design. Instead of a bolt (for the main caps) threading into the body of the center section, a high-strength Grade-9 bolt goes completely through the center section.

With a through-bolt case, no threads engage the center section, which means no chance of stripped fasteners. It also means the strength is increased many times.

larger the axle diameter/spline you can use, the larger the axle diameter and spline, the stronger the axle).

Another option is the "through bolt" aluminum case manufactured by Mark Williams. Isn't aluminum weaker than nodular iron? Not necessarily. This is a highly refined, extreme-duty component that has become pretty much the standard in NHRA Pro Stock. It's also used with regularity in slower-class drag race cars, "pro/street" cars, and any number of seriously quick street machines. It weighs 11 pounds less than Williams' comparable nodular-iron carrier or a stock Ford carrier. Cast from an ultra-strong aircraft alloy (30 percent stronger than 6061T6), the case is engineered with special "through bolts" that go completely through the center section to secure the main caps.

The actual main caps are machined from 7075 aluminum and include billet-steel carrier adjusters. The pinion pilot-bearing bore incorporates an extra-length bearing that is completely captive and retained by fasteners. Meanwhile, the pinion support is held in place by way of large-diameter 7/16-inch studs. The case is manufactured in three bore sizes (3.062, 3.250, and 3.812 inches, although for anything short of an all-out drag car, the 3.812-inch piece isn't necessary). All through-bolt case configurations have clearance for 9½-inch gears (9¼-inch actual diameters). Fluid passage ports for external lubrication systems are pre-drilled. In addition, the case is set up so that you can add a load bolt if necessary. What is a load bolt? Essentially, a load bolt is a bolt positioned close to the backside of the ring gear, but not in contact with it. It only contacts the ring gear if there is deflection under severe load. Load bolts were originally used on heavy-duty truck differentials. They prevented chipped teeth if the driver's foot slipped off the clutch when backing up. The bottom line here is, it might be necessary in *extreme* power applications, but for we mere mortals, it's not required.

Ford 9-Inch Carrier

When it comes to the carrier (differential) for a 9-inch Ford, three basic options are available: Spool, Posi-Traction, and Locker, and of course, a series of variants in each. You can also get an open carrier, but honestly, this isn't really a performance choice, at least for anyone

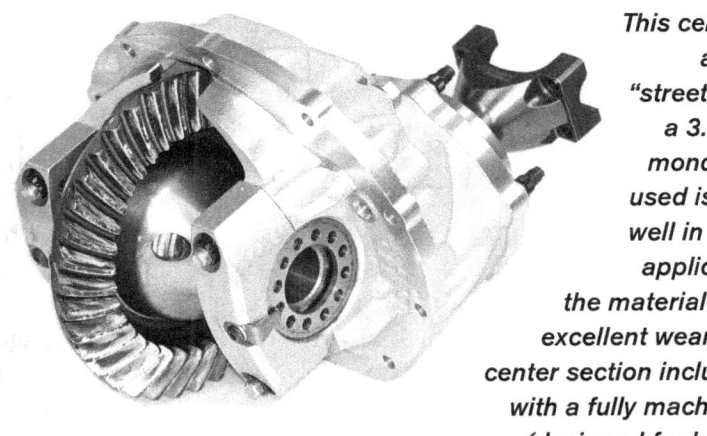

This center section is based around "standard" or "street" gears (in this case, a 3.89:1 ratio from Richmond Gear). The material used is 8620 steel. It works well in oval track and street applications. Furthermore, the material was heat-treated for excellent wear and service life. The center section includes a Detroit Locker with a fully machined billet-steel case (designed for huge 35-spline axles).

contemplating a drag race situation. Mark Williams notes, "An open carrier uses a set of gears to allow slip. The thing to remember with an open carrier is that torque is always equal between both wheels. This means that if one wheel is slipping, the other is only able to apply as much torque as the slipping wheel.

"A spool is a single piece carrier and does not offer any compensation for different rotating speeds in the wheels. Because of additional stresses created by a spool, it is not a good idea to run stock-spline axles with a spool. Spools should be run in race only–type applications and are not intended for use on the street.

"Lockers use a ratcheting technique in combination with a cam to ensure that both wheels are locked together. The locker does not allow the wheels to spin at different speeds as long as there is forward torque on both wheels. The unit allows the outer tire to ratchet while turning a large radius such as cornering.

"Torque Sensing differentials use mechanical means to control slip. They are rated with a bias, such as 5:1, that rates the amount of torque the unit is capable of applying to the non-slipping wheel. For instance, if you are spinning with 20 ft-lbs of torque, the non-spinning wheel is able to receive 100 ft-lbs in a 5:1 ratio. In a case where there is no torque on the loose wheel, the differential does not apply torque (this is why they recommend off-roaders apply the brakes when they slip). With an adjustable bias, you can tune the differential to your needs.

"Posi-Traction is similar to an open carrier and uses a set of clutches to apply torque to both axles. The clutches are pre-loaded by springs and the separating action of the spider gears increases the pressure on the clutch discs. Different clutch materials can be used as well as different static preloads to change the amount of torque needed to make the wheels slip."

For a street/strip Nova, it's difficult to beat a Detroit Locker. I dig deep inside the Locker elsewhere, but for a strip-only Nova, your best bet is a spool. Spools are available in both steel and aluminum. On the steel spool side, Williams' spools begin as 4140 steel forgings that are CNC-machined, and heat-treated using the same austemper process as axles. During the machining process, the ring gear register and the bearing diameters are precision ground to ensure zero run out on the ring-gear mount surface. The cross section beneath the ring gear register is increased to prevent ring gear deflection. Lightweight steel spools incorporate lightening holes drilled through the hub of the spool, as well as a profile-milled ring gear flange. This reduces weight by as much as 25 percent over the standard steel spool, and it doesn't sacrifice strength.

Standard steel spools for 9-inch Fords are available in 28-, 31-, 35-, or 40-spline axle configurations. Lightweight steel spools are available only in 35- or 40-spline configurations. The 35-spline spools require a stock 2.893-inch case or a 3.062-inch case. The 40-spline spools require a 3.250-inch-bore case, 45-mm wheel bearings, and matching housing ends.

Aluminum spools are manufactured from 7075-T6 alloy forgings (they're gold coated following

In the Ford rear, after the pattern and backlash have been established, you must set the preload on the differential bearings. This is accomplished using these adjusters. In practice, the adjusters are first snugged by hand only (both sides). Typically, each adjuster must be moved anywhere from .004 to .006 inch (depending on the bearings used). The holes in the adjusters are a guide. Rotating the adjuster from one hole to the next provides changes in preload. A spanner wrench is used to set the adjuster, and then it's locked in place.

machining). An aluminum spool is approximately half the weight of a profile-milled steel spool. They're available for 28-, 31-, 35-, and 40-spline axle combinations (keep in mind that the guidelines for case and wheel bearing sizes mentioned above still apply).

The 9-inch Ford pinion support assemblies are available for a number of applications, Novas included. The support housings for the Mark Williams components are CNC-machined from aircraft-quality aluminum and use either oversized tapered roller bearings or low-friction angular contact ball bearings. All pinion supports come preassembled. The bearing pre-load is set through the use of a solid, hardened pre-load spacer rather than a crush sleeve or stack of thin shims. The spacer is factory machined to the required pre-load for each assembly. Pinion seals are included. Housings are drilled to accommodate the 7/16-inch studs used in all MW cases. That doesn't preclude the use of these custom pinion supports in a stock Ford case. By using special reducer bushings from Williams and accompanying studs the housing can also be used with stock-style 9-inch Ford cases equipped with 3/8-inch threads.

Dana 60

If you want a big brute of a rear end under your Nova, look no further than a Dana 60. Even in the heyday of the muscle car, Dana 60s were renowned for their strength, along with being difficult to locate. Today they're incredibly easy to track down. For example, Strange Engineering and DTS offer a full range of heavy-duty, bolt-in rear-end assemblies for many popular applications, including our favorite, the 1968–1974 Nova. The truth is, in modified form, you can now build a better rear than a Dana (an example is the 12-bolt that I discussed earlier), but for street-driven cars it's a decent choice.

Dana 60s are equipped with a huge, 9¾-inch-diameter ring gear, and when fitted with a contemporary Posi-Traction setup (there are several, including Detroit Lockers), the axle splines increase to a hefty 35. The pinion is a large, 1⅝-inch-diameter affair (29-spline) that can be set up to accept massive Spicer 1350-series universal joints. Gear ratio choices prove to be plentiful too, ranging from 3.31:1 to 7.17:1. As you can

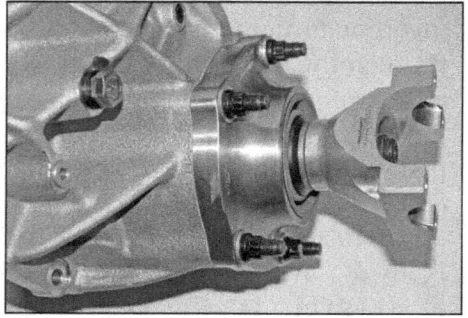

For a street-driven Nova, a tapered-bearing pinion support such as this Mark Williams version is what you need. This piece is engineered to work with OEM-style 1.313-inch-diameter 28-spline pinion gears. The aftermarket also offers Ford 9-inch pinion gears in 35-spline derivatives (1.875-inch diameter). Don't confuse the pinion spline with the axle spline. Large pinion gear sets are only available in 9310 alloys, which are specifically designed for the shock loads drag racing places upon them.

Mark Williams includes a special billet yoke machined from 4340 steel in its pro/street center section (in this case, "pro" doesn't necessarily mean fat back tires). They use special tooling to ensure that the yoke is machined concentric to the pinion spline (not always the case with pinion yokes). These yokes are engineered to accept a huge Spicer-style 1350 universal joint.

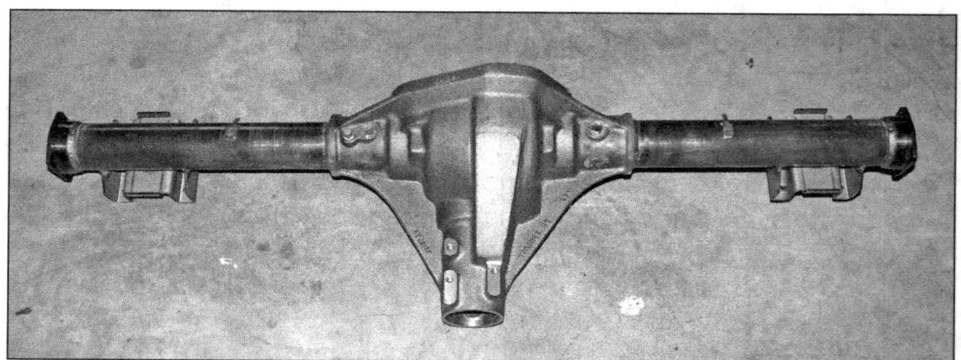

Strange Engineering came up with the idea of improving upon the vintage Dana 60. Its version is dubbed the "S-60," and it's full of neat tricks and rear-end innovation. As pointed out elsewhere, it's available in any number of configurations from a bare housing without ends and brackets to a bolt-in Nova housing (as shown here) all the way up to a complete rear axle assembly.

REAR AXLE

The Strange S60 center section is cast from premium nodular iron, and so are the large bearing caps. Like the 12-bolt shown earlier, this is one beefy rear end.

Production line Dana 60s have the axle tubes pressed into place and plug welded. The Strange S60, on the other hand, has the tubes cleanly rosette-welded and then each tube is totally welded to the case. Welding the axle tubes to the case prevents them from rotating under hard use.

Strange includes these internal adjusters as standard equipment in the S60 case. This allows for easy backlash setup.

Check out the material under the main caps. In a conventional Dana 60 this large support doesn't exist. Strange added this material where it counted and shaved bulk off the exterior of the case. Overall, the S60 case is thicker than a standard Dana 60.

The housing ends are similarly welded to the axle tubes. This is what a proper weld on a housing end looks like. For this Nova application, a small-bearing GM housing end is used. This allows the use of a stock GM drum brake backing plate.

see, the Dana 60 has always been the bully of the boulevard when it comes to rear-end housings.

But that's not the end of it. Strange Engineering's Dana 60 (dubbed the "S60") isn't exactly a piece-by-piece clone of the original. Instead, it's jam packed with interesting technology, much of it garnered from lessons learned in the drag racing trade. Essentially, the Strange Engineering team took the stock Dana 60 and filled it with a full complement of modern features.

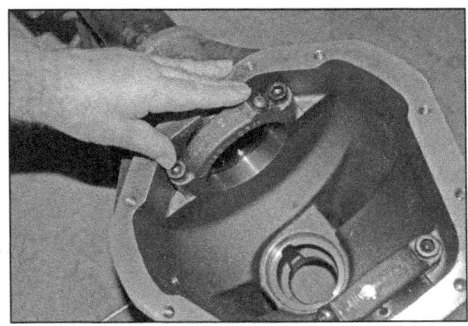

In a conventional Dana 60, it's not uncommon to replace the caps with billet-steel models because they add strength. When stressed (big power, big tires, sticky pavement), the car attempts to force the carrier right out of the back. The fix isn't required here. The extra material within the case prevents the carrier from migrating. Note the hefty Allen-head cap screws included in the mix.

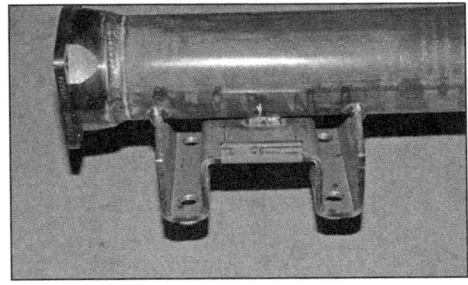

For a Nova application, Strange equips the S60 with OEM-style leaf spring perches. You can order any type of perch, including mono-leaf, multi-leaf, and Mopar style for Cal-Tracs bars. Each side is fully welded (wherever accessible).

Gear Sets

You can specify ring and pinion assemblies in at least two materials. They're most often referred to as a street gear or a pro gear. What's the difference? Mark Williams elaborates: "Pro gears are made from 9310 and then heat treated. It is a softer alloy than the 8620 street gears. The softer 9310 alloy allows the gear to absorb

CHEVY NOVA 1968–1974: HOW TO BUILD AND MODIFY

higher-impact loads that are generated in drag racing without developing cracks. A harder 8620 street gear could shatter under the same loads. As a side effect, the pro gears are not the best choice for street use because they wear faster. Also available in the pro gears is a large pinion with a 35-spline shaft for high-powered applications. This requires a bearing change in the pinion support as well as a 35-spline pinion yoke. Gears termed 9½-inchers are also available for the 9-inch third member. They offer a slight strength advantage over a standard 9-inch gear."

Axles

If you see a Nova that just pitched a wheel (most often with a chunk of the axle attached), you'll get a far better understanding of why axles are critical. It's also the reason why most race sanctioning bodies have rules that lay out what you can and cannot have when it comes to axles (case in point: some sort of positive axle retention device, which translates to *no C-clips*).

But let's start from the beginning. Original equipment automotive axles are most often manufactured from 1055 or 1541 steel, usually on the borderline between a medium- and a high-carbon steel with a relatively large manganese content. The 1055 steel has a carbon content between .50 and .60 percent, while 1541 has between .36 and .44 percent. The carbon content allows the shaft to be induction hardened. It's also easy to work with. These original equipment axles are induction hardened up to the bearing mount surface (next to the flange, induction hardening is used to selectively harden areas of a part or assembly without affecting the properties of the entire component).

With induction hardening, the axle shaft passes through an electromagnetic coil. Eddy currents are generated within the metal, which in turn heats the shaft. The shaft is then quenched. This hardening process leaves the shaft with a surface hardness of 55–58 Rockwell, penetrating to a depth of approximately .150 to .300 inch. The core of the axle remains relatively soft, but the surface is very hard, almost brittle. So far so good, but an axle with a soft flange is better suited for folks smacking curbs than it is to handle the shock loads of something such as a drag race car.

Curbs and potholes aren't the biggest concern for a dedicated Nova race car or, for that matter, a street/strip combination. More relevant factors for these applications include the load that will be placed on the axles at launch, the overall weight of the various drivetrain pieces, and of course, budget.

Calculating the amount of torque applied to an axle is easy. Take the engine torque output and multiply it by both the transmission first gear and rear-end gear ratios. If it's an automatic, the multiplication factor from the torque converter should also be added in the mix. In total, it's not unusual to see figures of more than 10,000 ft-lbs of torque transmitted to the axles. That's a bunch.

With these kinds of loads there's more to it than simply the tensile strength of the material. The ductility of the axle shaft itself plays an important role. The torsional load presented to the axle is so large that it must be able to twist and rebound like a torsion bar instead of being too stiff and ultimately snapping.

Rewind a couple of paragraphs. Recall that induction hardening used on OEM axles? While it might be great to combat impacts from curbs and potholes, something else is needed for race car and super-high-performance pieces. I turned to Mark Williams Enterprises for information on axle performance and, especially, ductility.

To achieve the kind of ductility necessary for racing purposes, Mark Williams Enterprises employs an austempering process on its nickel-chromium-molybdenum alloy Hi-Torque axles. This heat-treating process involves submerging the axle in a molten solution at more than 1,500 degrees F and then quenching the components in a molten brine solution. This results in a material structure known as

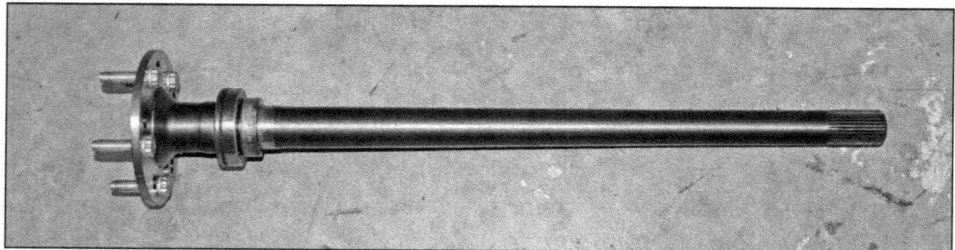

This is what a quality axle looks like after it is forged, machined, heat-treated, and assembled with bearings and wheel studs. Mark Williams Enterprises uses quality high manganese steel for its MasterLine series of axles and a more durable nickel-chromium-molybdenum alloy for the Hi-Torque series. A 300M alloy is also offered for extreme-duty use. This is a Hi-Torque pro/street axle.

Determine Axle Housing Width

Poll all of the chassis shops and they will quickly tell you that a car should be built around the wheels and tires (particularly the back ones). A good number of home-built cars are constructed that way too, but plenty aren't. If the business end of the car isn't built around the rear rolling stock, the wheel fit along with the ride height may never be right. Get the ride height wrong and you're asking for suspension grief. Ditto with the wheel fit. The bottom line here is to measure everything multiple times before ordering parts.

Fair enough, but where do you begin? The place to start is the rear-end housing. Each car is different. That shouldn't be a surprise. But if you have the back wheels and tires in hand (mounted), that's the only piece of the puzzle, aside from the car, that you need. In a few cases it's simply a matter of jamming the wheel and tire combination up inside the existing wheelwell, squaring the works up in the chassis, and measuring between the respective wheel mount flanges. You're pretty much done.

However, that's the easy route. What if you have to chop the floor, cut out the wheel tubs, or narrow or fab the frame before anything fits? And what if you don't want to cut anything up before you have a new frame or frame segment to slide under the car? After all, for some cars the floor is one of the few structural pieces that hold the body together. If you drag out the Sawzall too soon, you'll have to deal with a flexing, flopping carcass. That can make a simple job like moving the body around the shop rather difficult.

To figure out the rear width, you need some simple tools. Included in the mix are a couple of plumb bobs, a tape measure, a carpenter's square, and a straight edge. A wee bit of tape, a Sharpie marker, and a hand calculator come in handy too. Housing calculus isn't difficult. ∎

First things first: See the scribbles on the tape? First, the centerline of the rear axle in relation to the body is determined. In some cars, the back axle isn't centered in the wheelwell. Assuming everything is square, just measure between the leading and trailing edges of the lower fender and split the difference. That's the "C/L," or "center line," mark on the fender.

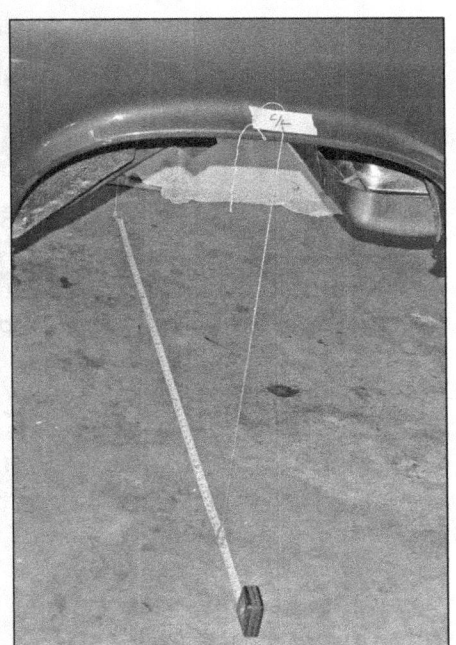

Overall, this Nova measures 72.40 inches wide. If you're wondering why I didn't measure from the inside wheel lip on each side, it's because I take clearance measurements into account later.

Drop a plumb bob down from the axle centerline on the outside edge of each fender. You can use an inexpensive carpenter's plumb or you simply use a heavy nut strung through some string. Run a tape measure from one plumb line to the other (on each side of the car).

The rolling stock is critical in determining the width of the rear-end housing. You really can't determine anything unless you have the exact wheel and tire combination in your hands. Here is a set of 16 x 10 wheels wrapped with a set of P285/60R16 tires. This setup is relatively wide and definitely tall. And no, the package doesn't fit inside a stock Nova wheelwell.

Determine Axle Housing Width CONTINUED

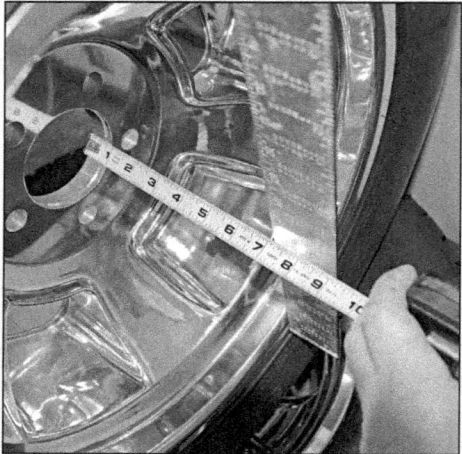 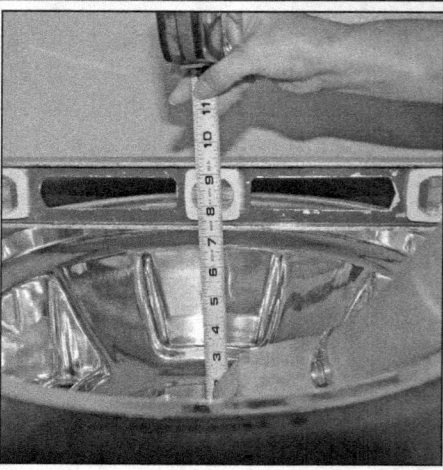

Next get the dimension from the wheel-mounting surface to the tire bulge on the curb, or outboard, side of the wheel/tire. You can use one of two methods to check the wheel face dimension. The first photo shows the tape measure stretched from the wheel mount flange (the part where the brake drum or the disc brake hat meets the wheel) to the bulge using a carpenter's square. The second photo shows another way to do it. Simply place a straight edge over the tire bulge and measure down to the wheel mount flange. Write down the number (in this case it's 7 3/16 inches).

It's a good idea to hang a square over the tire to determine overall width. It's easy on a square-shouldered radial such as this. The mounted tire is just over 12 inches in width (sidewall bulge dimension). When this figure is compared to the tire company dimensional data, the numbers prove to be a long ways off (they claim 11.4 inches for the section width). The catch: The tire specs assume the tire is mounted on an 8.5-inch-wide wheel. These wheels are 10 inches wide. The extra 1.5 inches in wheel width stretch the tire out a bit more. The point is, you really can't use printed tire dimensional data when it comes to rear-end housing measurements. Instead, measure the rolling stock you intend to use.

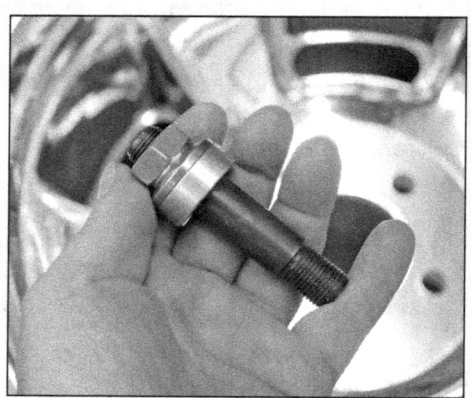 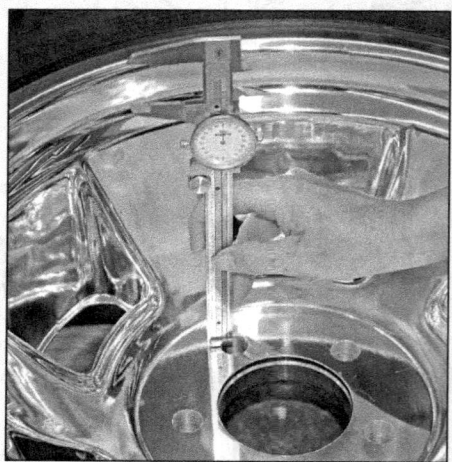

Several elements affect the clearance between the curbside of the tire and the inner fender, not the least being the thickness of the wheel at the mount flange. Case in point: the wheel studs (first photo). They're actually "drive studs," where the stud drives the wheel, not the shank of the lug nut. The drive studs in this photo measure 1.250 inches in length. Meanwhile, the wheel has a center flange thickness of 1.00 inch (second photo). That means there must be 2.250 inches of clearance between the curbside of the wheel and the inner fender to allow for wheel removal. The trimmed wheelwell lip in the back quarter measures .500 inch per side. I therefore have a minimum clearance figure of 2.75 inches per side. I add an extra quarter inch for a fudge factor. With the wheel installed, this also provides room to clear the curvature of the back fender.

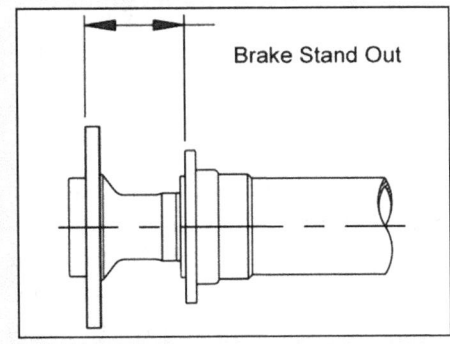

The next thing you need to figure out is the brake "stand out" dimension for disc brakes, or the drum thickness for drum brakes. Mark Williams offers several standout dimensions for its line of aftermarket discs based upon the housing end you select.

GM 10- to 12-bolt ends, 2.812 inches
Symmetrical ends, 2.834 inches
Olds ends, 2.834 inches
Mopar ends, 2.500 inches
Ford ends, 2.500 inches

Double-check these dimensions with your brake supplier. If the plan is to use a drum setup out back, take into account the drum width along with the thickness dimensions of the backing plate. (Illustration Courtesy Mark Williams Enterprises)

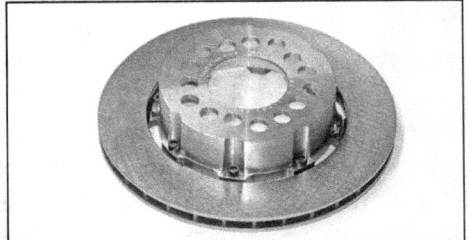

When measuring for a rear end, consider the thickness of the drum or the disc brake hat. A typical iron drum measures in the .100- to .125-inch range while disc brake hats such as those manufactured by Mark Williams have a hat thickness of .250 inch. Measure yours and write down the number.

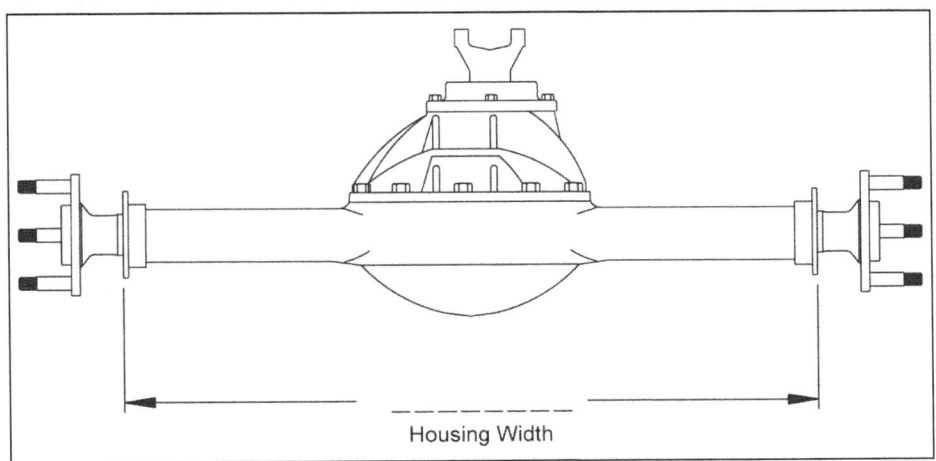

At this point, you can use your dimensions to figure out exactly what you have and what you need. (Illustration Courtesy Mark Williams Enterprises)

Bainite; it proves to be far superior to the Martinsite structure that comes with the ordinary heat treating and oil-quench processes that are commonly employed (that results in a more brittle axle). Other important benefits of austempering include higher impact and fatigue strengths, resistance to hydrogen embrittlement, a more uniform hardness, and increased wear resistance. In the end, the choice of materials coupled with the austempering process provide an axle with an ultimate tensile strength of 225,000 to 253,000 psi along with exceptional ductility (the ability to change shape or form without breaking). The shaft surface hardness is approximately 50 Rockwell, which proves to be far less brittle than an induction-hardened carbon steel axle.

If all of that is necessary to build good axles, why do you see "alloy axles" advertised so cheaply? The reality is, those components are produced by an OEM axle forging company. The main business of that company is to manufacture axles for the heavy truck and construction industries. And yes, the material used is carbon steel, common to original equipment axles. In this case, the manufacturer produces an axle blank. The companies selling those inexpensive alloy components cut the axle to length and then spline it. These axles are made from the same material as stock axles and receive the same heat treatment. The only real difference is that they are available in shorter lengths and with different splines. Now you know why they're cheap; you get what you pay for.

When you examine a set of axle splines, the outer edge of the spline defines the major diameter. The lowest portion of the groove within the spline defines the minor diameter. The minor diameter is what determines the strength of the axle shaft. The included angle of the spline (commonly called the "pressure angle") is important as well. Some pressure angles measure 30 degrees (which works out to a 60-degree included angle). But for racing applications, a 45-degree pressure angle (90-degree included angle) is superior. The reason is, the spline depth is shorter, which allows for a *larger* minor axle diameter (on a specific axle outside diameter).

Most modern axles are manufactured with a 24-pitch. If an axle has a 1-inch circular pitch diameter (the midpoint between the major and minor diameters), it has exactly 24 splines (or teeth). The distance between the centerline of adjacent splines remains constant, so as the diameter of the shaft increases, so does the number of splines. As an example, a 35-spline axle has a major diameter of 1.500 inches while a 40-spline axle measures 1.708 inches in diameter.

The actual shape of the spline is important too. Original equipment axles are manufactured with what is called an "involute spline." This means the face of each spline is slightly curved. This type of spline provides for an optimum contact patch along with even pressure while engaged. But there's a hiccup: You can't re-create an involute spline by way of fly cutting (re-splining). That results in a straight-cut spline. To manufacture an involute spline, you must hobb the spline. Hobbing is a machining process that incorporates a special type of mill. The teeth, or splines, are progressively machined into the component by a series of cuts made by a cutting tool, which is called a hob. It is possible to fit (and use) a fly-cut flat-axle spline into a spool or differential designed for an involute spline. But what happens is the spline on the axle(s) is stressed, often considerably. Reliability diminishes. That's why it's not a good idea to mix and match splines.

But can't axles with similar spline counts be interchanged? No! For example, if you compare an original equipment 35-spline Dana axle with something such as a special MW 35-spline axle, you find they are not interchangeable because the MW spline features a 45-degree pressure angle, which (obviously) differs from the stock Dana 30-degree pressure angle configuration. Mark Williams does, however, offer Hi-Torque forged-steel axles with OEM-type splines. Because of this, be sure to get the right axle spline for the right spool or differential assembly in your Nova.

Why do some axles have a reduced diameter after the spline? For a splined shaft to carry its maximum torsional load it is necessary to have a working shaft diameter smaller than the major spline diameter. The reduced section after the spline works like a torsion bar, allowing the rotational wind up to occur over a longer area. This prevents the axle from experiencing permanent set. Axles that are not undercut twist at the end of the spline engagement and eventually fail at this point.

The actual shape of a given axle has a major influence upon ductility. For example, the MW Hi-Torque axle(s) shown in the accompanying photos taper from the axle bearing shoulder (1.774 inches) down to the minor diameter of the spline. This effectively creates a profile in the shape of a triangle. In turn, this triangulation provides the axle with more resistance to bowing (it's not uncommon for the rear end in high-horsepower cars to bow, which creates an axle toe-in situation; obviously, this has an effect upon performance). Approximately one-third of the axle remains in the minor diameter to allow for torsion bar–like twisting. The triangulated profile of the axle prevents it from permanently changing shape.

You sometimes see axles with shorter spline areas. The reason is, many axle builders gang-run axles

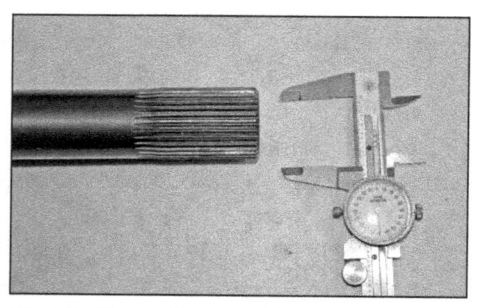

Here's the spline end (35 spline) of a Mark Williams Hi-Torque axle for a 9-inch Ford. This is actually a pro/street setup. As you can see, this 35-spline axle measures a full 1.50 inches on the OD. The axle tapers down slightly after the spline.

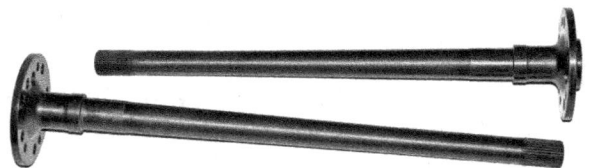

If you view the profile of the Hi-Torque axle, you see that the entire axle is tapered. There's good reason for this triangulation (which, as most know, is the strongest of geometric shapes). Williams builds axles that are designed to work like a torsion bar.

Measure for Custom Axles

In this chapter I discuss the intricacies of high-quality aftermarket axles for your Nova. It's a lot to digest, but when you're done reading and you need new (quality) axles, how do you measure for them? While that sounds simple enough, more than one person has made a critical error in axle dimensions. It's important to get it right, though, because once you have them, you have them.

Fortunately, a foolproof method exists to measure for axles. Before going any further, keep in mind that many housings make use of an offset pinion. Because of this, each axle is a slightly different length (sometimes considerably). The following method might take a bit more time to calculate than some of the quick and dirty means, but after the dimensions are established, there's no need to worry about axles being too long or too short.

This is a list of dimensions you need on a bare housing:

- A   Housing flange to flange
- B   Driver-side housing flange to pinion center
- C   Passenger-side housing flange to pinion center
- D   Wheel-to-wheel width
- E   Axle flange (driver side) to pinion center
- F   Axle flange (passenger side) to pinion center

The photos provide an easy measuring system. ∎

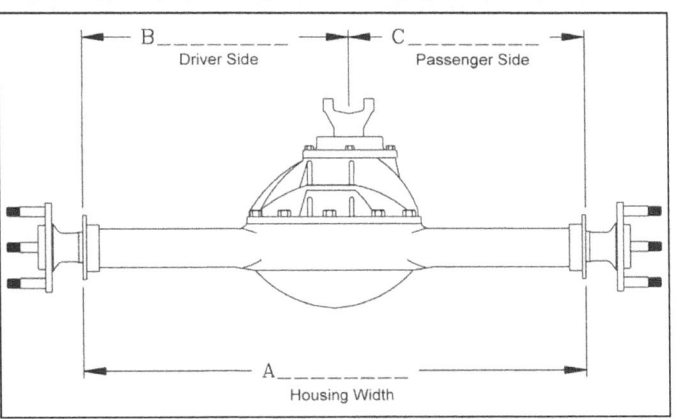

Many production cars do not have centered engines. They're often offset toward the passenger's side of the vehicle. To compensate, the pinion in some applications is also offset (for example, in some later-model Fords, the offset is just under 1.00 inch). Consequently, the passenger-side axle is shorter than the driver-side axle. By the way, Mark Williams points out that an offset to the passenger's side is normal, but a pinion offset to the driver's side is abnormal. In a race car application or one in which the driveshaft is very short, the pinion should be centered. The housing must then be constructed with the offset taken into consideration. (Illustration Courtesy Mark Williams Enterprises)

With the housing out of the car, I simply set it up on a set of axle stands with the pinion rotated to face upward.

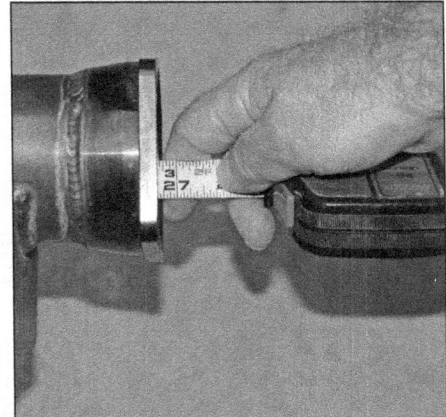

The first step is to measure the width of the housing, flange to flange. Simply run a tape measure through the bare housing to get the number. Here, I'm first measuring for offset; the total housing measures 52.75 inches wide.

Measure for Custom Axles CONTINUED

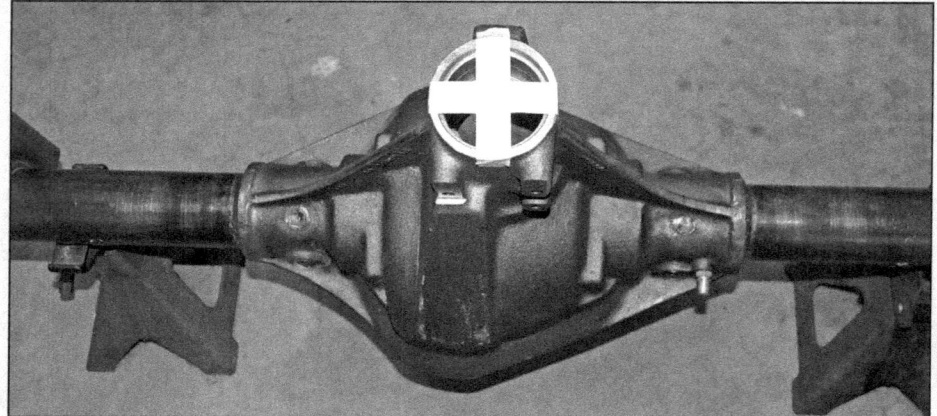

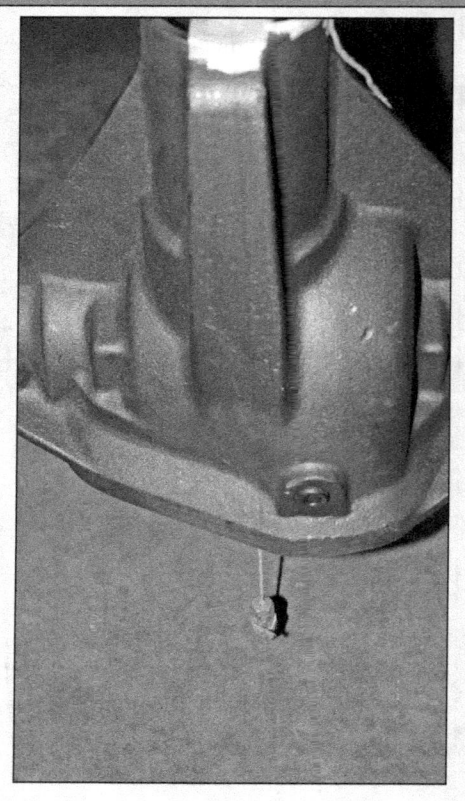

I found the centerline of the pinion and taped it over as shown here.

A plumb line was dropped from the pinion centerline out the back of the S60 housing. I measured from the axle-housing flange back toward the plumb line. The passenger's side measured 25.875 inches while the driver's side checked out at 26.875 inches. Even though the axle tubes welded to the center section are the same width, there's an inch difference in actual axles. The reason is the pinion offset. To double-check the numbers, add the pair of measurements together (25.875 inches + 26.875 inches = 52.750 inches). They should be the same as the axle flange–to–axle flange figure.

in batches in a few specific lengths. They manufacture those axles with very long splines. When the company receives an order, they simply cut off the excess spline. On the other hand, those companies with shorter splines build the axle to the correct length, which allows for 100-percent engagement in the spool or differential. If you have excess (unused) spline, the torsional capability of the axle is reduced.

On a similar note, some axles are shorter than others for a given application. The reason is, the spline location in some spools is located farther outboard. This allows for a larger (stronger) spline, but at the same time, the axles can be built shorter. This means the axles are lighter, and that's a bonus.

Finally, the shoulder of the axle bearing is another area to ponder. Standard 12-bolt Chevy axles typically

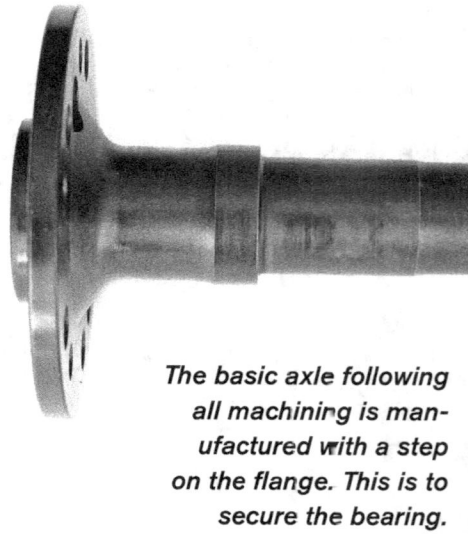

The basic axle following all machining is manufactured with a step on the flange. This is to secure the bearing.

This is a pair of axles for the same car. There's quite a difference in axle length because of the pinion offset in a Ford housing.

REAR AXLE

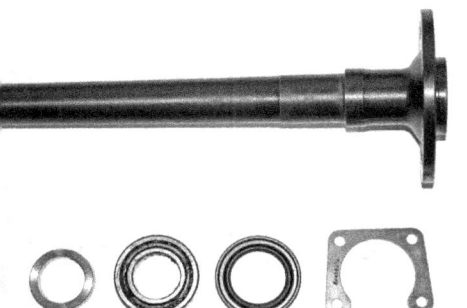

These are the basic components used to secure the axle to the housing (obviously, no C-clip is used). Below the axle and from the left are bearing lock ring, bearing, seal, and axle retainer. All are from Mark Williams.

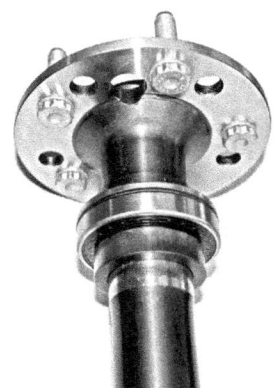

Viewed from the spline end, you can see how the bearing is pressed in place and secured. This setup uses a drag race–style wheel seal (the bearing incorporates an O-ring rather than a separate seal).

This is the flange side of the pro/street axle. Different applications mandate different flanges. A pro/street piece is thicker (heavier) than a dedicated drag race axle (for example, no worries about curbs on the strip).

have a 1.400-inch bearing (ID); a small Ford housing has a 1.378-inch ID. Most mid-range performance axles make use of a 1.562-inch ID bearing whereas a race axle such as the MW Hi-Torque is designed for a 1.774-inch ID bearing. That's a huge difference, especially when you consider that the larger the bearing, the greater the surface area to both carry weight and transfer the load.

The flange on an original equipment axle typically measures .375 inches in thickness. Wheel studs are of the press-in variety (with a knurled shank) and usually measure 7/16 inch (small GM vehicles such as the Nova and select early Mopars) or 1/2 inch (the rest). Later-model cars are usually fitted with metric studs, but again, they're of the press-in variety. Most aftermarket axles have a thicker flange. It is (most often) drilled and tapped to accept 1/2-inch-diameter screw-in studs. Quality race axles are set up for 5/8-inch-diameter drive studs.

What type of axle retention is required? Most race-sanctioning bodies require some form of positive axle retention. The original equipment C-clip (which fastens the axle on the inboard side at the very end of the spline) does not meet these requirements. Accordingly, MW offers a special bolt-in C-clip eliminator kit that provides the necessary retention. If, on the other hand, you plan on narrowing the housing, it's a good idea to change the housing ends. Weld-on aftermarket housing ends provide for a much larger (stronger) bearing and provide for positive retention by way of a hefty retainer. They can be mated to most popular brake applications (ranging from OEM drums to aftermarket disc brakes).

If you're a dedicated Nova drag racer, a big consideration should be weight. A set of lightened axles can reduce weight by at least 9½ pounds (depending upon the length of the axles and the type of rear end they're going into). As an example, one standard Mark Williams axle for a typical S/S car weighs 17.3 pounds. The same axle in a Mark Williams Super-Light configuration weighs 12.4 pounds. How is axle weight reduced? With a "gun" drilled axle. Using Mark Williams' pieces as an example, the core of the axle shaft is bored 11/16 inch to resemble a gun barrel. As you can well imagine, this requires special machine tools, but Mark Williams takes an extra step in the process (which is seldom, if ever, done by other companies): It precision hones the gun drill bore to remove tooling marks on axles produced from 300M steel. The gun drill found on the 4340 axles is actually smooth. This might seem like a small step, but the honing process improves the strength of a gun-drilled axle. Whenever Mark Williams gun drills an axle, it also includes round lightening holes in the axle flange. These two steps reduce axle weight by 17 percent over a standard axle.

This is the standard axle flange found on Mark Williams' Hi Torque axles. It's double drilled for conventional 1/2-inch studs and drag race–style drive studs.

CHAPTER 4

REAR SUSPENSION

Something many grizzled old Nova racers remember is the saying "hooks hard; goes straight." It was used everywhere, and was often attached to cars advertised for sale. It wasn't just a passing statement either. There were plenty of squirrelly cars out there (including Novas), and the truth is, there still are! Getting a car to hook properly isn't quite as easy as it looks, even with back-to-basics leaf springs out back.

All Novas used leaf springs on the rear. That makes bolting on rear traction devices quite simple. Unfortunately, simple doesn't necessarily mean adjustable. Simple doesn't always work that well either, especially if your car has serious horsepower under the hood. Furthermore, some of the traction bar information gleaned in years gone by has little or nothing to do with the way cars are set up today.

Bolt-On Bars

Ask anyone in the know about bolt-on traction bars and the first thing he (or she) will tell you is to forget the rest and go straight for CalTracs. Calvert Racing Suspensions manufactures a complete bolt-on system for 1968–1974 Novas that includes CalTracs traction bars, unique split mono-leaf springs, dedicated shock absorbers designed specifically for the CalTracs, and several tuning bits.

I look at the CalTracs springs in Chapter 5, but here's the scoop on the CalTracs bars: John Calvert and Larry Kieser designed them many years ago. Together, they developed a traction bar that hooks a (limited tire) NHRA Stock Eliminator car. The design is "tunable," easy to install and set up, and works far better than the "slapper bars" of old. It also had to fit the NHRA Stock regulations, which mandated a bolt-on bar only. For Nova applications, the CalTracs bar bolts to the front spring eye mount location and the bottom. It replaces the OEM spring seat.

Compared to a slapper bar, which pushes up on the spring when loaded, the CalTracs bar basically reverses the "pushing forces" on the car. For all intents and purposes, a slapper bar is engineered to prevent spring wrap-up. On the other hand, a CalTracs bar is much

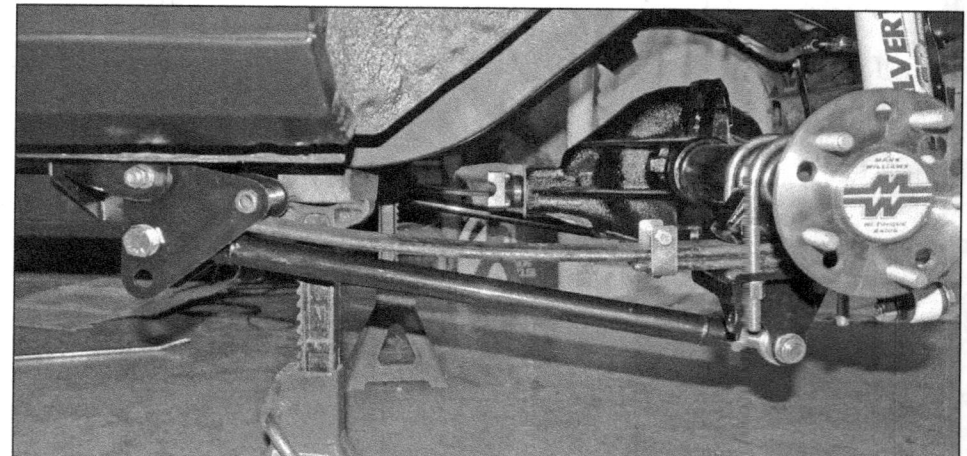

One of the best and most successful traction devices available for 1968–1974 Novas has to be the CalTracs bar. These traction bars have set the standard for most small-tire applications. Cars have run deep into the 8-second zone with CalTracs.

REAR SUSPENSION

This pivot arrangement mounts at the front of the CalTracs traction bar. When installed, it mounts over the top of the leaf spring pack. In operation, it forces down on the leaf. A conventional slapper bar primarily stops leaf wrap-up. To install the bar, the front leaf spring mount must be removed (note that in this photo, the pieces are upside down).

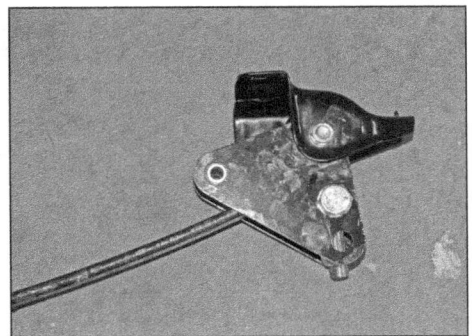

Here's another look at the front pivot; this time from the side, as installed inside the stock Nova forward leaf spring mount. Installation is simple, but keep in mind that the three OEM bolts that hold the production spring mount might be difficult to remove. If you break the captured nuts, Classic Industries has replacements in stock.

This Nova was fitted with a set of Competition Engineering subframe connectors. They bolt in for the most part; however, they do need minor trimming where they sandwich between the body (rear subframe) and the forward leaf spring mount.

This is another view of the front CalTracs pivot, as installed on the Nova (but prior to installing the lower link bar). See the smudges on the side plate on the bar? That's anti-seize. Use it on the threads every time you install a rod end; otherwise, you run the risk of galling threads (which is bad news from an adjustment point of view).

like the lower half of a four-link. The chassis instant center (IC) location is moved forward. This allows the car to pick up weight in a location near the front end of the Nova and transfer it to the drive wheels. In operation, the front pivot applies force to the front spring eye and loads with a down-force on the forward segment of the Nova leaf spring. As the rear end of the car rotates, the CalTracs bar creates a forward motion. This motion drives forward on the pivot and forward on the body. This is the opposite of a slapper bar, which drives motion upward. As a result of the forces manipulated by the CalTracs bar system, pinion angle is maintained and the Nova hooks. The Nova exhibits less body separation than with a slapper bar combination, but more weight transfer (effectively, this means serious hook). As pointed out previously, the bars feature multiple adjustment points, and it is possible to preload them as necessary. I'll get to tuning them in a moment.

Adjustment is easy, likely easier than a ladder bar or even a four-link. The bars can be moved for more preload, and depending upon the set you purchase for your Nova, they include two forward mount holes (you can

In operation (bar attached), as you load the tire with power, the link bar moves forward, which, in turn, loads the spring.

CHAPTER 4

The back end of the CalTracs bar is easy to work with too. It bolts in at the lower shock mount perch. This is much the same rear mount arrangement that's used with a good slapper bar. As you can see, the OEM factory mount location is maintained. You don't need the rubber spring seat that is sometimes sandwiched between the spring and the shock mount bracket. Obviously, the rear end isn't installed here.

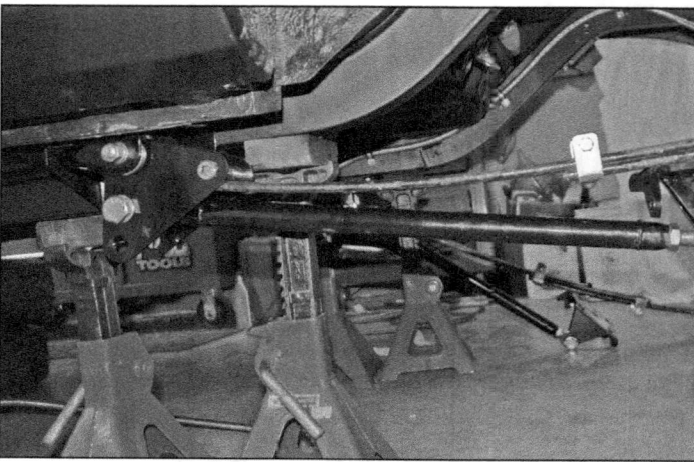

Under the front pivot is the chrome-moly lower link. A rod end is incorporated at this location, along with "wrenching flats" on the lower link for ease of adjustment. Left- and right-hand rod ends are used at both the front and rear.

purchase CalTracs bars with a single forward mount location, but that restricts tuning capability). When the force link bar is moved to the lower mount location, the IC moves farther forward. This allows nose-heavy applications (for example, an all-steel iron-head big-block such as an NHRA-legal B/Stock Nova) to transfer weight to the rear (and hook).

I'll tell you right now that a well-set-up Nova with CalTracs has outstanding traction capability without any extra fabrication. The bottom line here is, you simply bolt them on and tune the bars for the track or road surface and the horsepower conditions. Lots of folks run them on the track and, yes, an equally large number is run on the street (although they can be a bit noisy when the leaf spring is loaded under power).

Tuning CalTracs

Unlike a four-link Nova, which can be adjusted by way of the suspension links, shock, and strut settings, a stock Nova–style leaf spring suspension system is adjusted in a slightly different manner. The big change is the way you deal with the back end. As mentioned earlier, with CalTracs, changing instant center comes from the link attaching point (upper or lower hole). Preload settings have an effect upon the action in the back of the Nova, and preload on one side or the other helps steer the car while the front wheels are in the air, much the same as an upper bar in a four-link or an anti-roll adjustment.

For the setup, try this: Starting at the front of the Nova, ensure that the front end is not binding. "Stiction" in a bushing (for example, a poly bushing) tends to induce front-end binding. With a dedicated drag car or a street/strip Nova, what you really need is either a bearing or rod end, or a Delrin bushing in the control arm. Front springs should be "soft," which is achieved with either a special drag race spring or something like a 6-cylinder spring with a small-block or a small-block spring with a big-block (engine). You need something in the range of 5 to 6 inches of travel. This is a case where more is better. You need a "loose" shock. The CalTracs shocks for Novas are 90/10 jobs and they're perfect for the application. If you use adjustable shocks, set them full loose for the baseline. You can adjust them from this point.

At the back of the Nova, again check for binding. The most likely spots for suspension bind are at the rear spring shackle and/or the front mount bolt (the one that passes through the spring eye). In many

You can sometimes use a slider instead of a shackle, but for a street-driven car, it's best to stick with the tried and true rear shackle arrangement. Be sure the shackle and spring bolts are not over-tightened. That causes them to bind.

REAR SUSPENSION

Adjusting the length of the lower bar determines how much space you have between the load bolt and the spring. Shortening the bar increases the space; lengthening the bar decreases it.

This is the load bolt mentioned in the previous photo. When you set up the CalTracs bar, the consensus is to run a gap with the thickness of a dime as the baseline.

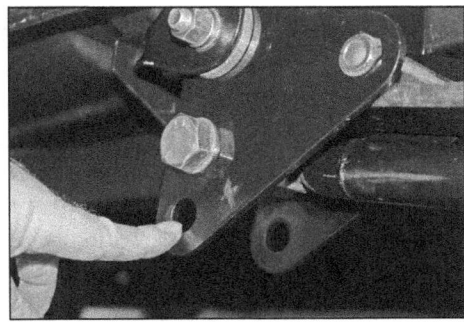

The upper front hole (where the bar is currently attached) makes for a more violent hook than the lower hole (where I'm pointing). If the car flattens the tire on the hook (squashes the tire to a flat shape), move the bar to the lower hole.

cases, the shackle bolts and spring eyebolts are over-tightened. Lube the bushings too. Without the shocks and the CalTracs bars in place, you should be able to easily push the rear of the car down several inches by hand. If the car doesn't move, the suspension is most likely binding.

Begin with the upper adjustment hole in the CalTracs bars. Set the preload on the CalTracs at 1/16 inch. Rather than use the 1/16-inch preload, some folks use a dime and set up the bars so that the dime just slides out from between the spring and the load bolt.

For now, set the rear shocks at full tight (extension). At this point, you're ready to test the car. What follows are several scenarios you're likely to encounter.

- The Nova works perfectly!
- The Nova hooks and wheelstands. If the wheelstand is huge, tighten down the front end. You can do this with the shock and/or a suspension travel limiter.
- The Nova hooks, but starts spinning the tires when it's past the Christmas tree. Loosen the extension on the rear shock absorbers. Try loosening them by one adjustment "click" until it hooks without blowing off the tire.
- The Nova hooks but it pulls to the right or to the left. Add a small amount of preload to the side the car pulls toward.
- If the Nova hooks too hard and wads up the tires (hits the tires too hard), move the bar into the lower front mount position and re-tune using the above steps.

If your Nova hooks and then wheelstands violently, you need to reduce front-end travel. See that long Grade-8 bolt on the top of the front control arm? To tie down the front end, the bolt must be tightened.

If the Nova hooks hard but then turns (spins) the tires, try loosening the back shocks. This is easy enough with an externally adjustable shock, as shown here (Calvert Racing single adjustable). Chapter 5 has more information on shock settings.

CHEVY NOVA 1968–1974: HOW TO BUILD AND MODIFY

The most common mistake a tuner makes with a CalTracs setup is to tune it like a big-tire car. For example, if you leave the starting line using a transbrake, don't leave with the RPM too high. That (obviously) turns the tires. If you leave the starting line off the foot brake, use a two-step. It adds consistency to the launch. With a stick shift combination, too much clutch air gap, too much clutch base pressure, and too much RPM (basically a violent clutch setup) make the tires spin.

Four-Links and Ladder Bars

If you've decided that bolt-on bars aren't for you, the logical options include a ladder bar setup or a four-link. Let's start at the beginning. When a Nova launches at the dragstrip the rear end wraps up. No news to anyone. The purpose of a traction device (ladder bar or four-link) is to turn that wrap-up into forward motion. Consider the case of a ladder bar. This is a simple device constructed in a triangle-like shape that connects the rear-end housing to a point on the frame. Excessive suspension wrap-up is prevented by pushing up on the frame at the point of forward connection on the frame rail (basically the point where the upper and lower bars of the ladder bar intersect). This intersection point is where the car is "picked up." A ladder bar car has two "pickup points," one on each side of the Nova.

Consider what happens when the ladder bars push up on the chassis at the pickup point. The respective bar on each side of the car also pushes down on the tires and wheels. This effectively "plants" the tires, which in turn make the car hook.

That all makes sense, but over time it didn't take long for racers and hot rodders to figure out that changes in that pickup point location can have a sizeable influence upon the way the car reacts. If, for example the pickup points were situated rather high and short (closer to the back axle), the car would launch violently. This regularly resulted in the tire wadding up at the launch. Following this hit to the tire, load transfer usually wasn't sufficient to maintain traction. The car would start to turn the tires again. The excessive initial hit to the tire coupled with the inability to maintain load transfer, caused the ET of the car to suffer. That wasn't the end of it either. A ladder bar with a short, high pickup point usually creates major body separation during the launch. With body separation, the rear of the body drastically rises above the wheels and tires. It looks wild, but it also can result is horrendous driveshaft alignment, and that can spell serious grief for universal joints, driveshafts, tail shaft housings, and even third members.

What if, instead of a short, high pickup point, you had a long, low pickup point? This arrangement tends to hit the tires with less violence, but it can still generate more total load transfer to the rear tires. For most Novas, this is generally an acceptable situation, but if you go too far, the chassis may squat markedly (again, not good for universal joint angles) or, worse, shake the tires.

If there is a downside to ladder bars and four-links, it is that ladder bars allow less body roll than a four-link and a four-link has less body roll than a bone-stock leaf spring suspension system. Neither a ladder bar nor a four-link is perfect on the street. To be perfect, the suspension must be capable of rolling independent of the body (for example, when one wheel hits a pothole). Basically, both setups allow for some of this roll, but less than a stock rear suspension system. Does that make them a bad choice? Not really, because there's a catch: The majority of street/strip cars (Novas included) equipped with a ladder bar or four-link suspension setup are tubbed and fitted with tall and wide tires. Those big tires actually add suspension to the car.

Tuning

The big question with a ladder bar setup is this: Is it possible to make the ladder bar adjustable so that you can tune it from a range of short, high pickup point to long, low pickup point? It's not that easy. It can be accomplished with several ladder bars along with several forward ladder bar mounting positions. If you begin with a four-link, pro chassis builder Jerry Bickel notes, it is entirely possible to create both pickup point extremes (short and high versus long and low). That's

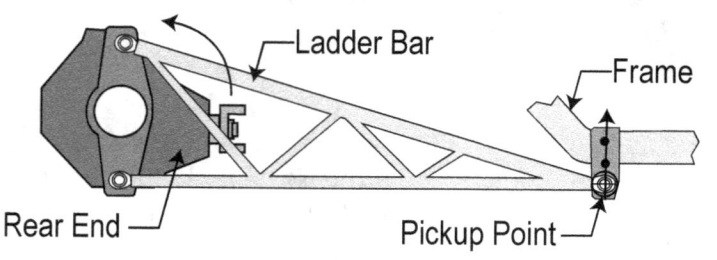

With a ladder bar, pickup points are limited. You can move them up or down. If you want to shorten or lengthen them, you need another ladder bar (shorter or longer). (Illustration Courtesy Jerry Bickel Race Cars)

REAR SUSPENSION

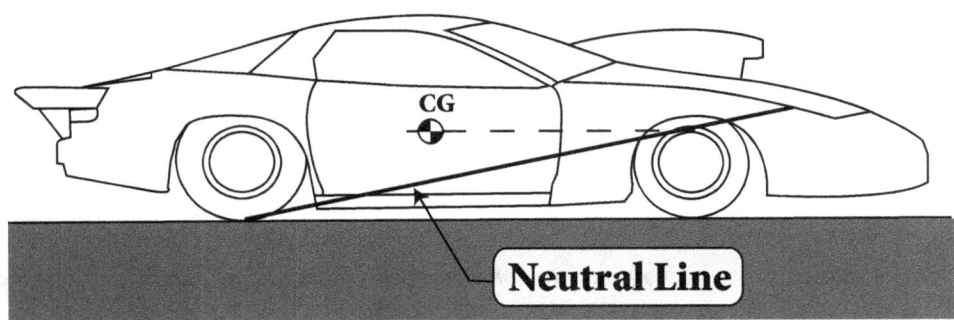

The neutral line in the chassis is where the car's body neither squats nor separates on the suspension. (Illustration Courtesy Jerry Bickel Race Cars)

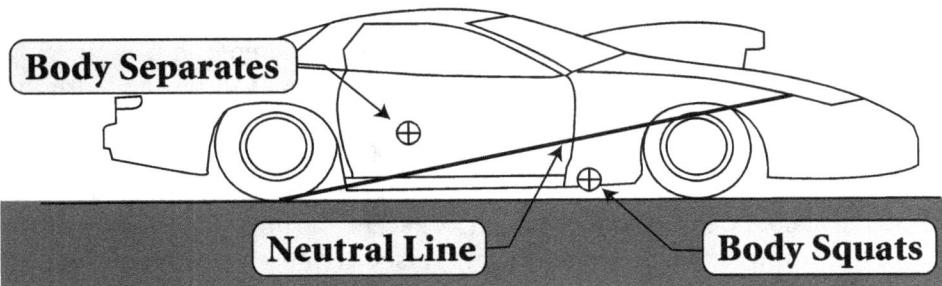

When it comes to "imaginary" pickup points, the ideal location would be somewhere close to the neutral line, as shown here. (Illustration Courtesy Jerry Bickel Race Cars)

why four-link suspension systems are more versatile on the track.

What is the ideal pickup point location? It depends on multiple factors; however, there is one constant. All cars have a neutral line that determines how the chassis behaves. If the pickup point is located about this line, the body separates upon acceleration. If the pickup point is located below this neutral line, the body squats.

In a perfect situation, the front pickup point should be located near the neutral line. This setup ultimately works well and proves to be very stable. The Nova neither shows squat nor encounters excess body separation. The question is, how do you figure out the neutral line location? Most pros feel that the neutral line of a drag car can be determined by extending a line level with the height of the CG (Center of Gravity) until it crosses a vertical line through the front spindle. The neutral line can be represented as a diagonal that intersects this location as well as the center of the rear tire–to–pavement contact point.

So far so good, but according to chassis wizard Jerry Bickel, there are several difficulties with this method, "It is difficult to measure the height of the CG accurately. Most racers use the camshaft centerline as the CG height, but without an accurate measurement, it is impossible to locate the neutral line with precision.

"Another problem with this traditional neutral line location theory is that many drag race cars wheelstand through low gear. After the front tires are in the air, I do not believe that they have an effect upon neutral line location. Experience has shown that the pickup point distance from the rear axles is at least as important as its height.

"In practice, I find that pickup point location must be changed, depending upon racetrack conditions and vehicle performance. You should rely on conventional neutral line theory only as a starting point for rear suspension setup."

Chassis Instant Center

Fair enough, but what you need is an idea of something called the "instant center." What's that? The instant center, or "IC," is an imaginary point about which the chassis

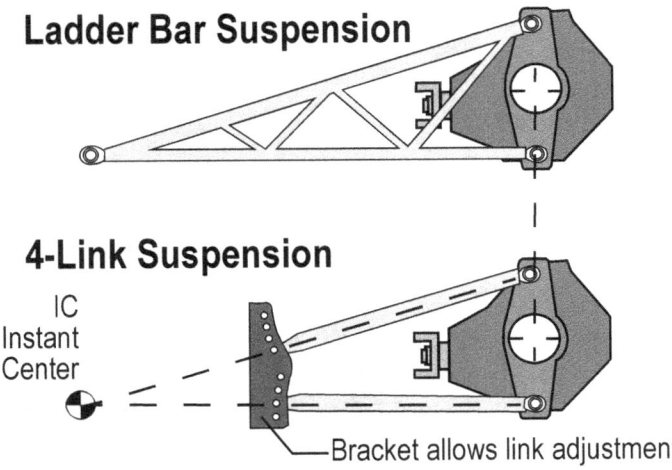

A ladder bar is very limited when it comes to setting up the instant center (pickup point), but a four-link offers many possibilities. (Illustration Courtesy Jerry Bickel Race Cars)

or a suspension member rotates (in a given or "instant" position) with power applied to it. You can find it by simply projecting lines along suspension members to a point of intersection. This is easy enough on a ladder bar. The intersection point is regularly the front rod end. However, it can move to any number of locations with a four-link. If you examine Jerry Bickel's drawing carefully, you can see that the four-link instant center is invisible, and that invisible point is the actual "pickup point" for the rear suspension.

Because the respective brackets found on something such as a four-link are under load during acceleration and braking, they must be robust. When the Nova accelerates, the rear end wraps up, placing the upper bars in tension while the lower bars are held in compression. As you brake, the forces are reversed. But I digress.

Establishing Four-Link IC Location

When you or your chassis builder install the rear end in your Nova with a four-link setup, that's the time to decide exactly which bracket holes you use for the links. The location where the four-link (front mount bracket) is installed determines the length and height of the instant center. That in turn determines how the car works. Bickel says that if the tire is driven down too hard by way of the IC location, it tends to fold up the sidewalls, which in turn makes for poor surface contact. If the four-link doesn't apply sufficient force to the tire, it spins. If you look closely at Jerry's illustration, it's easy to see the many possible IC locations in a four-link. Pick the one that works best for your car, but it's not cut and dry.

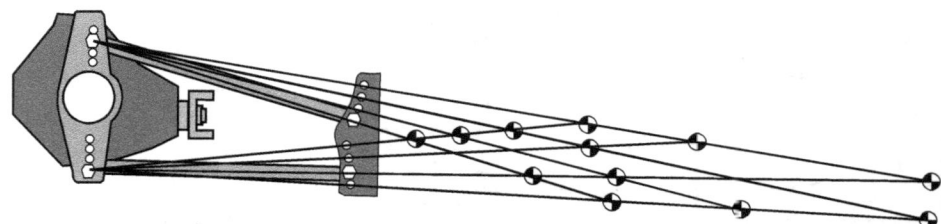

This is a look at the many possible combinations you can come up with for tuning the instant center on your Nova. (Illustration Courtesy Jerry Bickel Race Cars)

So where do you begin? Jerry offers a very simple explanation to choose the IC pickup points, "Long, low-intersect points create traction for the longest time, but react slowly. Short, high-intersect points create traction for the least time, but react fast."

Figuring Instant Center Length

IC can affect the overall vehicle reaction time (this includes the Nova and you). If you have good reactions to a light, a long IC point (50 to 60 inches) works better than a short one (50 inches or less). The long IC plants the tires smoothly and tends to keep them planted for a considerable length of time. Earlier, I noted that if you lay down too much initial power coupled with a long IC point, you will likely end up with tire shake. Tires "shake" when they become oval shaped and consequently become unbalanced under power.

That brings me to the torque output of the engine in your Nova. Bickel has an example, and although the first one probably doesn't apply to a four-link Nova, it does offer a lot of insight into how this all works. "Racers of high-powered Pro Mod cars often use tires that were initially designed for solid suspension Funny Cars and Top Fuel dragsters. The sidewalls of these tires are tall and very flexible, acting like a sort of spongy suspension system. They work best when you limit the rear movement to as little as possible with an IC point on or near the neutral line of the car.

"Further to this, I like to run a long, low IC point in an application such as a high-RPM low-horsepower

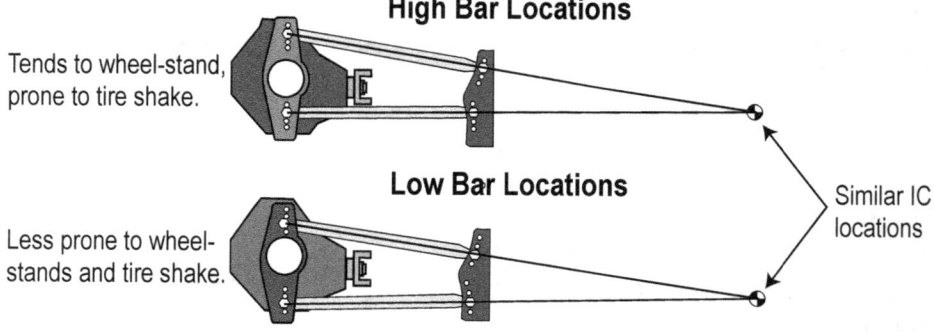

This is where four-link tuning gets interesting! As you can see, there are several ways to come up with the same instant center (or at least instant centers that are close). One tends to wheelstand and/or rattle the tires. The other does not. (Illustration Courtesy Jerry Bickel Race Cars)

small-block clutch car. This combination seems to help overcome the impact from the high-RPM launch and the engine usually doesn't have enough power to shake the tires."

Remember when I initially discussed location of the bars in the four-link? If you have a side view of a four-link, the location of the bars in relation to the centerline of the rear axle makes a difference in performance, even if the IC point remains the same. The closer to the housing the upper bar is, therefore, the less the car tends to wheelstand. When the bottom four-link bar is located lower in the car the suspension maintains better traction control, and at the same time, is less prone to tire shake.

Figuring Instant Center Height

The neutral line (examined previously) slopes within the car from the front to the rear. Bickel states that, should you decide to change the length of the IC, you must also change the height to maintain the same anti-squat characteristics.

When it comes to IC height settings in your Nova chassis, the farther forward you move the Instant Center, the lower it must be. The farther back you move the IC, the higher it must be.

Some other food for thought is this (again, taken from Jerry's tuning bag of tricks): Automatic-transmission cars along with lower-torque stick-shift cars work best when the IC point is from 1 to 2 inches above the racing surface. Big-power stick-shift cars typically need to stay 3 to 7 inches above the racing surface.

The bottom line here is, you must take your time setting up a four-link for your Nova. Jerry recommends you follow the above methodology and make only one change at a time.

It's very important to keep notes of the changes too.

Before moving on, there's something you should consider if you chose to use a ladder bar or four-link in your Nova and you want to retain the factory leaf springs: With this arrangement, the suspension is placed in a bind as it travels up and down. If it binds it bends the ladder bars (or four-link) or the leaf springs. Or both. There are a couple of solutions: You can use ladder bars with slotted front mount points or a housing floater. With either of these setups (and leaf springs), the ladder bars (or four-link) control suspension movement and front to rear, rear axle placement. However, they do not control side-to-side motion, at least not very well. You still need some form of lateral link (more on this later). In the end, though, using leaf springs and ladder bars (or a four-link) isn't much fun; it's a noisy, bulky setup, and if you've gone this far you're far better off with coil-over springs out back.

Pinion Angle

The rear suspension in a Nova under power experiences "wrap up," and with it the pinion is driven upward (out of whack). Rear axle and driveshaft manufacturer Mark Williams notes that the optimal angle for any driveshaft to run at is 1/2 degree, where many vibration and friction problems are non-existent. To minimize power loss and vibration in an offset configuration, the pinion centerline and the transmission centerline need to be parallel. In general, the largest angle for high-performance applications should be 2 degrees, and the centerlines should be parallel within a few tenths of a degree.

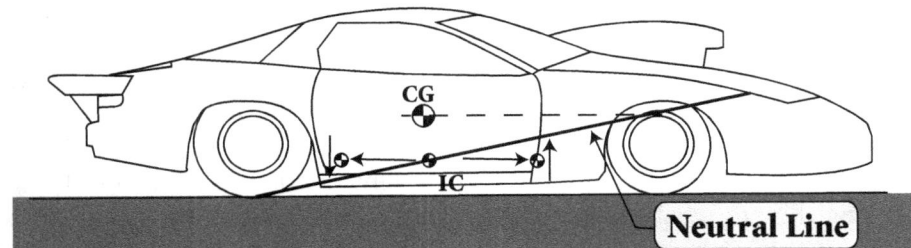

This drawing shows why changes in the instant center length must be accompanied with a change in instant center height. (Illustration Courtesy Jerry Bickel Race Cars)

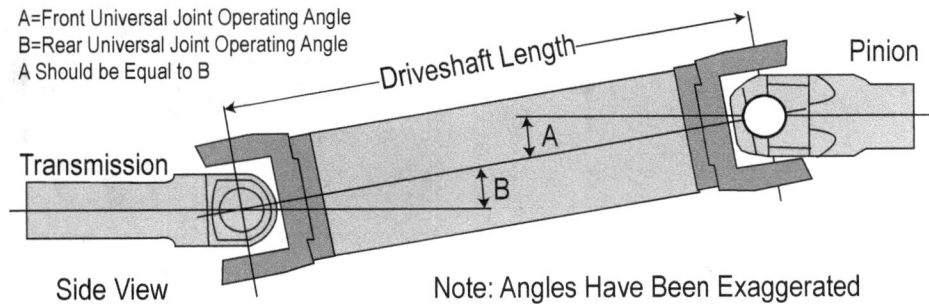

Pinion angle is critical in any car, and your Nova is no different. If you don't get the pinion angles sorted out, you'll be chasing trouble (which usually translates into broken parts) for a long time. (Illustration Courtesy Mark Williams Enterprises)

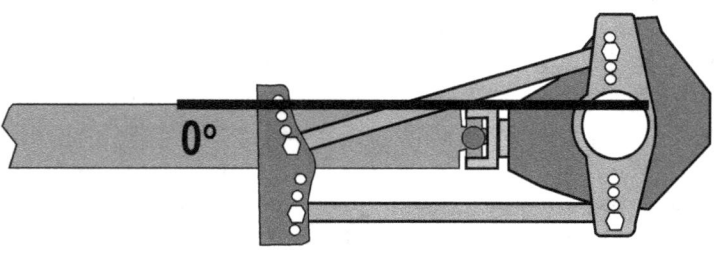

Under power, the pinion angle should be zero.

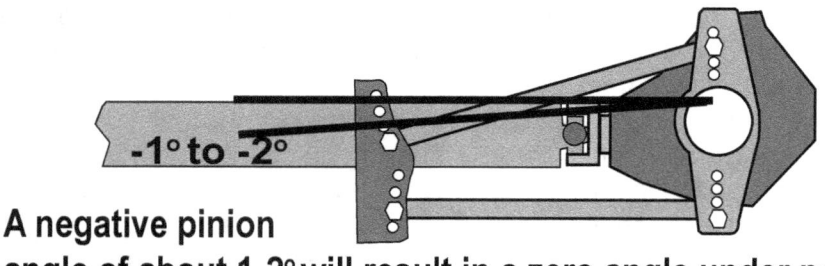

A negative pinion angle of about 1-2° will result in a zero angle under power.

Bickel goes on to show that with a race-style four-link, you most likely need a pinion angle nosed downward of 1 to 2 degrees to obtain a pinion angle of zero while under power. (Illustration Courtesy Jerry Bickel Race Cars)

Jerry Bickel is quick to point out that under power, you must ensure that the pinion angle is zero. (Illustration Courtesy Jerry Bickel Race Cars)

If the chassis has some type of a parallel traction bars system, the angles should remain parallel throughout the suspension travel.

Drag race chassis builder Jerry Bickel adds, "There should be no pinion angle (0 degrees) on acceleration, or vibrations, power loss, and universal joint breakage can result."

Keep in mind that with suspension movement the operating angle increases but should not exceed a few degrees. If the parallelism of the centerlines changes, the U-joints travel at uneven operating velocities, causing vibration (this is the same problem induced by poorly phased end yokes). This vibration is hard to distinguish from an unbalanced driveshaft.

To ensure that the pinion is in the correct location under power, it is typically set nose down static. Mark Williams notes that some of the most common information (or perhaps misinformation) on setup was derived from the very early years of Mopar racing. The very early Chrysler cars had a thick spring that was subject to wind up. To try to make allowances for this wind up the pinion was dropped down a few degrees in an effort to have the centerlines running close to parallel when under power. If the car has OEM-style rubber suspension bushings, a pinion angle of -3 to -4 degrees is likely more appropriate. Williams notes that this nose-down attitude was originally done to compensate for the compression of the rubber bushings.

To set the pinion angle on a four-link car with adjustment capability (for example, a Nova with a four-link), you lengthen or shorten one or both of the upper bars to move down or up. If the Nova has stock leaf springs, you can use wedge plates (wedge-shaped aluminum shims) to move the pinion up or down. The wedge plates effectively rotate the pinion upward or downward depending on which way the wedge is facing. The wedge plates are designed to sandwich between the rear-end housing perches and the leaf springs.

Pinion angle should be checked and adjusted any time there are changes in the chassis that affect the ride height or the length and location of the suspension link bars. Prior to setting up the pinion angle, you should have the four-link instant center set, the rear end aligned, the chassis at correct ride height, the weight distribution set, the tire rollout checked, and the tire pressure set.

So far so good, but the other thing to keep in mind about the

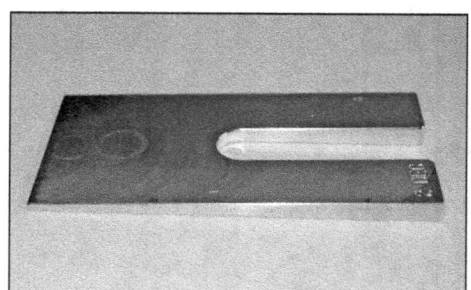

Classic Industries offers several offset wedges for leaf spring Nova applications. This particular example is a 2-degree aluminum job for a split mono-leaf (Cal-Tracs) spring. It can be used to move the pinion down (or up) 2 degrees.

The upper bars in a four-link typically are used to set the pinion angle. If you look closely, you'll see wrenching "flats" on the left-hand side of the bar. After the jamb nuts are loosened (on both sides), you can turn the bar out.

driveshaft is critical speed. Critical speed is the speed at which a spinning shaft becomes unstable. This is one of the single largest factors in driveshaft selection. When the whirling frequency and the natural frequency coincide, any vibration is multiplied, so much that the shaft may self-destruct. Another way to think of this is that if a shaft naturally vibrates at 130 times a second, and one point on the shaft passes through 0 degrees 130 times per second (7,800 rpm) then the shaft has hit a critical speed. The critical speed of a driveshaft can be raised by several means. You can make it lighter, stiffer, or increase diameter without increasing weight. This is the reason carbon fiber makes a good driveshaft; it is stiff and light and can be made to any diameter or wall thickness. Aluminum, while it has a higher critical speed than steel (same diameter and length shaft) is not quite as strong as steel. Steel, with good strength characteristics, has a lower critical speed. Because of this, it's important to check with a driveshaft manufacturer before you decide upon a specific driveshaft for a specific application.

Laterally Linked

If you've installed a four-link or ladder bar in your Nova, you must ponder a way to control the side-to-side movement of the axle housing. The only exception is if the Nova car is equipped with conventional leaf springs fitted without a housing floater. All other suspension arrangements encompass some form of coil-over spring and, as a result, a means of positively locating the rear axle laterally is required. You must be able to control this motion as the rear suspension moves completely through its travel.

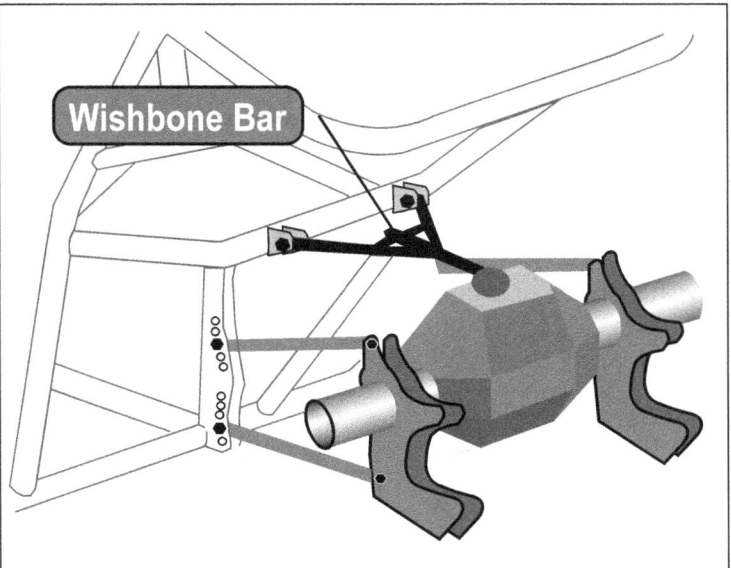

Bickel likes to mount the wishbone above the rear housing. This location provides for much easier access to the third member. It also gets the wishbone away from the road surface. (Illustration Courtesy Jerry Bickel Race Cars)

The control of lateral movement is imperative. Take, for example, a four-link setup coupled with coil-over springs (obviously, a very common arrangement); there is absolutely nothing to hold the rear axle housing from moving side to side. Without some form of lateral control to keep the housing in check, it can shift itself right out of the car. You can't drive the Nova without controlling the lateral motion.

So, what are the options for controlling this motion? Several designs are in use today. Included in the mix are diagonal bars (often called a "track locator"), Panhard bars, wishbone track locators, Watt's linkage systems, and angled trailing arms. What's best?

Before I begin, one form of suspension (the triangulated four-link) doesn't need a lateral link of any sort, but fitting one to a Nova is rare, and if you do, fabrication is a real chore.

Panhard Bar

A Panhard bar is designed to link the axle housing to the frame. Panhard bars are simple devices. They're effective too. They can be light in weight, but beefy mounting brackets usually offset that. The brackets must be large and strong and that usually translates to heavy. In operation, the arc the Panhard bar travels in must be kept as small as possible. Accordingly, the Panhard bar must be built as long as possible. The travel arc is created during suspension travel. It produces a slight side-to-side movement of the axle housing (typically you see movement of between 1/16 and 1/8 inch). If your Nova has large amounts of wheel travel and you run a Panhard bar, it's a very good idea to increase the length of the Panhard bar. There's a catch: When you build a long Panhard bar, it must clear the

Panhard bars are a good way to maintain side-to-side motion (between the car and the housing). This big, curved job is designed so that it can clear the "bump" on a rear-end housing.

differential. This can be troublesome if the housing is back braced. The most important factor when installing a Panhard bar is to ensure that the bar is parallel to the rear-end housing at ride height. For a closer look at a great Panhard bar setup, take a look at the setup used in a 1982–2002 Firebird or Camaro. The size and heft of the associated bracketry is considerable, but the geometry is spot on.

Watt's Linkage

The Watt's linkage system eliminates the small side-to-side movement that occurs when you use a Panhard bar. The downside to a Watt's link is that it is often difficult to package at the appropriate height for many chassis setups (Novas included). You need to get it set up at the Nova ride height, plus it's difficult to mount on the nose of the rear axle assembly (although it is possible). Why? A Watt's link requires a bell crank system to work. If you choose to mount the Watt's link behind the axle, the brackets must be extremely robust to handle loads that may be very high. Factor in the need for third member access and/or a back brace on the rear and you can see why there aren't many Watt's linkage systems in use today.

Diagonal Bar

Compared to a Watt's linkage, a diagonal bar is an extremely simple component that connects between the respective lower links of the suspension (most often the lower two bars in a four-link). By connecting the bars diagonally (and, of course, by using rod ends on either side of the diagonal bar), the housing cannot move from side to side, but it's free to move up and down. In some applications with considerable travel, there is some side-to-side deflection. With a diagonal bar installed in the car, at least one end must be removed to service the third member in something like a 9-inch. It's also important to note that in any application that sees cornering forces, you should not use a diagonal bar. As you go around a corner with a car using a diagonal link, the loads placed upon the front of the bar are incredible. Diagonal links sometimes bend when used in a street-driven application. For any Nova that sees any amount of street use, a Panhard bar (or even a wishbone) is a far better option.

Wishbone Bar

A wishbone bar typically connects to one bracket on the rear-end housing along with a pair of brackets on the chassis. Rod ends allow the wishbone bar to pivot as the rear-end housing moves up and down during suspension travel. The single rear rod telescopes to prevent binding, but it cannot move laterally. Wishbones are really the best choice for applications where the frame is narrow (for example, a Nova with big tubs). A point to consider with a wishbone is the clearance in the slip joint. The joint must be machined to keep clearances tight. If the joint is sloppy, you're assured some amount of side-to-side movement. Access to the third member is difficult when conventionally mounted under the housing. Equally important, a bottom-mounted wishbone is susceptible to damage on the telescope rod from debris. That's why the top-mount setup championed by Jerry Bickel is a good idea. However, with the wishbone mounted upstairs, exhaust clearance is an issue.

Controlling the Roll

If your Nova has coil-over springs on the back, it needs an anti-roll bar. If it doesn't have coil-overs (let's say it's equipped with factory leaf springs), there's a good chance it could still use one. Why is it so important? First, let's look at why you need an anti-sway device on the back of a car that mainly sees straight-line use (and keep in mind that the anti-sway bar does a far different job than a track locating device). The first thing to do is to consider the torque loads placed upon the rear housing. If you haven't considered these factors, you should, along with torque loads.

The torque produced by your Nova engine is not constant. It varies with the RPM of the engine. Basically, the engine produces a torque curve, and that curve might peak with 500 ft-lbs at 5,000 rpm. Easy enough but remember, too, that as engine speed increases or decreases from this peak in the curve, the torque produced is lower. Furthermore, if the Nova in question is equipped with an automatic (as shown in our mathematical example below), the true amount of torque delivered to the drive wheels (and, of course, through the chassis setup) is huge.

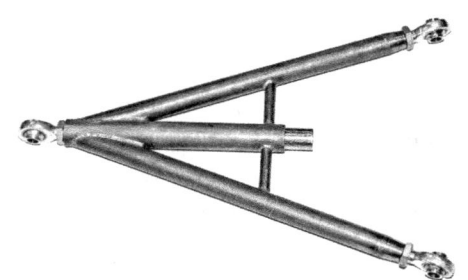

One of the best choices for rear-end control is a wishbone. The center tube contains a machined rod that telescopes as the suspension in the Nova goes through its travel. You must keep it lubed and, obviously, free of debris.

REAR SUSPENSION

> ### Calculating Maximum Torque Load
>
> Here's a hypothetical set of relatively mild (and easily attainable) Nova specifications.
>
> | | | |
> |---|---|---|
> | A | Engine Torque | 450 ft-lbs |
> | B | Torque Converter Multiplication Factor | 2.2:1 |
> | C | Transmission First Gear Ratio | 2.52:1 |
> | D | Rear Axle Ratio | 3.73:1 |
>
> Plug these numbers into the following formula:
>
> Rear Axle Torque Load = A x B x C x D
> That's 9,305 ft-lbs (450 x 2.2 x 2.52 x 3.73).
>
> Gulp. The loads working through the rear axle assembly (and, ultimately, attempting to twist it right out of the car) prove to be considerable, and that's with a mild combination. If the car dead-hooks, you could easily encounter breakage, or at least bending forces somewhere.

The maximum torque load passed through the rear axle is very easy to calculate.

I should point out that stick-shift cars do not have the benefit of torque multiplication; however, they tend to leave the starting line at a higher RPM (when compared to their automatic-equipped counterparts) and they tend to have much smaller driveline parasitic power losses. That's the reason automatics and sticks sometimes have similar performances.

Torque Rotation

Let's back up a bit and see exactly how physics forces things to happen inside a car. When you dump the clutch or leave the line with an automatic (foot brake or transbrake), something happens in the Nova. A huge amount of engine flywheel torque reaction is transferred to the chassis. And as our friend Jerry Bickel is quick to note, Sir Isaac Newton's Third Law of Motion states that for every action, there is an equal and opposite reaction.

When the engine in your Nova is running, the pistons and, eventually, the connecting rods apply torque to the crank. When you view this from the front of the car, the crankshaft rotates clockwise. Taking Newton's Third Law of Motion into account, something opposite to this must happen. That opposite thing is the engine block in your Nova. It's applying torque in the opposite direction of the crankshaft. In other words, the engine is rolling (twisting) counterclockwise.

Inertial Torque

The inertia forces created by spinning power train components should not be overlooked. Inertia is the force that causes an object to resist changes in motion. If your Nova is equipped with a manual gearbox, the engine, crankshaft, flywheel, and clutch could be spinning at 5,000 rpm or more as you sidestep the clutch at the starting line. Combined, the spinning mass of these components might weigh more than 140 pounds, storing a considerable amount of inertial energy. When you dump the clutch at the starting line (or even if you take off gradually at a stoplight), this added inertia tends to boost chassis roll.

The same applies to an automatic transmission. If you deliver too much power (and, consequently, too much inertial energy) too quickly into the drivetrain, the tires spin (no secret). That's why clutch setup and adjustment along with torque converter selection play an important role in chassis setup. The bottom line here

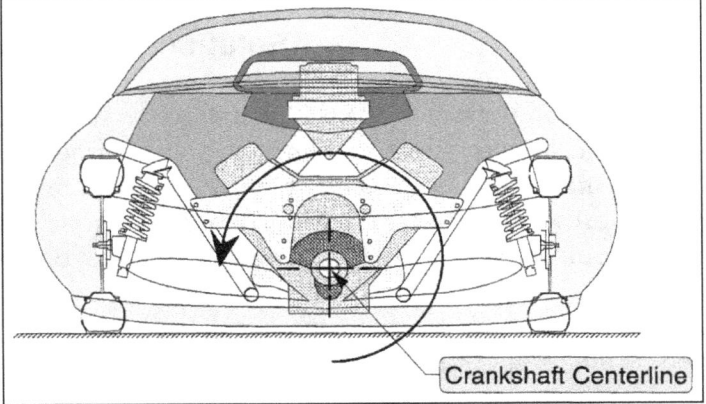

As each cylinder in the Nova engine fires, the pistons (and consequently the connecting rods) apply a force to the crankshaft. The crank rotates and applies a clockwise twisting force (when you view it from the front). Fair enough, but then our pal Mr. Newton's Third Law of Motion enters the equation. As the crank spins, an equal amount of torque is applied in the opposite direction. That occurs within the cylinder block. Obviously, that upsets the chassis. (Illustration Courtesy Jerry Bickel Race Cars)

is, with today's cheap and readily available horsepower, it's not hard to overpower the chassis with too much torque.

Rear-End Torque

The gears inside the rear end in your Nova turn the driveline power 90 degrees to the axles. This in turn produces rear-end torque rotation. What happens is that a certain amount of inertia in the chassis resists the rotation of the wheels, axles, differential (or spool), and ring gear. The resistance causes the pinion gear to convey rotational force or "torque rotation" to the rear-end housing.

This causes a car to have more traction on the left rear wheel and less traction on the right rear wheel. Rear-end torque rotation is also the reason most cars want to move right when you accelerate.

Remember Newton's Third Law of Motion? The roll in the chassis caused by engine torque should be equal and opposite that of rear-end torque reaction. A Nova constructed with a completely rigid chassis should, in theory, allow these two forces to counteract each another. As a result, the Nova could rocket straight and true down the racetrack. Unfortunately, it's not a perfect world, and you almost always end up with a certain amount of flex in the chassis. That's not to say you should build a "flexi-flier." They simply do not work and they're almost impossible to tune. What you should strive for is a chassis constructed as rigid as possible to harness the opposing twisting forces created by the torque. With a rigid platform for your Nova, spring and shock rates can be set and tuned so that you're able to compensate for weather and track conditions as well as racetrack irregularities.

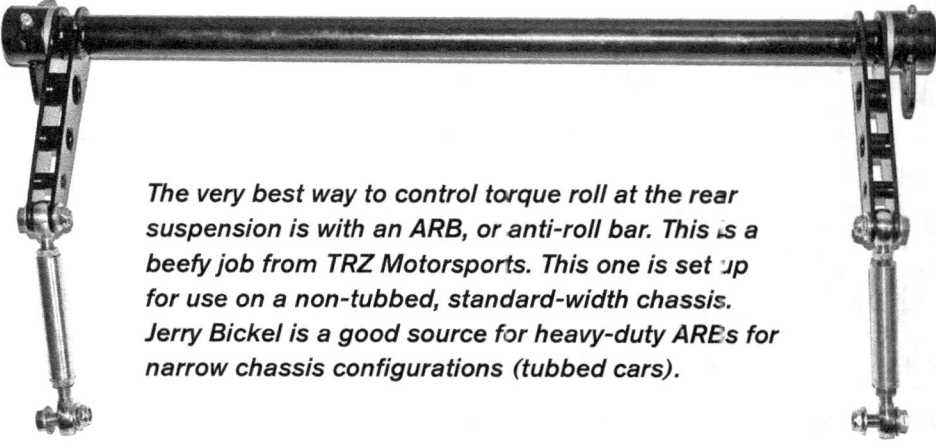

The very best way to control torque roll at the rear suspension is with an ARB, or anti-roll bar. This is a beefy job from TRZ Motorsports. This one is set up for use on a non-tubbed, standard-width chassis. Jerry Bickel is a good source for heavy-duty ARBs for narrow chassis configurations (tubbed cars).

How to Control Torque Factors

Just how can one control chassis roll? One approach is to install extremely stiff springs. Another approach used in the past and still rather common today is to install an air bag or two in or over the back springs (stock spring applications). This approach may limit roll, but it creates a very rigid suspension system that cannot comply with racetrack irregularities. If you have a big-power Nova with a ladder bar or four-link suspension and it has coil-over rear springs, you should use a rear stabilizer bar (sway bar). The bar provides significant resistance to roll, but at the same time, doesn't really affect the normal travel of the rear suspension system.

Solutions

What if you have a small-tire, stock mounting point suspension arrangement Nova and you're trying to make it hook? Or what if you have a Nova with a four-link or ladder bar setup? Several years ago I built a high-horsepower coil-spring street-driven car. It certainly wasn't a Pro Stock car, but it sure did have plenty of rotation out back. Enter TRZ Motorsports. They had (and still have) a very nice weld-in ARB (anti-roll bar) kit. FYI: Our pal Jerry Bickel also offers a wide range of ARBs designed for narrow-chassis, large-tire cars.

The anti-roll bar shown in the accompanying photos is a chrome-moly tube that pivots on bronze bushings captured within the end brackets. As with other configurations, it connects to the rear end through attaching levers and links fitted with rod ends. The stabilizer bar itself is bolted to a tubular chrome-moly cross brace that welds between the respective frame rails. On straight up and down suspension travel (no chassis roll), the attaching levers move together. The stabilizer bar simply rotates on the bushings and suspension movement is unaffected. Chassis roll, on the other hand, causes the links to pull the attaching levers into different angles,

TRZ's ARB is engineered with a bronze bushing on each end, and as you can see, it comes with grease fittings (zerks) installed.

REAR SUSPENSION

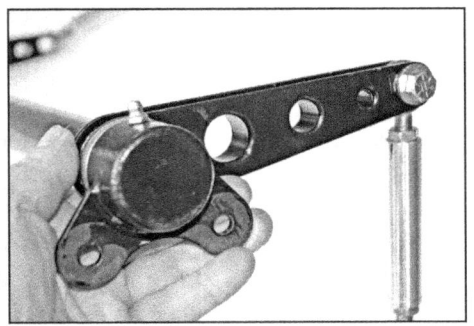

The mount pad below the bushing bolts to a tubular crossmember, which in turn is welded between the frame (or subframe) rails. TRZ supplies the mount crossmember and components with its kit.

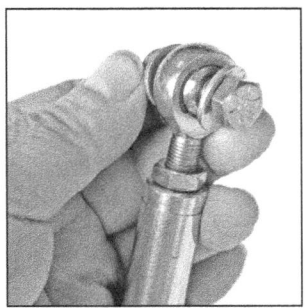

Each of the ARB arms incorporates two rod ends. A pair of rod ends bolts to a set of tabs (supplied) that are welded to the rear-end housing. One rod end per side is right-hand while the other is left-hand. You can therefore adjust the ARB by loosening the lock nuts and turning the respective links in or out.

The Basics of Rod-End Construction

What makes up a quality rod end? Basically, a rod end consists of a spherical ball engineered to rotate inside a housing. This ball does the bearing "work" while the housing wrapped around becomes the race. The rod-end ball has a machined flat on each side, and it is bored with a hole right through the center. That, of course, is the basics of rod-end construction, but as you might expect, quite a bit more goes into the equation. When scouring the marketplace for rod ends, you regularly find "economy" or "commercial" examples. Many economy rod ends are available, but the only type you should even think about are the fully "swaged" two-piece examples. When these rod ends are manufactured, the body is swaged around the ball so that the race that the ball rides on is part of the body. When it comes to the cheaper rod ends, you will find that two-piece swaged-construction rod ends are the only examples that can provide good axial strength along with decent radial or pull strength. What is "axial strength"? It's the resistance of the ball being pushed out of the side of the body.

Top-of-the-line rod ends are manufactured in a precision three-piece

Although not a Nova, this G-Body, I built several years ago shows how the ARB is installed. Adjusting the ARB links allows you to preload the chassis (which is all dependent upon how your car reacts). It works fabulously.

which, in effect, twists the stabilizer bar. The bar resists this twist and chassis-rolling force is delivered directly into the rear-end housing.

What about the installation? Is a weld-on bar difficult to install? It's not difficult, and in the photo that follows you see how a system was mounted in a real-world application. Keep in mind, this was done on a GM G-Body, but the process is exactly the same with a Nova.

Rod Ends

Inside any modern high-performance Nova, one thing is certain: You're going to find more than a couple of rod ends or spherical bearings. All rear suspension components I discuss in this chapter make use of rod ends. And they're incredibly important. Rod ends are regularly used in places where they must absorb considerable loads. Basically, it comes down to the strength of the rod end versus the demands of the load. Should a rod end break in your Nova, you can appreciate the trouble this can cause. Given the potential ramifications, each and every rod end tends to become a critical component.

This is a three-piece, or "aircraft," rod end. That means it is constructed with three separate primary components. There are all sorts of ways and combinations to put this together.

format. In these cases, the race is formed around the ball. Next, the race insert is staked into the body. What makes this so vital? That's easy. This manufacturing process provides for a much closer fit as well as a much higher degree of precision between the ball and the race. Essentially, the three-piece design is what is commonly called an "aircraft" rod end. Because three pieces are used in the manufacture, the rod end can be built with different materials. For example, races can be built of mild, alloy, or stainless steel. Don't bother with brass or aluminum bronze races; they don't have the strength necessary for any race application. Similarly, the rod-end body can be manufactured from mild steel, alloy steel, stainless steel, aluminum, or even titanium.

More Material Types

Rod-end balls are most often heat-treated steel (most often chrome-moly steel, stainless steel, or 52100 bearing steel). So that they remain round, the balls must be tremendously hard (it is common for the rod balls to be chrome plated to provide a smooth bearing surface).

Given the heat treatment along with the overall hardness of the

How to Clock Rod Ends

When a pair of rod ends is used in a single component (using that four-link bar as an example), the orientation of the rod ends on either end is important. This is what chassis builders refer to as "clocking" the rod end. Stop right here for one second. When you make very small adjustments in a suspension link that sees preload, it turns out you can make a huge difference in the way the car works or handles. According to pro chassis builder Jerry Bickel, one-sixth of a turn at a time is all that is required to see a change in the way the car works. Keeping this in mind, counting the number of "flats" (the flat side of the rod-end jamb nut) you turn on a link is critical.

Included are a couple of illustrations. The first one shows how a typical link is configured. One side of the link is fitted with right-hand threads while the other end of the link is fitted with left-hand threads. By simply loosening the jam nuts, you can lengthen or shorten the entire four-link bar.

What about clocking? It's easy. When the rod ends are properly "clocked," then they are aligned. When aligned you don't encounter binding in the suspension. At the same time, a link with clocked rod ends makes it easy to determine if the link is under tension. Simply grab the link by hand and rotate it back and forth. You can tell if the link is neutral or under load. ■

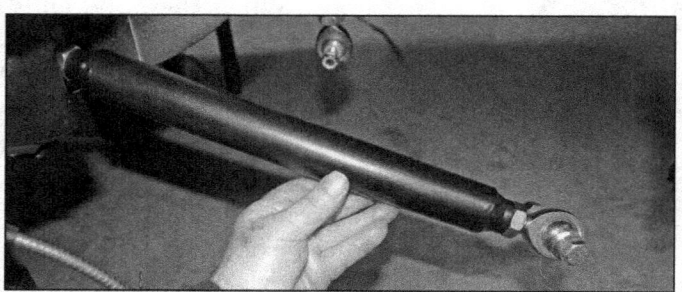

Rod ends used in conjunction with four-link bars (as shown here) should be "clocked." That means you should align them after adjusting (or otherwise changing) the link length.

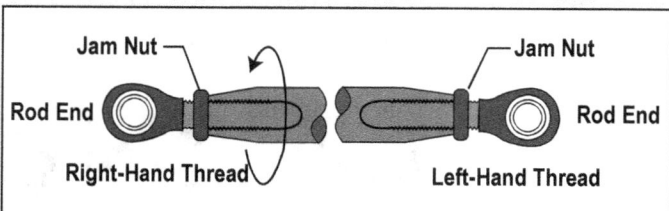

When you adjust something such as a four-link bar, you loosen the jamb nuts on each end and turn the link (bar). That moves the link in or out. It can also change the orientation of the rod end after you re-tighten the jamb nuts. Each rod end can become "cocked," or twisted sideways. (Illustration Courtesy Jerry Bickel Race Cars)

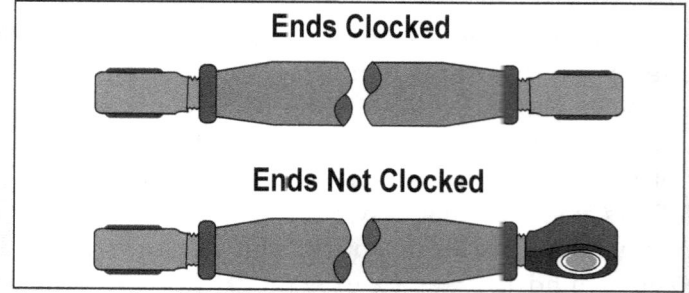

You must "clock" the rod ends when you've completed the length adjustment on the link. This drawing compares a clocked rod end to one that is not clocked. Properly clocked rod ends on a given link allow the rod end to function without binding. (Illustration Courtesy Jerry Bickel Race Cars)

ball, the race must also be hard, but it can't be as hard as the ball. It is common to find three-piece rod ends manufactured with a race built from through-hardened steel alloy or a stainless steel. In either case, the outer race is heat treated for strength and wear resistance.

Is there such a thing as less expensive rod ends? Certainly, but as you see, there are limits. Economy rod ends are usually built with bodies manufactured from low-carbon grades of mild steel. It is not possible to through-harden this material (through-hardening, or quench and temper, is a process used to increase the hardness and tensile strength of a given material). While this less costly material works reasonably well under lightly loaded applications, a rod-end body built from chrome-moly or heat-treated stainless steel is far superior in racing applications. When the manufacturer builds the rod-end body from chrome-moly or stainless steel, the physical size of the rod end can be reduced because the material is stronger. Some rod-end bodies are built from 7075-T6 aluminum. This is a beefy grade of aluminum with a tensile strength that is actually slightly greater than mild steel. But when carefully analyzed, aluminum is not as forgiving as mild steel. It does not stretch or bend as much before breaking. Compare the strength of an aluminum rod end with a heat-treated chrome-moly or stainless component; the steel jobs have almost double the strength.

Teflon Liners

A common (and good) option for rod ends is the Teflon liner. The liner allows the rod end to be self-lubricating. This feature is important because it eliminates the need to grease a rod end after it is installed on your race car. What about a rod end with a grease fitting? Stay away! They're not a good concept, because drilling a hole in the rod end for a grease fitting weakens it (much the same as a driveshaft universal joint with a grease fitting). Besides, grease or oil on the rod-end ball attracts dirt, which in turn promotes wear on the ball/race.

Use a Teflon liner and the need for lube is pretty much history. Please note that Teflon is a DuPont product. DuPont invented it, and Teflon is its name brand. DuPont is not the only company that manufactures polytetrafluoroethylene (PTFE) products. A Teflon liner consists of a carrier component, often a fabric that provides compressive strength, a Teflon component for lubricity, and various bonding resins. The Teflon liner is bonded to the race, which means the rod-end ball physically rotates on the liner. As the ball moves, Teflon rubs on the ball. That, of course, provides lubrication. Rod ends with Teflon liners are manufactured in

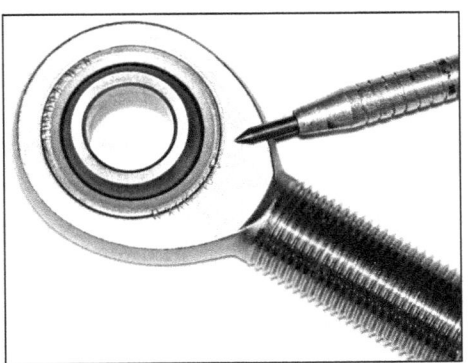

What you're looking at is a very-high-quality, extreme-strength, made-in-the-USA Teflon-lined rod end. Aurora Bearing is the manufacturer. Teflon provides the lubricant necessary to maintain free movement. By the way, you can't go wrong with Aurora Bearing when it comes to rod ends.

two- or three-piece configurations, but watch out for cheap rod ends assembled with virgin Teflon. Virgin Teflon is comparatively soft. It has a compressive strength of (+ or –) 10,000 pounds psi. Compare that to a high-quality composite Teflon liner, which usually has a compressive strength of somewhere between 40,000 and 60,000 psi, and you can see there's a huge difference. A quality Teflon liner provides another bonus as well: It eliminates extra clearance between the ball and race. This means the ball and race have a much tighter fit.

Here is something else to consider: If a manufacturer adds a Teflon liner to a rod end, it doesn't always mean that it's a precise piece. In addition, it doesn't mean that it's a high-performance piece. When you shop for rod ends, you'll probably come across a phrase that includes the words "beating out." Beating out usually refers to the deformation of low-strength "self-lubricating" liners. Some cheap rod ends are built with races constructed from molded plastic (sometimes they're mixed with a fiberglass filler). They can also add a small amount of Teflon for increased lubrication. Sounds fair enough, but cheap rod ends such as this might look and sound like trick, but they usually have a compressive strength of 15,000 psi or less. Under a given load, the race can deform, and you might not see it because the body can be undamaged.

Rod-End Alignment

The misalignment of a rod end is important. A bolt, stud, or other form of fastener goes through the hole bored through the center of the rod end. That means the ball inside the rod end has limited rotation (a full 360-degree rotation is obviously out of the question). Accordingly, all rod ends have definite limitations on how far they can be "misaligned" before the sphere becomes bound up in the housing. What you're dealing with is the "angle of misalignment" and it's important when selecting a rod end for a given task. As it turns out, not all rod ends are designed to accept the same degree of misalignment. That's why misalignment angles are published in the specifications of most high-quality rod ends. What, then, is the consequence of exceeding the manufacturer's recommended maximum misalignment angle? At the least, you end up with early rod-end wear. At worst, you bind and break the rod end.

That's not good, so how on earth do you figure out the misalignment angles? It's not difficult. Remember that grade school protractor you had? You can use it to check the geometry. Compare that to the "angles of misalignment" laid out in the manufacturer catalog. By the way, you can attempt to shortcut the job by simply using a big honking rod end, but in truth, that won't fix the problem. That's why manufacturers build high-misalignment rod ends.

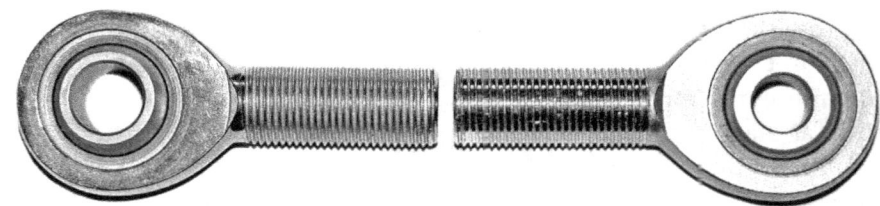

Two Aurora Bearing rod ends. Two identical shanks. The rod end on the right has a small bore size; however, it also has a much larger body and is therefore much stronger than the rod end on the left. Quite often, these are referred to as "racing rod ends."

Is Bigger Better?

Is a bigger rod end better? From a size point of view, a rod end can be constructed two ways. The first example incorporates a shank (the threaded segment) that is the same diameter as the hole in the ball (as an example, a 1/2-inch bore coupled with a 1/2-inch shank). The next setup is built with shank one size larger than the bore (a common example here is a 1/2-inch bore mated to a 5/8-inch shank). The second configuration (small bore, large shank) comes with benefits, particularly when the rod end encounters bending loads. You don't have to look too far to find this in a custom-built Nova. Think four-link. Here I have a four-link that acts as levers. They transfer (often) huge forces from the chassis to the rolling stock, transmitting considerable forces from the chassis to the tires (and vice versa). Because of this, the larger-than-normal shank gives the rod end more ultimate strength, but it also adds a large margin of additional reserve strength to the respective four-link bar.

The oversize shank rod end is most often built by installing an insert one size smaller in the body of a rod end. A 1/2 x 5/8–inch rod end always demonstrates higher load capacities than a 5/8 x 5/8–inch rod end, assuming both are built with similar materials and specifications, because of the amount of body material found around the insert. Rod ends of this configuration give you added wrench access too. The reason is, the fastener that goes through the bore of the rod-end ball is smaller. An asymmetrical rod end can be built by adding a larger shank to a smaller body. It serves the same purpose, but you end up with less material surrounding the ball, which in turn, makes it less desirable.

It should be no surprise that you get what you pay for. Quality rod ends, such the pieces we're showing in the accompanying photos, aren't cheap. What you're paying for is an extensive engineering background, arduous research, development, and equally demanding testing agendas. The bottom line here is, when you buy into a manufacturer's product, you trust them to keep you safe.

This is what the "alignment angle" mentioned in the text looks like. Essentially, it shows just how far a rod end can go before it is misaligned. FYI: This is actually a special high-misalignment bearing manufactured by Aurora. It is engineered to operate successfully at angles such as this.

You get what you pay for when it comes to rod ends. When a component such as this is charged with holding major suspension and steering components in check on a modified Nova, don't even think about getting cheap here!

CHAPTER 5

SPRINGS AND SHOCK ABSORBERS

Springs and shock absorbers do more than hold the car up and keep it from bouncing uncontrollably. Springs can be used to your advantage to determine ride height, help launch the car down the quarter-mile, and help with lateral acceleration. Shock absorbers (or perhaps better, "dampeners") are capable tuning devices that can be used to control the motion of the suspension. I delve into the why's and how's in this chapter.

Springs

Springs? What's so important about the front coil springs on your Nova? Quite a bit actually. Springs tend to be one of the most important and often the most misunderstood components on a modified Nova, whether it is a street or race application. A lot of issues can arise with springs, many in the "out of sight, out of mind" category. For example, springs tend to settle with age. How old are the springs on your car? Equally important, far too many Novas operate with springs that have been improperly modified (coils cut by way of a torch, springs that are coil bound, sagged springs, and so on).

Crude modifications to springs can do more harm than good, obviously. A drag Nova with a stock-style front suspension system is an example. It's common to install a set of race front coils, but sometimes the ride height is too tall. The quick "fix" is to cut the springs. A month or two later, the car sags. Instead of buying correct springs, the next "fix" is to slip in a set of black plastic spacer donuts on the spring to restore the ride height. Not a good idea. This stiffens the spring rate to the point where the car is seriously over-sprung. The spring rate has been messed up by shortening it. More often than not, the ETs change and the Nova develops quirky handling characteristics. The real fix is to use a quality spring that isn't cut (even if it means having a set of springs custom wound).

Coil-overs aren't exempt from this either. It's just as easy to install springs with the wrong rate when using coil-overs. Springs of all configurations are correctly picked by way of calculations based upon the geometry of the car (short-long control arms, MacPherson strut, etc.), the corner weight of the car, the dimensions of the spring, and a series of component measurements. There is no magic one-size-fits-all when it comes to springs. Each car requires a different spring and spring rate. Spring rate refers to the amount of weight needed to compress a spring 1 inch.

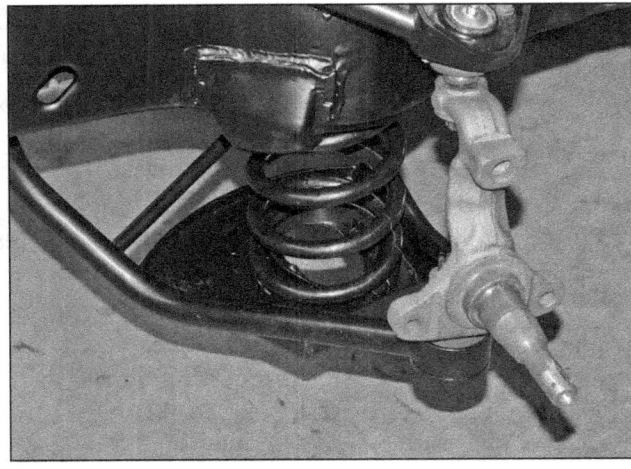

Coil springs are not all created equal. And they're not as simple as "they look okay; they fit." This chapter lays out how to select springs correctly.

CHEVY NOVA 1968–1974: HOW TO BUILD AND MODIFY

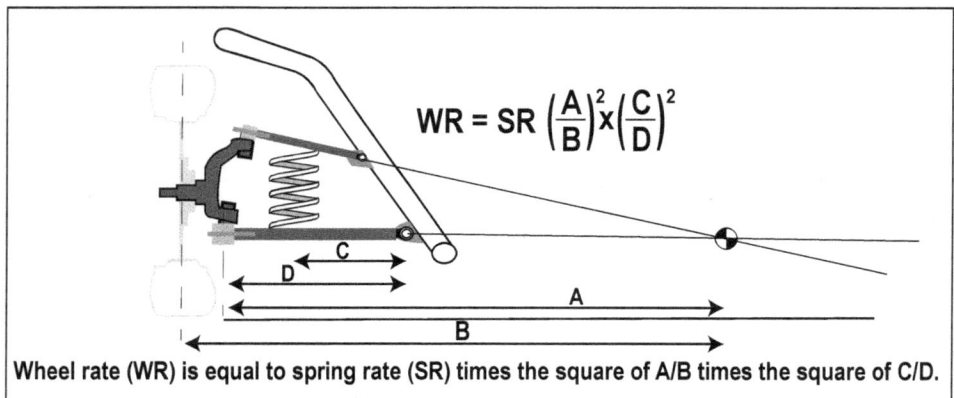

Here's an easy-to-use formula for approximating front wheel rate (WR) versus spring rate (SR). (Illustration Courtesy Jerry Bickel Race Cars)

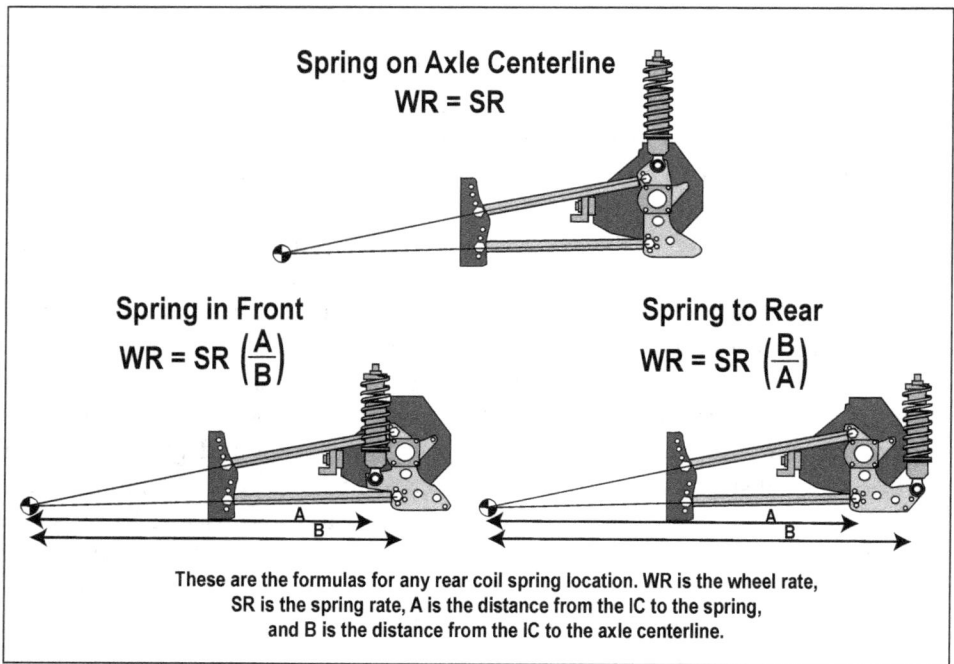

These are the formulas to determine rear wheel rate for a drag race car. (Illustration Courtesy Jerry Bickel Race Cars)

the spring increases, the spring rate decreases. A spring with a closed end has a coil that is "squashed" into the next coil in the stack.

To figure out spring rates, the first thing you should do is determine the exact corner weights of your Nova (left front, right front, left rear, right rear) with the car at running weight or race weight (including the driver weight, fuel, oil, etc.). Spring rates are determined by the amount the spring deflects versus the weight placed upon it. The actual suspension geometry can influence how much the spring deflects. You must compensate for the geometry when determining the correct spring rate for your race car. Here's an important quote from Jerry Bickel on the topic: "When you buy front springs, the listed spring rate (in-lbs) is not the same as the rate at the wheel. Front control arms are lever systems that alter the motion and applied forces between the coil springs and the wheels. The front wheels gain a mechanical advantage against the coil springs, so the wheel rate is always less than the spring rate."

Jerry points out: "If the car has MacPherson struts, the top line should be drawn from the top strut mount at 90 degrees to the strut. Actual wheel rate is extremely difficult to calculate with accuracy. This is because the angles of suspension members change continuously though the normal range of travel and the front coil springs are not perpendicular with the pavement.

"Fortunately, front spring rates are not quite as critical in drag cars as they are for road race or stock cars. If your spring and wheel weights are within the correct range, little or no performance gain should be expected from changing them. Remember this

(For example, a 250-pound-per-inch spring with 250 pounds resting upon it compresses 1 inch). Three factors influence spring rate.

Wire Diameter: This affects rate since a greater wire diameter is stronger than a smaller-diameter wire. When the wire diameter of the spring is increased, the spring rate increases.

Mean Spring Diameter: This refers to the overall outside diameter of the spring, less one wire diameter. When the mean spring diameter increases, the spring rate decreases.

Active Coils: Determining the number of active coils varies with the configuration of the spring. For springs where both ends are closed, count the total coils minus two. For springs with one end closed and one end open, count the total coils minus one. As the number of active coils in

SPRINGS AND SHOCK ABSORBERS

Front Spring Selection

Here is a handy front spring selection chart for drag race cars equipped with MacPherson struts. Remember, this is only a rough guide for spring rates. The correct rate for your car may be somewhat higher or lower than those listed below.

Gross Vehicle Weight (lbs)	Front Spring Rate (in-lbs approx.)	Rear Spring Rate (in-lbs approx.)
2,000	185	85
2,350	200	95
2,500	215	120 to 140
3,000 to 3,500	250 to 350	150 to 200

rule when selecting spring rates: *The farther the spring is from the tire, the lower the wheel rate will be. The closer the spring is to the tire, the higher the wheel rate will be.*

"All of our Pro cars are equipped with MacPherson struts in front, with the springs very close to the tires. This is why the front spring rates I use are low compared to those used on cars with unequal-length control arms.

"Rear suspension members may also create leverage against the rear coil springs and affect wheel rate. This depends on the type of rear suspension system and the location of the coil-over-shocks.

"Depending on the builder, the rear coil springs may be located in front, on, or behind the rear axle centerline.

"The same formula can be used for ladder bar suspension systems. Simply use the front pivot as the IC reference point. I prefer to mount the coil-over shock behind the axle centerline. This keeps it from interfering with the four-link bars and lowers the top mounting location."

As it turns out, the approximate spring rates provided by Jerry Bickel are similar to those required in many drag race Novas, even those without MacPherson strut front suspension systems. Many companies out there can build you a trick drag race spring (Moroso being one of them). Typically, springs of this sort are manufactured with a small wire diameter. They're also built rather long. As a result of these two factors, the spring helps promote front-end lift, which makes for better weight transfer. Moroso says that many factors, including wheel offset, influence the front-end height of a car. A front wheel offset to the outside tends to increase leverage of the lower A-arm against the coil spring. The result is a lower ride height. Disc brake spacers do the same thing. Of course, moving weight around on your car can do the same thing too. Replacing a steel hood with a lift-off fiberglass job, moving the battery to the trunk, replacing the water pump with an aluminum job, swapping to aluminum heads, and so on can radically change the front corner weights, allowing the nose of your Nova to sit higher. Believe it or not, in some cars, taking out as little as 50 pounds can affect ride height.

All sorts of custom springs with all sorts of different spring rates are available for Novas. The front-end weight is the ultimate decision maker when the time comes to select front springs. This is something you should consider for all Novas (drag race, street/strip, pro-touring, and so on). A good chassis builder nails down the exact corner weights on a car during the setup phase.

In the end, it's easy enough to see that there are many front suspension arrangements (modified MacPherson strut, short-long control arm, etc.) and that the geometry of each design differs considerably. Because of this, spring rates can differ dramatically too, even when overall front-end weights are similar. So, what can you do to get it right? Get the corner weights of your Nova right and take the time to do the math.

Split Mono-Leaf Springs

What's the story with "split" leaf springs? According to the folks at

The spring might look "bowed" in this photo, but it's not. What worked for this Nova was a stock small-block spring for a car with power steering and a few other options. The car will eventually receive a big-block.

CHAPTER 5

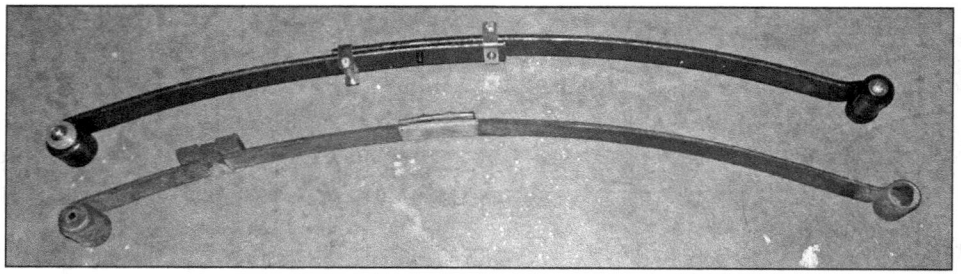

At the rear of a Nova, it's easy enough to run stock mono-leaf springs or stock multi-leaf springs (or custom versions of each). Or you can opt for what is likely the best bet: a split mono-leaf.

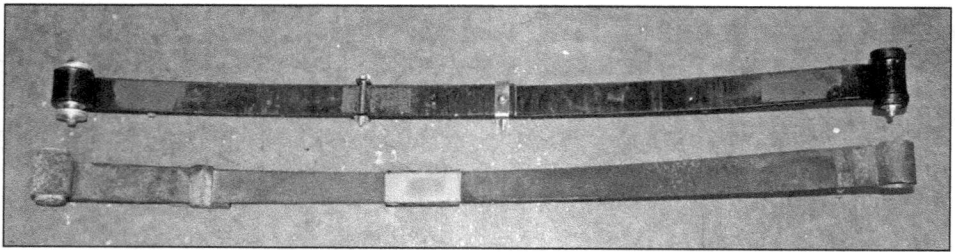

From the top (or the bottom), the split mono-leaf follows the same shape and size as a stock mono-leaf. The split segments are the difference (and what make it work).

Here's a look at the side of the spring. Not only does the split mono-leaf spring work better (when it comes to hook), it's also easy to change ride height. It's a simple matter of exchanging spring segments.

Calvert Racing (the folks who brought the design into popularity), split mono-leaf springs are considerably lighter than factory leaf springs (especially multi-leaf jobs). This reduces unsprung weight, and at the same time, the new spring package allows you to select the ride height you need for your car. In addition, split mono-leafs are designed to work with the CalTracs traction bars. Calvert also points out that it has tested countless different leaf spring configurations over the years. Included are stock mono-leaf, multi-leaf, multi-leaf with a single added thick leaf, multi-leaf with very heavy leafs, biased multi-leafs (such as an old Chrysler SS spring), parabolic mono-leafs, and finally, split mono-leafs. Overall, cars have performed the best (in drag racing or street/strip applications) with the split mono-leaf springs. A big reason for this is the fact the front segment of the spring can be manufactured super-stiff. Coupled with the way the CalTracs works, it allows the suspension to mimic a four-link.

Split mono-leaf springs can be built for a wide range of combinations, including a number of ride heights: stock, +1, and -1 are the basics (special orders are possible). You can also get the springs tailor-made with regard to spring rate (the rate ranges from approximately 200 to 225 pounds).

Now, if you're wondering, these springs are at home on the street. That's one of the basic tenets of the CalTracs "system." Many Calvert customers with leaf spring vehicles still use them as double-duty machines (street and strip). If those cars were converted to something such as a ladder bar or a four-link, the suspension hardware required to get the job done (panhard bar, anti-roll bar, Watts linkage components, and so on) could limit their usefulness on the street. The complete CalTracs setup doesn't have those issues.

Those split mono-leaf springs we're talking about do look quite a bit different than the setups you're used to.

Shock Absorbers

The truth about making a quick Nova work on the street or on the strip is that the shock absorber is a key ingredient. The reason is simple: If you can control wheel motion, you can control the dynamics of the car. The better the control of the wheel motion, the better the control of the dynamics of the entire car. Interpretation? In the world of acceleration this boils down to hook. It also means your tuning capabilities are amplified manifold.

What really is a shock and what does it do? A shock is a hydraulic device that resists chassis movement by passing oil through a set of orifices and valved passages. Manipulating the fluid movement through the valving of an adjustable shock changes its dampening characteristics.

SPRINGS AND SHOCK ABSORBERS

All sorts of shock absorbers are built for third-gen Novas. This is a complete set from Strange Engineering. The fronts are single adjustable (right) while the rears (left) are double adjustable.

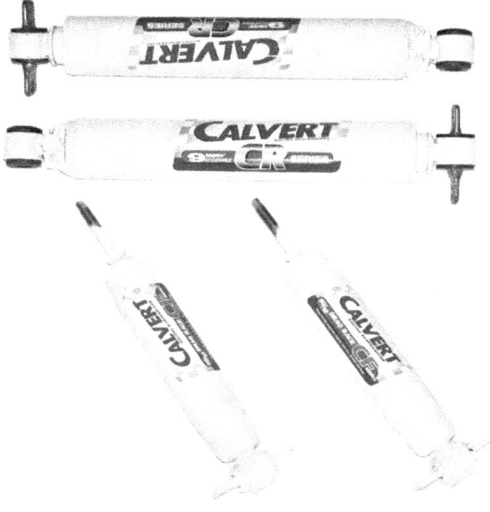

Calvert Racing offers a pretty neat (well-tested) set of shocks for Novas. These are an inexpensive option. The fronts are non-adjustable (bottom) while the rears are single adjustable (top).

Rebound (extension) is the shock's resistance to being pulled apart. It can be used to control chassis separation, the point at which the axle housing is pushed away from the chassis and the tires are applied to the track. During separation, many things occur. Forces push the Nova up and forward and the axle housing sees the opposite force (don't forget the tire sidewalls are also wrapping up). While the car moves forward, torque is created as the tires generate traction to start this movement. Too much body separation can lead to undesirable side effects. Wheel hop can occur as the tire tries to return to its original form (the tire unwraps). Stiffening the rebound can control wheel hop. Tire shake is similar to wheel hop and can be addressed similarly. For the most part, something such as a "bald" starting line or unprepared surface mandates a softer rebound setting to apply the tires with more force. On the track, a good starting line can use a stiffer setting. A stiffer rebound setting on a well-prepped track can provide quicker vehicle reaction times. Essentially, too much separation is an ET and energy waster.

Bump (compression) is the shock's resistance to the chassis moving down or the axle housing moving up or into the chassis. The bump adjustment is important since it determines how long the tires are held down on the track after chassis separation. When you use a soft rebound setting on a double adjustable, try using a slightly stiffer compression setting.

"Bump-Rebound-Compression-Extension." Whew. It all gets a little confusing. Let's take a closer look at the terms used by the shock manufacturers. Different shock companies use different lingo. Quite often the words "bump," "rebound," "compression," and "extension" are used interchangeably. A shock absorber travels in two directions: It gets shorter (compresses) and it gets longer (extends). Some shock absorber manufacturers call this "bump" and "rebound," but that can get confusing. To get a grasp of what this is all about, pretend you drive your car over a good old-fashioned speed bump. The speed bump "bumps" the shock that in turn compresses it. After you drive over the speed bump, the shock rebounds and extends. That's where you get the term "bump" and "rebound."

In the old days, a loose front shock (worn out stocker or a special 90/10 valving shock) was used to allow the nose to rise quickly. That transferred as much weight as possible to the back wheels. It was simple because there were virtually no rebound forces at work (the "10" in the 90/10) coupled with a whole bunch of bump at work (the "90" in the 90/10). With the 90/10 up front, the nose remained in the air. You can imagine how this messed with the race car aerodynamics. But that was then. Today, Calvert Racing has a new 90/10 designed specifically for maximum weight transfer. Internally, it comes equipped with modern dual-stage valving on the compression side that allows the nose of the car to settle on the top

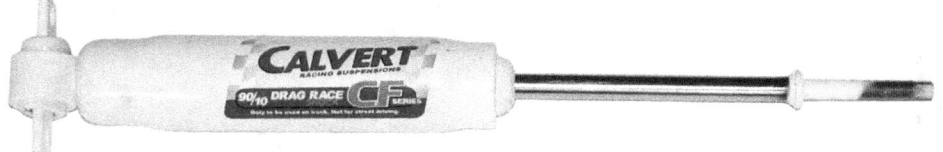

Calvert Racing front shocks have a traditional 90-10 valving arrangement. These differ from the old-school 90-10 valving packages in that they settle down quickly at speed.

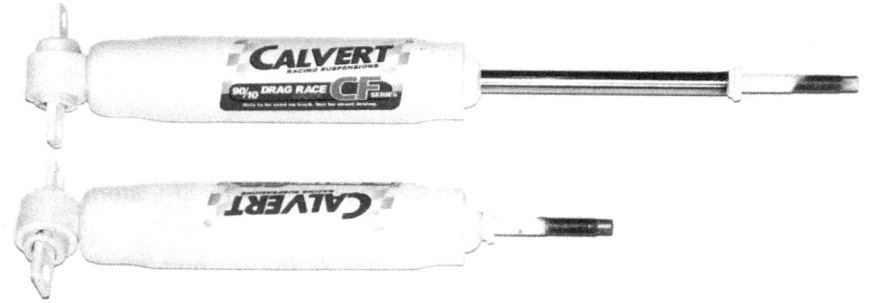

90-10 means the shock extends quickly. It compresses slowly (but again, with dual-stage valving, the nose of your Nova settles down much faster than the old 90-10).

end. They work well (they're very well-proven) and you don't have to fiddle with them.

On the other end of the spectrum are shocks such as those manufactured by Afco, Strange Engineering, Penske, Calvert Racing, and others that are available as single-adjustable and double-adjustable assemblies. A single-adjustable shock with external adjustment allows adjustment of the rebound while the shock assembly is still mounted in the car. A double-adjustable shock with external adjustment allows adjustment of the compression valving and rebound valving. Because of the increased sophistication of the internal valving, the double-adjustable shocks cost more than their single-adjustable counterparts.

With a Strange double-adjustable shock, the compression is adjusted by turning the knob from 1 (softest) to 12 (firmest). Because of the precision of the adjuster, only a click or two change is necessary to make a noticeable change in tuning the chassis. On a Calvert Racing single-adjustable shock, the range of adjustment is from 1 (softest) to 9 (firmest). There's more on setting up Strange and Calvert shocks later.

With an adjustable shock, where do you begin? It all depends upon how sophisticated the Nova is and how deep your pockets are. Many adjustable shocks are similar when it comes to adjustment. The shock absorber doesn't have to be removed for adjustment. After it's installed in the car, all changes are handled externally by way of the adjustment knob. After installation, the knob is accessible through the side of the spring (on typical front applications).

Using the Strange Engineering shocks as the example, setup works like this: Turn the knob fully counterclockwise. The "end" of the adjustment (where it does not turn or click any farther) is the softest setting, position 1. By turning the knob clockwise, each click increases the shock resistance. The full stop counterclockwise (front shock baseline) has valving like that of a 90/10. As you can see, this offers a

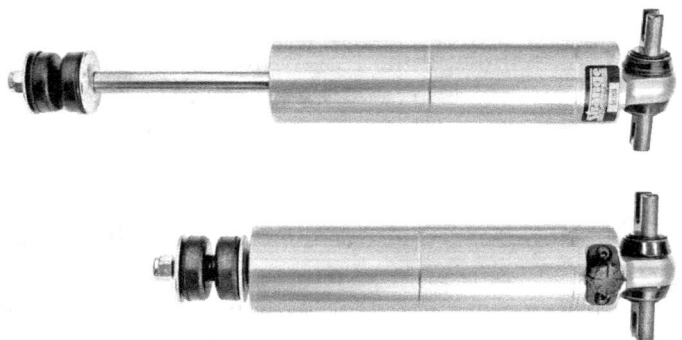

Single-adjustable front shocks such as these examples from Strange Engineering allow for external rebound adjustment.

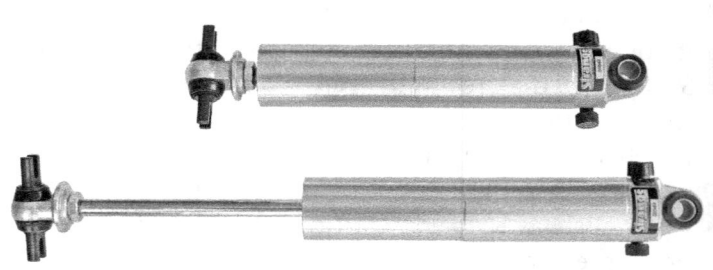

Double-adjustable shock absorbers such as these rear models from Strange Engineering allow for external rebound and bump adjustment. The shock has a separate adjustment knob for each.

SPRINGS AND SHOCK ABSORBERS

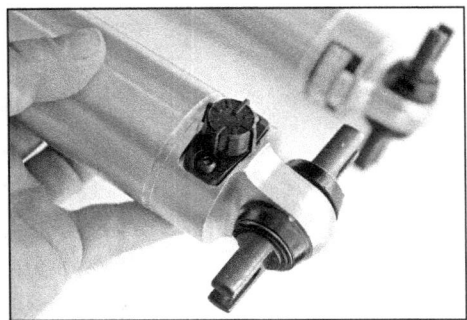

This is a good look at the adjustment knob on a single-adjustable shock absorber. While adjustments between shock manufacturers are often similar, each has its own take on where and how adjustments begin.

> ### Single-Adjustable Front Shock
>
> Strange provides the starting point for adjustment on a single-adjustable front shock as follows:
>
> **Drag Race**
> - Turn to position 2 or 3 (position 1 is full counterclockwise).
> - To increase weight transfer (front-end travel) rotate counterclockwise.
>
> **Street**
> - Turn to position 4 or 5 (position 1 is full counterclockwise).
> - For a firmer ride, rotate clockwise.
>
> Calvert Racing offers the following setup advice for its single-adjustable shock:
>
> **Drag Race**
> - Foot Brake: Firmer settings are typical, usually between 6 and 9.
> - Trans Brake: Softer settings are typical, usually between 1 and 3.
>
> **Street**
> - Adjust your Calvert Racing shocks to settings from 2 to 5.

very large range of adjustment. On the single-adjustable models, after you go past 6 clicks clockwise, the adjuster works primarily on extension (rebound). Moving all the way to the right (clockwise) makes the shock stiff.

On a single-adjustable Calvert Racing shock (available for rear applications only), the adjustment sequence goes like this: Begin the shock adjustment process by turning the adjustment knob fully counterclockwise until it reaches the 1/9 setting on the indicator. This is (obviously) setting number 1. Turn the dial clockwise until you achieve designated adjustment. The firmest setting is one revolution from the softest setting.

What about back double-adjustable shocks? A double-adjustable shock allows adjustment of the compression valving and rebound valving. In a Strange Engineering double adjustable, the compression is adjusted by turning the marked knob from 1 (full counterclockwise) to 12 (full clockwise). The rebound adjuster is extremely sensitive to change. Just 1 click makes a significant change in tuning the chassis.

 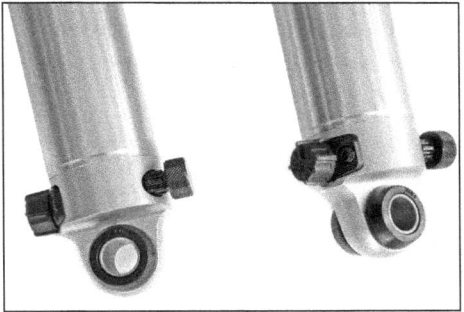

Here are the double-adjustment knobs up close on the Strange shock. When installing these shocks, it's a good idea to plan the orientation on your Nova. As you can see, one adjuster is larger than the other. With some suspension arrangements, it could be better to have the small adjuster inboard.

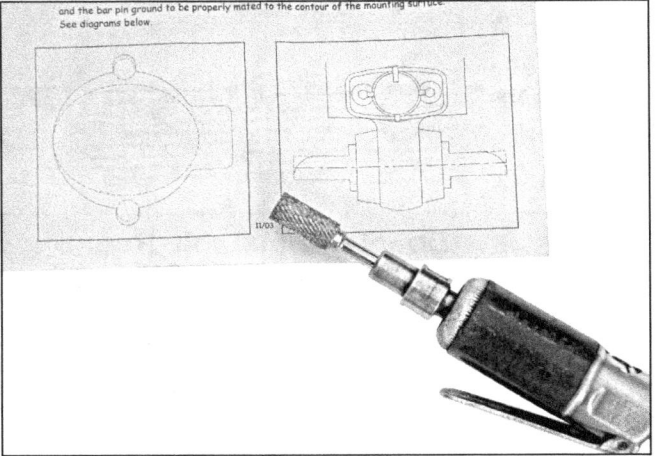

Fit up front is another issue when the shock absorber has a large adjuster knob. Strange Engineering includes a diagram showing how and where the lower front A-arm must be clearanced for shock fit.

CHEVY NOVA 1968–1974: HOW TO BUILD AND MODIFY

CHAPTER 5

Each car requires a different setting when it comes to sophisticated double-adjustable shocks. Chassis builder Jerry Bickel notes, "A good starting point for rear shock adjustment is to set the rebound adjustment tight and the bump adjuster loose. Remember that the final

Some aftermarket lower control arms come pre-notched for a shock absorber with an external adjuster. This is a TRZ Motorsports A-arm for a Nova.

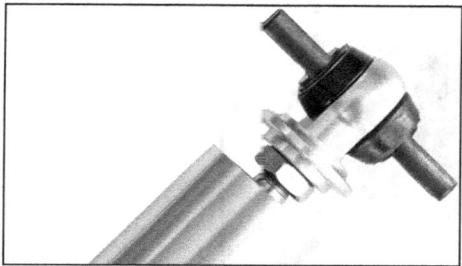

Tie bars are used on both the front and the back shocks on a third-gen Nova (bottom on the front and top on the rear). These Strange Engineering shocks use a hard durometer to keep the tie bar in place (note the snap rings on either end too).

This is a good look at how a rear shock fits a stock Nova. These Calvert Racing shock absorbers are a bolt-in. Note the use of Grade-8 bolts too. While not necessary, the zinc plate fights corrosion.

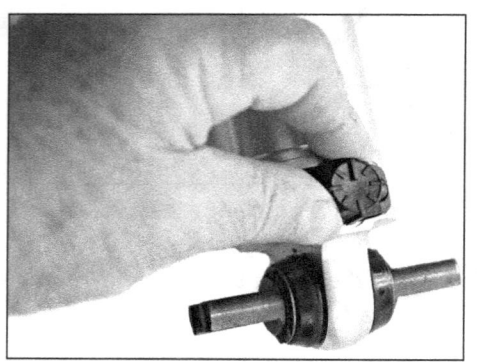

On a single-adjustable Strange Engineering shock absorber, it's best to start the adjustment process by turning the adjuster to full counterclockwise first. That's position number 1.

This Nova has obviously been mocked up without the rear end in place. Notice how the adjuster on this Calvert Racing shock is on the wheel side. And yes, it's a good fit.

This is Calvert Racing's single-adjustable rear shock.

Double-Adjustable Rear Shock

For a double-adjustable rear shock, Strange offers the following basic setup information:

Drag Race
- Turn to position 5 (position 1 is full counterclockwise).
- To plant the tires harder, rotate counterclockwise.
- To decrease wheel hop, rotate clockwise.

Street
- Turn to position 4 or 5 (position 1 is full counterclockwise).
- For a firmer ride, rotate clockwise.

SPRINGS AND SHOCK ABSORBERS

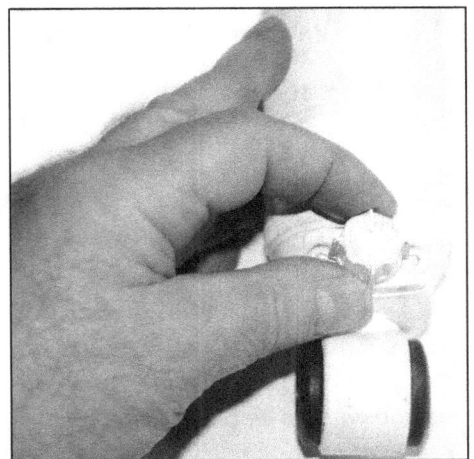

Calvert Racing shocks are numbered on the dial. Softer settings are lower numbers, and as the number of clicks increase, so does the stiffness.

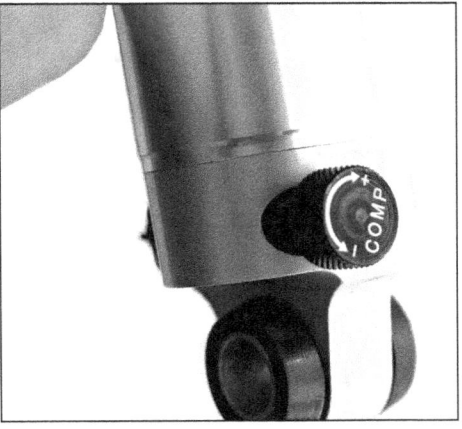

This is the compression (or bump) adjuster for the Strange double-adjustable shock absorber. Turn to full counterclockwise for the softest (lowest) setting and work your way up.

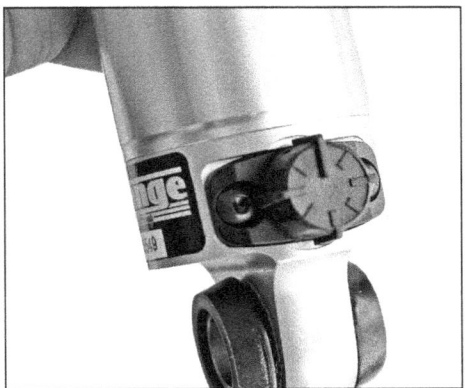

The rebound or (extension) adjuster on the Strange double-adjustable shock is on the opposite side of the lower body. It's best to start the adjustment process in the full clockwise (stiffest) position and tune from there.

setting that is best for your car must be found with some thoughtful trial and error and may change with track conditions."

Which End Do You Adjust First?

You have the shocks, you know how to adjust them, and you know how to install them on your Nova. Now what? Try the following steps.

If the Nova wheelstands excessively or bounces on the gear change (more likely), adjust the front shocks first. If the car rattles the rear tires, wheel hops, or has way too much body separation, adjust the rear shock absorbers first.

The idea is to get a smooth transition in the front-end movement as the car launches right through the first gear change. Bouncing and jerking motions do not help the launch, or the ET for that matter. If the car is violent on the launch and physically jerks the front wheels off the ground, the shock setting is too soft or loose. If the car bounces on the gear change the shock needs to be stiffer. When the car bounces on the gear change, it's coming down on the front suspension travel limiter, and then bouncing back up again. Obviously, if the shock is set too tight (stiff), the front doesn't move sufficiently to transfer weight. On a similar note, a too-stiff setting on the front shock bounces the car on the tire after the launch. Don't get this confused with bouncing off the front suspension limiter.

When it comes to the back shock absorber, the idea is to hit the tire as hard as possible (track conditions permitting). Keep in mind that it's the shock that controls how much force or "hit" you're applying to the slick. If the shock is too loose on the extension (rebound), you might get way too much rear body separation. If the shock is too tight, the car flattens the tire excessively or simply causes the car to spin. Generally speaking, start soft on the rear and keep tightening up the valving until the car slows down.

Shackles and Bushings

The stock rear leaf springs in your Nova were fitted with rubber bushings front and rear. For any

On the bench and on the floor, these photos provide a good look at the complete package of solid bushing, spring pocket mount, and Caltracs bracket for a third-gen Nova. Even if you don't have a set of Caltracs traction bars on your car, a solid front bushing is a good idea.

CHEVY NOVA 1968–1974: HOW TO BUILD AND MODIFY

CHAPTER 5

Calvert Racing manufactures solid aluminum front spring eye bushings. Others, such as Competition Engineering, make them too. The Calvert bushings are three-piece jobs with large spacers designed for use with its traction bars.

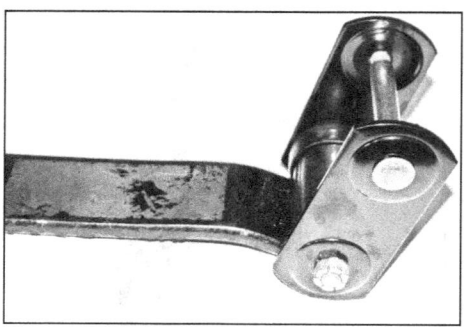

On the backside you don't need a special bushing or a special shackle. Good old-fashioned stock (length) shackles work perfectly. Never use a shackle to increase ride height. That's the job of the spring arch.

Stock bushings or urethane bushings as shown here work perfectly in the rear leaf spring segment. Obviously, a urethane bushing is more rigid than a stock or replacement rubber job.

performance work, it's advisable to replace the front bushing with a solid aluminum job. The reason is, when you're working the car hard (with decent power under the hood and particularly with a good traction device), the front bushing deflects. That's why quality springs, such as a Calvert split mono-leaf, come with aluminum bushings pre-installed. Even if you're not using a split mono-leaf, it's a good idea to replace the front spring eye bushings with solid bushings. Calvert Racing, Competition Engineering, and others offer direct replacement solid aluminum bushings.

At the rear segment of the leaf spring you should simply replace the stock upper bushings with new rubber ones. Companies such as Classic Industries offer exact reproduction bushings. Urethane bushings work well on the bottom end. Why not use solid bushings at the back end? Simple. That part of the leaf is along for the ride. There simply isn't a significant load (from the traction bar point of view) placed upon the rear of the spring.

What about shackles? Two schools of thought exist about the rear of the leaf spring in Novas: use stock shackles or go with a spring slider. What's a slider? Your local round-track store more than likely has a set hanging on the wall. They have been used in circle track for years. With a slider, the rear of the leaf connects to a box with a roller bearing that slides fore/aft. The box assembly bolts or welds to the rear subframe and the spring can then move with the roller. They need to be lubricated regularly, and they tend to be noisy. The idea is that sliders maintain a consistent load on the spring while going down the track. Do they work? You get a mixed bag of answers, but most confess, unless you're building stratospheric horsepower, you're better off with a standard shackle and fresh (OEM-style) rubber bushings.

Upstairs, the spring can be installed by way of stock rubber bushings. With this car, the stock bolts have been zinc-plated. The shackles were cleaned and powder coated.

CHAPTER 6

BRAKES

If you're into Nova drag cars or Pro Touring, you know that specialized brakes are nothing new. They've been around for all sorts of applications for decades. However, all of those systems had one thing in common: They were designed from the beginning for purpose-built cars. For drag cars, that meant that the rotors were usually thin, non-vented designs; calipers were usually built as small as practical (many were tiny two-piston affairs). The idea was to keep the weight down and to rely upon the back brakes and perhaps the drag chute to do most of the stopping. Those systems work great for stripped down race machines, but not so great for dual-purpose Novas.

In the case of Pro Touring Novas, the brakes are just the opposite: They're built with massive vented rotors and equally huge calipers. They'd probably bring the old space shuttle down from warp speed to a grinding halt safely. But there's a wee problem here too. Those big honking brakes mandate equally huge wheels to clear the works. In a nutshell, you can't fit them on a car with 15- or even 16-inch wheels (many are so large you need 18-inch-or-larger-diameter wheels).

When it comes to street/strip Novas, they're often much heavier (nose heavier too) than a dedicated drag race–only counterpart. How much heavier? Where the common drag car might weigh 2,400 to 2,800 pounds, today's trend has street/strip cars tipping the Toledos at 3,500 or more pounds. That's not the end of it either. Plenty of these heavy street cars run elapsed times and MPH figures that would embarrass a decade-old legal NHRA Pro Stocker. Using brakes designed for lightweight cars on something portly certainly doesn't allow you to make the first turn-off road at the strip, and in most cases, the thin rotors crack or warp because of the excess heat. Calipers are stressed to the max and often flex at the mounts due to the strain. The bottom line is, these new-angle street/strip Novas usually have a wide range of street equipment on

There's no question disc brakes are the answer when it comes to bringing your Nova down from speed. Today, there are all sorts of disc brake kits out there. One of the best for street/strip cars is the package from Baer Brakes.

CHEVY NOVA 1968–1974: HOW TO BUILD AND MODIFY

This is the complete Deep Stage Brake kit. As you can see, it's a comprehensive kit. Baer follows the old-school principle of "made-in-the-USA," which is important.

board, they're portly, and they really do mandate a different type of brake arrangement.

What's needed for these Nova fat flyers (that's not an insult; those new-wave machines are very cool) is some form of brake that fits inside a skinny drag race wheel, but with a larger vented rotor; something that reliably dissipates the heat with sufficient capability for hot laps at the dragstrip yet functions as a street car.

Stop for one minute before I move on. Believe it or not, plenty of brake packages (race, Pro Touring, and otherwise) are manufactured in China. Worse, some are repackaged, so you might not even know the source. I can assure you that the quality of some of those pieces is rather suspect. It's buyer beware.

Back to Nova brakes. What if you have a car with old-school 15-inch rolling stock? Baer Brakes offers a high-quality, affordable, made-in-the-USA brake systems (the Deep Stage Brake lineup) designed specifically for high-power, fast street/strip cars.

When the folks from Baer took note of what was happening on the racetrack, they sat down and engineered a new brake system that fit the application. For the front (where I concentrate now) Baer began with its tried and true SS4+ package and reworked it with an eye to drag racing. Keep in mind, they had to make everything fit inside drag race–style skinny 15-inch front wheels too.

The rotors are a very important part of the equation. Here, Baer's system features an 11-inch-diameter

Multiple options exist when it comes to rotors. This set has been zinc-plated and includes milled slots and drilled holes.

two-piece rotor. The actual rotors are 1-inch thick, cast from high-silicone cast iron, and follow the directional vane configuration. Rick Elam of Baer Brakes contends that this setup is superior to a straight vane or solid rotor in that it cools the brake while rotating. Something most don't consider is that a directional vane is actually longer (when compared to a straight vane). This effectively adds to the stability of the rotor. Depending upon the options you tick off on the order sheet, the Baer Deep Stage Brake rotors can be drilled, slotted, and zinc-plated. You can specify the whole works (slotted, drilled, and plated) or slot only with no zinc plate, or plain (no slots, no holes, no zinc).

Because the rotors are directionally vaned, they must rotate in the correct direction to obtain proper airflow. When you open the boxes containing the brake kit, you find the rotors are clearly marked "left" and "right." If you miss that, just remember that the internal vanes curve toward the back (not the front of the car). That provides the proper

Here's a good look at Baer's reverse slot and hole layout, which prevents carbon build-up inside the slots.

These rotors are directional. That means they are "sided" to the car. They're labeled for the respective side of the car.

Look carefully at the rotor and notice that the internal vanes are curved. Curved directional vanes improve the cooling and, at the same time, strengthen the rotor.

These two photos show the front side and the backside of the rotor and hat assembly. This is a two-piece arrangement. That means the rotor can be serviced (and replaced as necessary) separate from the hat.

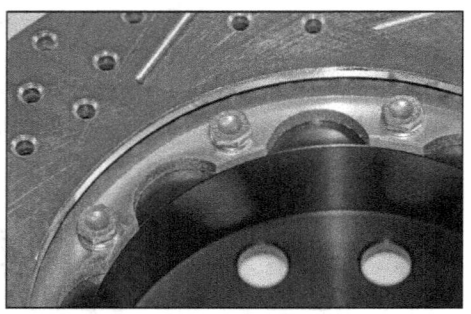

The rotor is affixed to the hat with 10 NAS fasteners and mechanical lock nuts. With this system, no fasteners thread into the aluminum hat.

The hubs are machined from billet aluminum, and after anodizing, they're fit with U.S.-sourced bearings and races. There's no need to pack bearings or add grease. Baer does that for you. It's ready to go.

orientation. The rotors have what is called a "reverse slot" or a "reverse slot and drill" pattern. While it looks "backward" to the uninitiated, it's actually correct. Baer Brake's Rick Elam says this is current race car practice, and it lowers the potential for "carbon smearing," or transfer from the pad material to the trailing side of the slots on the rotor. This is rather important since carbon smearing affects the rotational balance of the rotor. That imbalance can cause shake you can feel while braking.

Since the Baer Deep Stage Brake package is based upon a two-piece rotor (rotor "ring" and a hat), it's easy to replace the rotors when necessary. Baer has them in stock and they sell for under $200 each.

The rotor hats are machined from 6061-T billet aluminum and then anodized black. Baer never screws hardware directly into the aluminum hats. Instead, it incorporates 10 NAS (National Aerospace Standard) stainless-steel bolts and mechanical lock nuts to affix the rotor to the hat. Baer notes that in theory, NAS hardware is reusable multiple times, but if you're replacing rotors, it's best to be on the safe side and replace the lock nuts every second time a rotor is changed (which, from experience, isn't often). Keep in mind that rotor replacement isn't something you have to do on a regular basis, but it's nice to know it's possible and easy to accomplish.

A step is machined into the rotor to allow the hat to recess flat. This lowers the weight of the iron rotor/aluminum hat configuration without compromising strength. Typically, a fully assembled rotor and hat combination weigh no more than 12.4 pounds (that's the heaviest combination with the deepest hat).

The hub is CNC-machined from 6061-T6 billet aluminum and is then hard anodized black. The hubs come pre-fit and preassembled with American-sourced races, bearings, and seals (typically Timken or SKF hardware). If you look closely at the hub, you see the cap is an O-ring-sealed billet job that simply snaps into place. The hubs come double drilled with a 5-on-4.5-inch (Ford and Mopar) pattern as well as a 5-on-4.75-inch (GM) bolt pattern. The wheel studs are press-in, and in the case of a Nova kit, they're high-end ARP 1/2 20-inch jobs with a quick start nose.

The folks from Baer pre-pack the bearings with synthetic grease. You do not have to add more grease to the bearings! However, during the install, it's a good idea to add grease to the hub seal surface prior to installation. Simply use a tiny amount of synthetic grease for the job.

Another consideration is the actual caliper mount. Mounts must be robust, because if the caliper is cocked or flexes, stopping power is eliminated or, at the very best,

Baer's hubs are double drilled for Ford- or GM-pattern wheels. This set is complete with press-in ARP wheel studs of the long variety.

The cap in this brake package is a billet-aluminum snap-in design complete with an O-ring seal.

reduced. Baer Brake's front mount setup for a 1968–1974 Nova incorporates a base bracket machined from billet aluminum and black anodized. It's a beefy piece, measuring .550 inch in thickness, and is held in place by two 1/2 20-inch Grade-8 bolts. FYI: In this application, the bracket mounts using the same holes in the spindle as the steering arm (but on the wheel side). Where some brake caliper mounts for some applications require machining to install, the Baer setup for Novas is a basic bolt-on (instructions are clear and virtually all of the hardware is included). The caliper is designed to mount to the rear of the spindle.

Added to the base bracket is what Baer terms an "intermediate" bracket. This too is a heavy-duty, black-anodized, billet-aluminum component. It's a honking .650-inch thick and it's held in place by way of a pair of 1.5-inch-long 9/16-inch Grade-8 bolts. Essentially, this piece mounts the caliper to the base bracket. The reason for using a two-piece caliper bracket is to allow for caliper shimming. Why the need to shim the caliper? To ensure the caliper sits centered atop the rotor. The shimming practice (which is spelled out in Baer's instruction sheets) compensates for variances in the factory spindle due to vehicle production line machining tolerances.

Baer Deep Stage calipers aren't converted race pieces; instead, they're heavy-duty, four-piston, purpose-built designs. These calipers are deeper than many you find because they include road-going dust shields that are recessed in the bore. They're sufficiently deep so that they never contact the backside of the brake pad. The seals are square-shoulder configurations (in contrast to the O-ring style used by many manufacturers). The reason for using this type of seal is to produce the maximum amount of retraction. This provides the least amount of brake drag and simultaneously eliminates the need for a pair of inline residual pressure valves. By the way, the seals are both dust/weather and pressure sealed. They meet DOT specifications.

Part of the benefit of a deeper-than-normal caliper is that it allows for deeper (longer) pistons. A longer piston is far less prone to cocking in the bore. In fact, when the pads are completely removed, the piston remains in the bore. With many race calipers, the piston tends to fall out of the bore when the pad is removed. Each of the four pistons within the calipers is hard-anodized aluminum. In addition, each caliper half is fastened by way of four 10-mm cross bolts. This provides maximum caliper stiffness.

The fluid crossover design of this caliper incorporates internal fluid passages. There are no external fluid lines from each half of the caliper. Typical of an original equipment manufactured caliper design, the Baer S4 caliper accepts a banjo fitting with a crush washer on the inlet side. The thread is a 10-mm affair that is compatible with any number of late-model brake hoses (no pipe threads are used on the components). In addition, Baer includes a 10-mm to -3AN conversion fitting with the brakes. That means you can also use a very common high-performance AN brake hose. Baer even includes a special hardline adapter for Novas (with factory disc brakes). In any case, it's a super-clean plumbing arrangement with these calipers.

Pads for Baer's S4 configuration caliper are loaded from the bottom of the caliper. The design is such that the pad cannot exit through the top. Baer uses stainless-steel abutment plates to eliminate wear on the aluminum caliper body. These plates minimize pad migration and, as a side benefit, eliminate excess pad noise. Pads used on these calipers are easy to source (common) four-piston jobs. Good replacement examples include Hawks no. HB100 or a no. DR1 pad.

Two brackets are used to mount the Baer caliper: a large base bracket followed by an intermediate bracket. This allows you to shim the caliper. The shimming process places the caliper square in relation to the rotor.

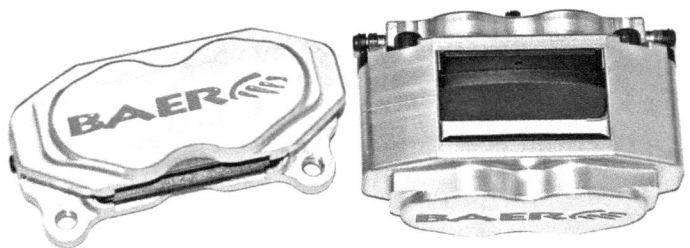

The caliper used in the Deep Stage kit is Baer's S4 (four-piston) job. The calipers are machined from 6061-T6 billet aluminum. This example has been clear anodized, although Baer provides a wide range of color options.

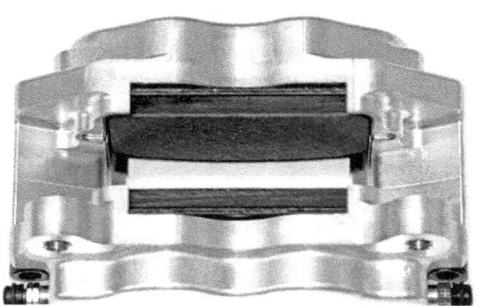

The brake pads are common four-piston examples (for example, Hawk Brake pads). They are installed through the bottom (only).

Each caliper is engineered for a specific rotor thickness. The standard rotor thickness is 1 inch in the Deep Stage Brake systems.

Caliper halves are held together with four 10-mm cross bolts (two are tucked behind the respective bleeders).

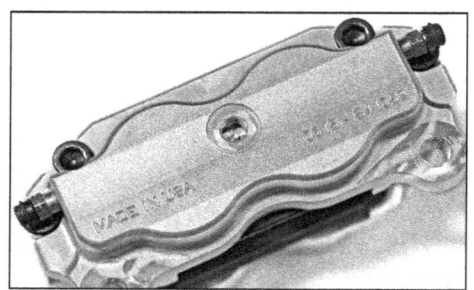

The brake fluid ports measure 10 mm. This allows you to use a common banjo-style brake hose with a copper washer, or you can use the supplied 10-mm to -3AN adapter fitting included with the kit.

Each caliper for the Deep Stage series is engineered to a specific rotor thickness. Baer notes that it does not use spacers between the caliper halves to make up for a thicker rotor. Most Deep Stage kits are designed for use with 1.00-inch-thick rotors. For specialized applications, however, the Baer S4 caliper can be supplied for rotor thicknesses as small as .400 to 1.375 inches. Each of the front calipers for the standard 1.00-inch-thick Deep Stage rotor weighs 4.10 pounds. Rear set calipers are slightly lighter at 3.78 pounds. Yes, they're heavier than common drag race calipers, but they're obviously more robust too!

When it comes time to order a Deep Stage Brake kit, you have several caliper options (I covered the rotor options previously) in more than a dozen color choices. If that's not enough, Baer can provide you with a wide range of custom colors. The calipers shown in the accompanying photos are clear anodized with a red Baer logo.

How to Build Drum Brakes

Drum brakes are a common commodity on Novas. All of them had drums on at least one axle. Plenty had drums all the way around too. Sure, drums are old-school tech and, yes, they get a bad knock. They can fade. They're definitely affected by water. Some require periodic adjustment. Moreover, there's no question that a set of disc brakes not only hauls the car down from warp speed in a more efficient manner, but they also use far few pieces. A typical pair of drums for a Nova might contain more than six dozen (!) individual parts you have to deal with.

What can you do about it? Throw away a set of correct drums and switch to four-wheel discs? Get someone else to assemble them? Buy the backing plates already "loaded"? Likely none of the above. Building up a set of drum brakes really isn't difficult. Certainly, plenty of parts are involved, and some of the many pieces are on the fussy side. Several special tools are required, but they're inexpensive and easy to source. In the end, after the drums are turned (by a brake shop, and when necessary), the job isn't really all that difficult. You can do it in an evening or two. In the photos that accompany this chapter, you can see just how it's done.

Drum brakes are common in Novas. They all had them on at least one axle. They still work perfectly in many combinations when coupled with discs on the nose.

BRAKES

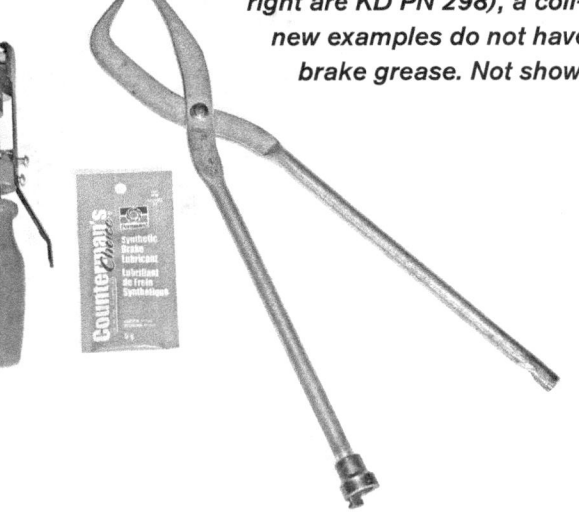

When working on Nova drum brakes, you need a pair of brake pliers (the silver pliers on the right are KD PN 298), a coil-spring shoe retainer tool (the red handled tool is KD PN 285; new examples do not have the external levers), along with a small packet of synthetic brake grease. Not shown is a spray can of brake cleaner.

The place to start is with a set of undamaged, clean backing plates. This set of GM backing plates was powder coated semi-gloss black prior to assembly.

If you remove the anchors from the backing plates, you need to re-torque them during assembly. The torque spec is 80 ft-lbs for the anchor nuts.

Drum brake backing plates are "sided," meaning the plate is designed to mount on a specific side of the car. The opening for the e-brake cable faces forward. Keep in mind that many of the small parts are sided within the assembly too.

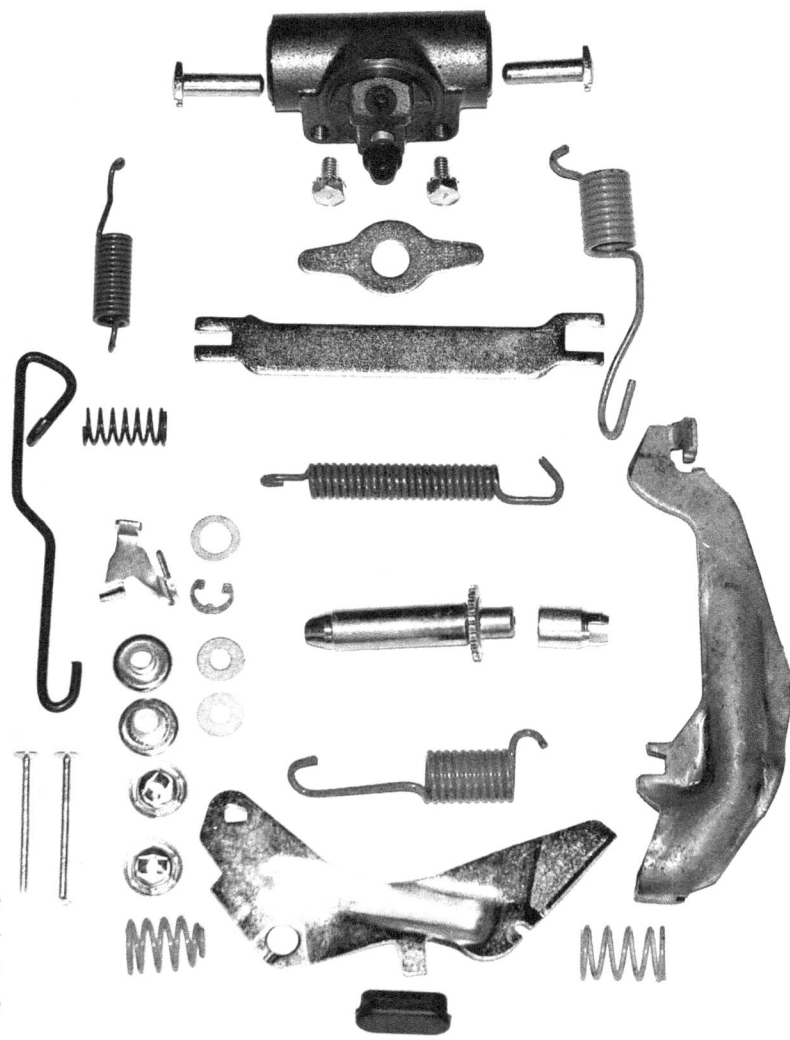

This is most of the small parts required to assemble (and thoroughly rebuild) one rear drum brake. Everything shown here, from the wheel cylinder (at the top) down to the drum brake adjuster plug, is available from Classic Industries, Inline Tube, and other sources.

CHAPTER 6

When rebuilding drum brakes, begin with the wheel cylinder(s). They're installed as shown here. Basically, they can only go in one way. Classic Industries catalogs the wheel cylinders along with the impossible-to-find mount pushrods for each wheel cylinder.

It's a good idea to lubricate the backing plates before going any further. Each backing plate has a raised surface complete with dimples. That's where the lube goes. Apply a small amount to each lubrication point. Lube should not contact the brake shoe surface (if it does, clean it with brake cleaner).

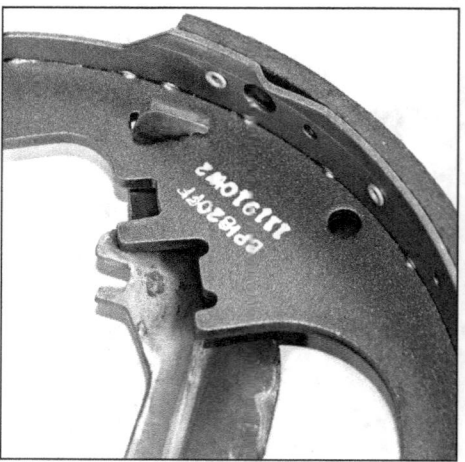

The park brake lever fits into the trailing (longer) shoe. It is hooked in from behind. It's a good idea to install it before the shoe is assembled onto the backing plate.

The easiest way to install the adjuster mechanism is to hook up the spring first with the shoes off the backing plate. Next, hook one end of the adjuster into one shoe. With a little bit of finesse, you can install the second side of the adjuster in place on the opposite shoe. Note that the adjuster wheel is close to the park brake lever. Each backing plate is different. The spring can only be installed one way (as shown here) so that it clears the adjuster wheel.

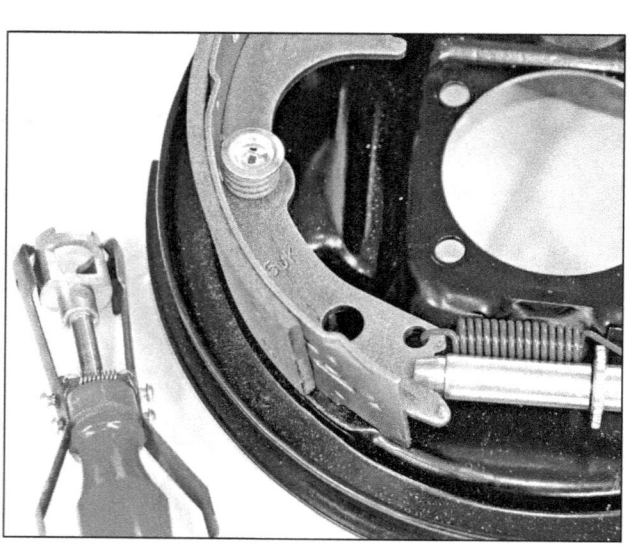

Both shoes (leading and trailing) are held in place by a coil spring. The leading shoe incorporates a beehive-style spring. The KD installation tool is used to compress the spring while you hold the nail (which passes through the back end of the backing plate) in place. A quick turn of the tool seats the nail in the spring retainer recess.

The self-adjuster actuator lever is located on the face of the trailing (back) shoe. The lever is two pieces (a small secondary hook slipped into the top). The hook, or "pawl," is for the return spring; it must be installed now. The coil attachment spring differs from the leading shoe job. Here it's a flat-bottom affair that works in conjunction with a spring seat. The spring seat installs in the actuator lever and is followed by the spring and retainer. Use the same spring tool to compress the spring as you hold the nail in place. Seat the nail correctly in the retainer. The secondary shoe is now in place.

Note the small flange on the actuator. This is where the small bumper spring resides. It slips into place. When it is fully assembled, the other springs in the assembly keep the bumper spring under tension.

Install the park brake strut next. The spring at one end only fits on the leading shoe side. Slide the strut into the trailing shoe. The slot in the strut also engages the park brake lever. Spread the shoes apart slightly and install the sprung end of the strut into the primary shoe.

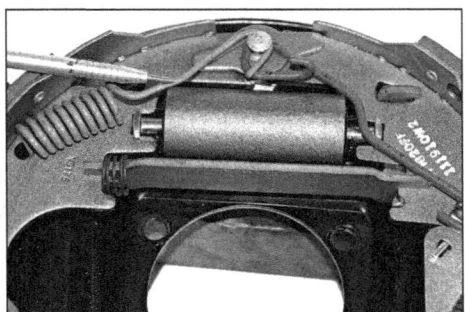

The actuator pull back spring is installed at this point. Install the lower hooked end first, and then with one end of the brake pliers handle inserted through the spring eye, stretch the spring out and over the tab on the pawl. The actuator lever body is dished for the spring body. This ensures the spring can only be installed one way.

Install the actuator link next. Place the anchor guide (the flat plate with a hole in the center) over the anchor pin and then hook the actuator link to the pawl.

The leading shoe spring can now be installed. Hook the shoe end in first, and with the help of brake pliers, work the spring over the anchor pin.

The spring for the trailing shoe is the last piece to be installed on the backing plate (aside from the park brake cables, and of course, the drums). The spring is first attached to the shoe, but instead of hooking directly to the anchor pin, the opposite end attaches to the open end of the actuator link.

Here's the finished product. Assembling drum brakes just takes time. It's something anyone can do at home with the right tools. (Note that this assembly is on the passenger's side of the car, and the front of the car is on the right-hand side of this photo.)

Master Cylinder and Proportioning Valves

Master cylinder choices are too numerous to be able to zoom in on all of them in this book. The pick of the litter (at least at this writing) is Baer's Remaster cylinder. This is a fully machined, billet-aluminum job, and unlike some other master cylinders available that are "universal" (with left- and right-hand outlet port fittings), the Remaster is built for the application. You can specify which side of the master the outlets are located and you'll get a cleaner look for the brake lines. For a Nova, the outlet ports are on the driver's side.

The Remaster is a short, compact design that fits both power booster and manual brake applications. The master is shorter than most. The 15/16-bore job for a Nova has an overall length (to the firewall) of 6.050 inches. It's just under 5 inches tall to the filler cap and it's 3 inches wide. The 1-inch-bore Remasters are the same overall size; however, the 1⅛-inch-bore jobs are slightly larger. In any case, it's a tightly wrapped package.

The actual mount pattern is such that General Motors and Ford applications can make use of the

The master cylinder filler caps are knurled billet aluminum and they simply screw on.

Look closely at the mount. It bolts on and can be replaced. This means the master can be re-purposed if necessary.

same master cylinder. The firewall mount is engineered to fit both. For long-pushrod applications, Baer includes a special insert adapter (bullet adapter). Another neat feature is the two-piece mount arrangement. Baer designed the master with a removable-mount block. If you change configuration (or even cars), you can take the master with you. All you need to change is the mount block.

The filler cap is a screw-on assembly. Each billet cap is engineered with a knurled edge. You don't need any special tools to check or add fluid. Simply unscrew the caps to gain access to the respective fluid chambers.

All Baer Remasters accept bolting a proportioning valve block to the bottom of the master cylinder. You don't need a special bracket to mount the prop valve, plus it really simplifies brake line routing on a Nova application. In addition, if you already have a Baer proportioning valve, it's a simple matter of specifying your master to accept it.

Speaking of prop valves, you need one for your Nova. Baer recommends it on any disc brake conversion (with rear discs or with rear drums). Keep in mind that some Novas have had the original factory distribution and proportioning valves eliminated. These OEM valves were often called "combination valves." They included a brake pressure warning light sender along with a fixed rear brake-proportioning valve. Although I don't have room to go into all of it here, with a front disc/rear drum setup, too much brake pressure is applied to the drums without a prop valve. Adding taller tires on the rear (for example, slicks or tall DOT tires) also upsets the brake balance, simply because the taller tire provides more leverage when you hit the brakes. With these variables on cars without a prop valve installed (and adjusted), what you regularly encounter is back brakes locking up way before the front, and with a really fast Nova, that's no fun. The solution is to reduce the brake line pressure to the back wheels.

This is Baer's Remaster master cylinder. It's a compact unit, measuring just more than 6 inches from the firewall forward.

This master has ports on the left side (correct for a Nova). Baer also offers it with right-hand ports.

BRAKES

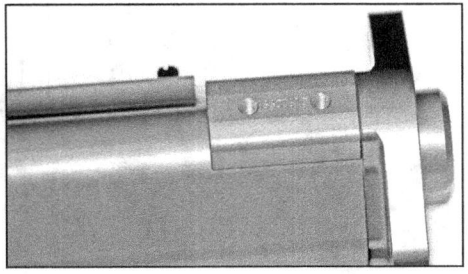

On the bottom side, Baer has included a special built-in mount bracket for the proportioning valve. There is no need for an extra bracket.

This is the proportioning valve Baer Brakes has available for its Deep Stage Brake package. It's adjustable.

Adjustment of the proportioning valve is accomplished by simply turning the knob. It's all very simple.

And that's where the adjustable proportioning valve comes in. According to Baer, "Our prop valve has approximately nine turns, lock to lock. Turning the valve all the way counterclockwise will make the outlet pressure approximately 57 percent of the inlet pressure. With the valve in the full clockwise position, the outlet pressure will be approximately 90 percent of the inlet pressure.

"Starting with the valve set approximately 4½ turns, test the brakes. When set properly, the rear brakes should lock up just *after* the front brakes. If the system is not set properly, readjust the valve and test the vehicle again. Continue adjusting until you are satisfied with the front/rear brake bias for your vehicle."

One last thing: Just like with the calipers, Baer can color coordinate your Remaster to your calipers or to match the underhood accessories in your Nova. Baer does all its coloring in-house, so custom mixes are possible.

Roll Control

Performing a burnout in a Nova isn't that difficult with an automatic. We've all done it; one foot on the brake and the other on the gas. Sure, it raises havoc with the back brakes, but it still cooks the tires nicely. Doing the same thing with a stick is another matter. It's next to impossible, unless you have a line lock, or roll control. It's basically the piece of the puzzle that allows you to perform a burnout seamlessly.

In terms of layout, the roll control consists of an electric valve plumbed into the brake line(s), a micro switch to operate the system, and a red "On" warning lamp. When drag racing the roll control is used during burnouts and staging (you never do a burn out on the street, right?). To set up the operation, the brake pedal is pumped a couple of times to ensure line pressure to the front brakes, and with the brake pedal depressed, the roll control switch is engaged. At this point, the foot brake pedal is released. Pressure to the front brakes is maintained, but pressure to the rear brakes is released. This means the front brakes are locked (the warning lamp glows after the roll control is engaged). You can put the Nova in gear, and if it's a stick, hit the gas and release the clutch. Or, with an automatic, simply nail the gas pedal. Obviously, you're now performing a burnout.

Installation is simple, but given the fact it involves the brakes, take the installation seriously! Brakes are critical components!

The first step is to mount the "valve" in the engine compartment.

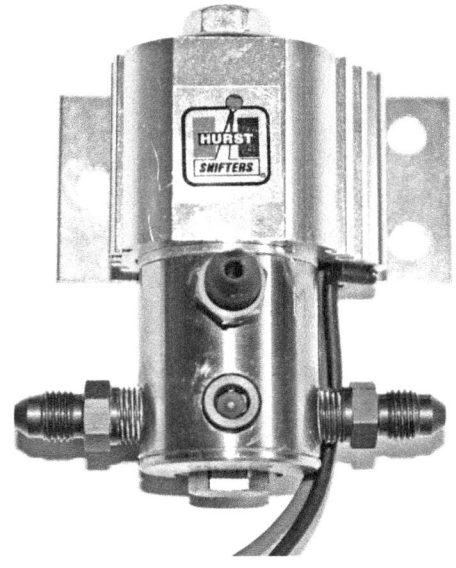

A roll control (or "line lock") is a pretty simple device. When a switch engages it, the solenoid maintains brake fluid pressure at the front wheels on your Nova. In turn, the back brakes have no pressure, allowing you to perform an effortless burnout.

CHAPTER 6

The Nova offers a lot of potential roll-control mounting locations, but this spot on the inner fender is one of the best (and easiest). Three bolts hold it in place.

Plumbing is a bit more complex. Each brake combination can differ, but with the Baer setup, this is how it's laid out. The front brake line runs to the roll control, and from there it splits to each of the front wheels.

It's a good idea to pick a mount location that's relatively close to the master cylinder. This makes for easier plumbing. For a Nova, the most obvious spot is on the driver-side inner fender well. If it's a Hurst roll control you'll need three mounting fasteners.

As far as plumbing is concerned, there isn't one accepted method of hooking up the system. An aftermarket brake system with a prop valve will certainly result in different plumbing than something such as a 1968 Nova with drum brakes on all four corners. Hurst provides a series of diagrams showing the plumbing requirements for most common master cylinder arrangements. Because several lines require fabrication, you need a flaring tool along with a tubing bender. When hand building your own line, be sure to use seamless steel or seamless stainless tubing designed specifically for brake use. The preferred size is 3/16-inch line.

When plumbing a roll control, keep in mind that most of the solenoid valves have the respective ports machined in pipe thread. If you're using AN fittings (as shown in the accompanying photos), you need AN-to-pipe thread adapters. When installing any pipe thread fitting (including adapter fittings), the pipe-thread side requires Teflon tape or Teflon-based thread sealant. You must also ensure that none of the sealant gets inside and contaminates the lines or the roll control valve.

The electrical hookup isn't difficult, but it takes time to route the wires. Electrical wiring obviously must start and end somewhere. The place to begin is the switch. Hurst roll control assemblies have a pair of wires that originate in the micro switch. It doesn't matter which wire is "hot" (routed to the fuse panel) or which one goes to the roll control valve. The switch works in either case. Nova fuse panels already have provisions for such accessory instal-

If you use the steel inner fender as the mount, you can ground the roll control solenoid to the fender. Then you need to route a power line to the car. Shown here is a quick connector. This is used to allow for easier servicing down the road.

lations. Virtually all 1960s, 1970s, and later fuse panels have a readily marked spare "LPS" terminal, a spare "BATT" terminal, and a spare "ACC"

BRAKES

Inside the car, the roll control switch is routed to the shifter tunnel (and in this case, eventually installed on the shifter handle).

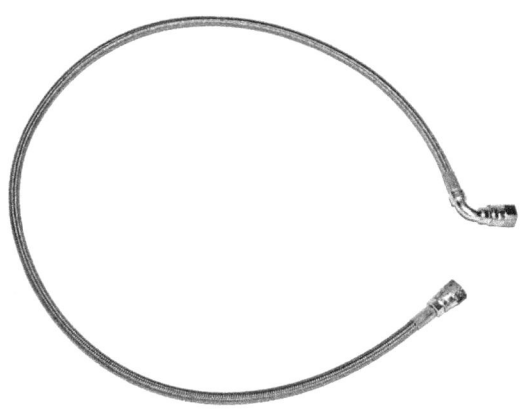

If you're going to use braided-steel brake hoses, this is what you need: a Teflon-core braided-stainless hose. Never use neoprene-lined AN hose for brakes. Under brake system pressure, a neoprene-lined hose expands, which increases brake pedal travel.

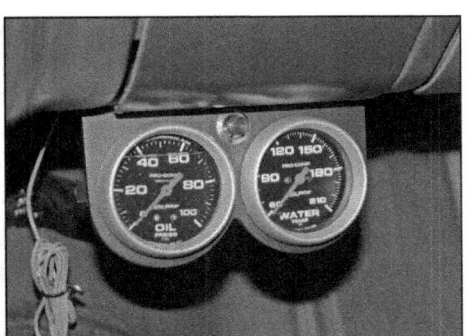

Hurst's roll control includes a red warning lamp. This tells you the system is armed. It's important to include it in the installation. This Nova has the lamp installed right over the accessory gauges.

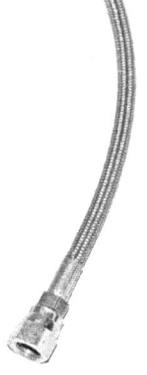

Rather than building your own hoses (and taking the chance you assembled them incorrectly), consider using factory assembled brake hose. The hose ends are installed by one of two methods by the manufacturer. The end is either crimped or swaged in place. That means the hose end attachment is permanent.

terminal. Use the spare spade terminal on the ACC side. ACC stands for accessory. It's hot when the ignition switch is clicked to ACC or ON, or when the vehicle is running.

Hurst includes a red "On" indicator lamp with the system. Use it! The last thing you need is to accidentally engage the roll control when you're on the brakes. Lamp wiring is basic. The lamp is spliced between the wire leading from the solenoid valve and the activation switch. After it's wired, whenever the system is engaged, the roll control light comes on. Finally, you should be certain that the ground is adequate. In most Nova applications, the roll control valve is mounted to a metal inner fender. If that's the case, the system is simply grounded directly to the fender using one of the roll control mounting bolts. One way or another, be sure the ground connection is sound and clean. You're done.

Brake Flex Hoses

Here's a scary thought: You stand on the brake pedal of your Nova at the end of a quick pass down the street or the quarter-mile. The fluid pressure exceeds 1,000 psi. Then the pedal goes to the floor. There's no need to explain what happens next (let your imagination be your guide), but the cause of the grief could very well have been a fitting that was blown off the end of a braided brake hose.

Sound impossible? Not so. One of the most perplexing scenes you may ever see is someone building AN (braided stainless-steel reinforced) brake hoses. More often than not, the hose is assembled incorrectly. The sad truth is, it's not hard to assemble the hose correctly or incorrectly. When planning (and building) brake flex hoses, you have only a few choices: OEM rubber flex hose, home-assembled -3 AN Teflon core hose, and preassembled -3 AN Teflon core hose (with and without a DOT-approved label).

Of those options, the best bet is a preassembled -3AN Teflon core hose assembly. Here's why: You *cannot* use neoprene-lined AN hose for brakes. Under brake system pressure, a neoprene-lined hose expands, which in turn soaks up brake pedal travel. Instead of forcing the brake piston (inside the caliper) against the brake rotor, the hydraulic forces take the path of least resistance and expand the hose. In the mid-1960s, Earl's Performance Products pioneered the use of armored flex hose with an extruded Teflon core to solve the problem. The stiffness of the Teflon liner combined with the tightly woven high-tensile stainless-steel outer braid fixed the dilemma of brake pedal travel, but it also offered another advantage. By eliminating hose swell (which is still present in OEM brake hoses to some degree), pedal firmness and feel improve significantly. Of course, the stainless-steel outer braid improves the abrasion resistance, and the design of this hose increases the temperature capacity as well.

Before you run out and buy some bargain basement Teflon hose, remember that there are two types of Teflon-lined braided stainless-steel hose on the market: commercial specification and aircraft specification. The difference is in the wall thicknesses of the Teflon. Commercial hose has a .030-inch thickness while the aircraft specification hose has a .040-inch thickness. Furthermore, some hose is manufactured with a stainless braid that is loose on the Teflon liner. This type of hose offers good pressure capacity, but it's limited in its resistance to expansion. For our purposes, we're dealing only with aircraft specification hose that is bonded tightly to the stainless-steel braid.

So far so good. Given the benefits of the -3 AN hose for brake applications, it seems like the way to go. And it is, unless you mess up the hose end

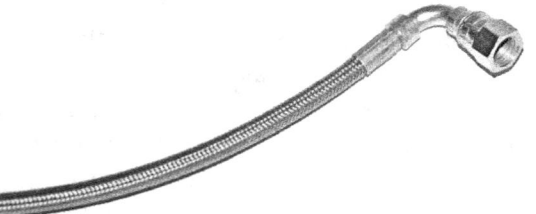

You can purchase stainless-steel braided brake hoses with any number of end fitting combinations. As you can see in this photo, each end of the hose has a conventional -3 female end.

installation. Although there's nothing complicated about the hose end installation (and no special tools are required), improper hose end installation can result in a catastrophe of the worst kind. During the assembly, the problem usually occurs when installing the sleeve (sometimes called an "olive") between the stainless-steel outer braid and the Teflon core. A small tool is available for this job (Earl's sells one under PN 007), but a small screwdriver or scribe can be used. Unfortunately, separating the braid from the liner is more difficult than it sounds. This can become a tedious job and you must be careful not to mark the Teflon. You also must be absolutely positive that none of the braid is trapped between the Teflon core and the sleeve. When you've reached that point, you then must be sure that the Teflon core is completely bottomed against the inside of the sleeve. Finally, you must be sure that the sleeve is square in relation to the Teflon core.

Part and parcel of the operation is usually a succession of holes punctured in your fingertips. It's inevitable. The stainless-steel outer braid is sharp. And the more you handle the cut hose, the better the chances of wounding yourself. To complicate matters even more, if you don't follow the instructions carefully, there's a very good chance that the hose end will back out under pressure. Unfortunately, folks often become frustrated with the process and the bleeding fingers that go along with it. Most of the time, the "that's good enough" attitude prevails, even if the internal sleeve isn't installed correctly. Then the hose is assembled and Lady Luck is your only friend. Evidence of an improperly assembled hose end on -3 Teflon hose is the final

gap between the face of the socket and the hex of the nipple. According to Earl's, it should be between .023 and .046 inch (a feeler gauge must be used to check this measurement). If you've been around the block, you see plenty of assemblies that exceed these dimensions significantly.

Given the above, it's easy to see why preassembled crimped Teflon brake hose is the best bet. Aeroquip, Earl's, Russell, and others have offered it as a service for years. With this type of brake hose, the hose ends are installed by one of two methods: The end is either swaged in place or it's crimped. In either case, the hose end attachment is permanent. After the manufacturer attaches the ends, *each hose* is pressure checked. They typically use a hydrostatic pressure test that goes to 4,000 psi on each hose. Obviously, this far exceeds the pressures of a brake system, and for the home-based Nova mechanic, there's no way to test the hose to this pressure.

What types of hose end combinations are available? Typically each hose manufacturer offers racing brake hose packages in countless configurations. You can specify -3 straight female swivel ends, -3 90-degree female swivel ends, 10-mm 3/8-inch banjo (.425-inch-thick) ends, 7/16-inch banjo (.425-inch-thick) ends, 3/16-inch tube inverted flare (3/8-24 thread) female ends, 3/16-inch inverted flare (3/8-24) male ends, 10-mm x 1 female ends, 10-mm x 1 male ends, and several -4 AN configurations (for pressure gauge and hydraulic clutch applications). You can also mix and match each of these end configurations; in each hose configuration, you can also specify the length. If that's not enough, the manufacturers can build a custom hose in any configuration and in any length. Bottom line? Whatever the type of brake hose end and length required, it's readily available.

After installation, the hose must be kept clean and free flowing. There must not be any possibility that the installed hose assemblies can stretch, crimp, or kink under any conditions of wheel travel and steering angle. It's also a good idea to inspect all brake hoses periodically for condition (this is a good idea for any form of brake hose).

Brake Hard Lines

When it comes to replacing brake hard lines on a Nova, you have two choices: Fit reproduction lines on the car or build them. Reproduction brake lines more or less fit, depending upon the manufacturer and how they're packaged. Expect some aggravation. Enough said.

The other option is to build lines. If your Nova has custom features (for example, aftermarket brakes and aftermarket master cylinder, or a roll control), you need to fabricate at least some of the lines. Nothing beats the look of a carefully fabricated hard line. Done right, it's drop dead gorgeous. Done wrong, it can be a dangerous mess. So how do you do it right and where do you begin?

When building brake lines, .020- to .025-inch-wall stainless steel works well (although the thicker tubing is quite a bit harder to flare). The next thing is very important: Only use hard line with an ISO certification. This is usually of United States, Canada, Japan, German, or other European origin.

When it comes to fabbing hard lines, there are no tricks. It's just a matter of trial and error coupled with time. The key is, keep safety in mind. Your lines must be functional and leak proof. At the same time, you can make them look good too. Mistakes can and do happen with regularity when forming hard line, but that's part of the process.

First you must determine where each line is routed. Because every Nova application differs, there really isn't one way to do the job. When figuring out where the lines go, keep the scrub line in mind. The "scrub line" is the imaginary intersection point where a part of the chassis or a piece of suspension hardware might contact the pavement in the event of a mishap (for example, a blown tire).

Another concern is potential damage in the event a piece of the driveline or the engine decides to take a vacation. What you need to do here is ensure the brake lines aren't routed near the bellhousing or close to the driveshaft.

Two other things to consider are maintenance and excess heat. You want to be sure your brake lines aren't compromised whenever you jack up the car. It's just common sense to keep the lines away from a high heat source such as headers or exhaust pipes.

General Motors typically routed brake lines on the inner side of the front subframe, and then they ran on the inside of the rocker panel lip until they reached the rear subframe. From that point they again went on the inner side. Given the routing, the lines are well protected from potential on-road damage. Moreover, the factory routing tends to keep the brake line as far away as possible from the exhaust system and rotating driveline parts. The bottom line here is, you have several hours tied up in just the planning phase of brake line construction.

As far as material is concerned, you can build lines from .028-inch wall thickness, or .020-inch-wall-thickness 3/16-inch OD seamless tubing (some better auto supply stores sell it and so do aircraft parts houses). It's available in a number of lengths; however, you need something in the range of 30 feet for a complete car (this takes mistakes into consideration). When working

---

Getting Away with Single Flares

Automotive brake line fittings have a 45-degree double flare. AN fittings have a 37-degree single flare. Aircraft, various military applications, and race cars typically incorporate 37-degree AN fittings for brakes.

For the most part, stainless brake hard lines need to be flared at 37 degrees (which requires a special flaring tool) and not 45 degrees. One reason is that stainless-steel hard line is too hard to double flare, and it will most likely split if you attempt it. A single flare at 37 degrees, on the other hand, can easily be formed in stainless steel, provided you have the correct tools. But how does it seal? Simple. The 37-degree AN flare is designed to seal with a special tube nut and ferrule assembly. You cannot interchange 37- and 45-degree fittings. If you use a 37-degree flare where a 45-degree fitting is incorporated (and vise versa), it does not seal properly.

CHAPTER 6

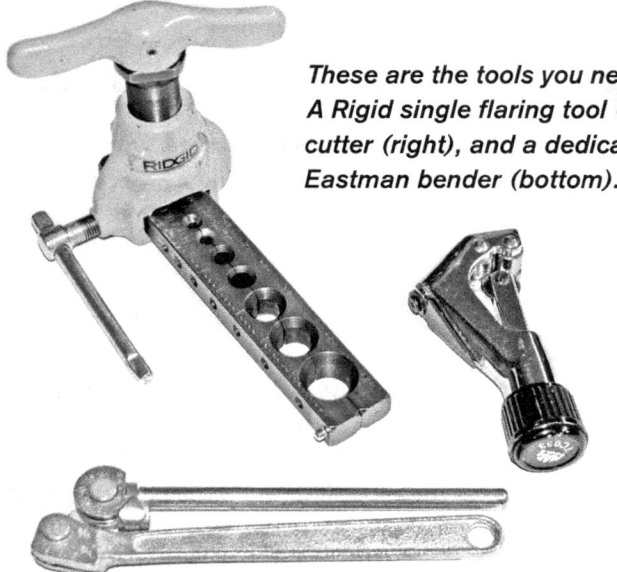

These are the tools you need to fabricate brake line: A Rigid single flaring tool (top), a Mac Tools tubing cutter (right), and a dedicated 3/16-inch-line Imperial Eastman bender (bottom).

with the tubing you discover that .020-inch-wall stainless forms far easier than the thicker stuff. You also need a supply of AN tube nuts and sleeves. Earl's and other hose manufacturers sell them.

When it comes to tools, you need several specialized items. Included in the mix are a tubing cutter, a 37-degree flaring tool, and a tubing bender. It's easy enough to find tools that work great on soft materials (for example, aluminum), but when dealing with stainless, the tools must be robust. Good options include a Rigid tubing cutter, a Rigid flaring tool, and Imperial Eastman benders (a dedicated bender for 3/16-inch line works far better than the universal options out there).

Hard lines, like wiring, must begin and end somewhere. Begin at the source and work from there. That means starting at the master cylinder. What you need to do is to convert all fittings (master cylinder, prop valve, roll control, and calipers) to AN. For example, a common replacement master cylinder for high-performance applications is the aluminum/plastic Mopar setup. It has two outlet ports (one for the front brakes and one for the back brakes) that happen to be different sizes. The leading port is 9/16-20 inverted flare while the rear port is 1/2-20 inverted flare. Wilwood can supply you with inverted flare fittings for this combination, but you should try to keep everything in a single configuration. In this case, Lamb Components machines a -3 AN adapter fitting just for the job. On a similar note, Hurst roll controls are built with 1/8-inch female pipe thread ports. This means you need an adapter to convert over to -3 AN. Every setup is slightly different, but all the major AN hose companies have adapters to fit almost anything.

Finally, you need some way to figure out how much line you need for a specific spot in your Nova. The easiest way to measure line is to fab up a pattern with easy-to-bend mechanic's wire. After you make the appropriate bends in the mechanic's wire, straighten it and measure it, or use a piece of string on the pattern and measure the string. That way, the mechanic's wire pattern can be used to fab up the stainless line.

In the accompanying photos, you can see how the line is formed.

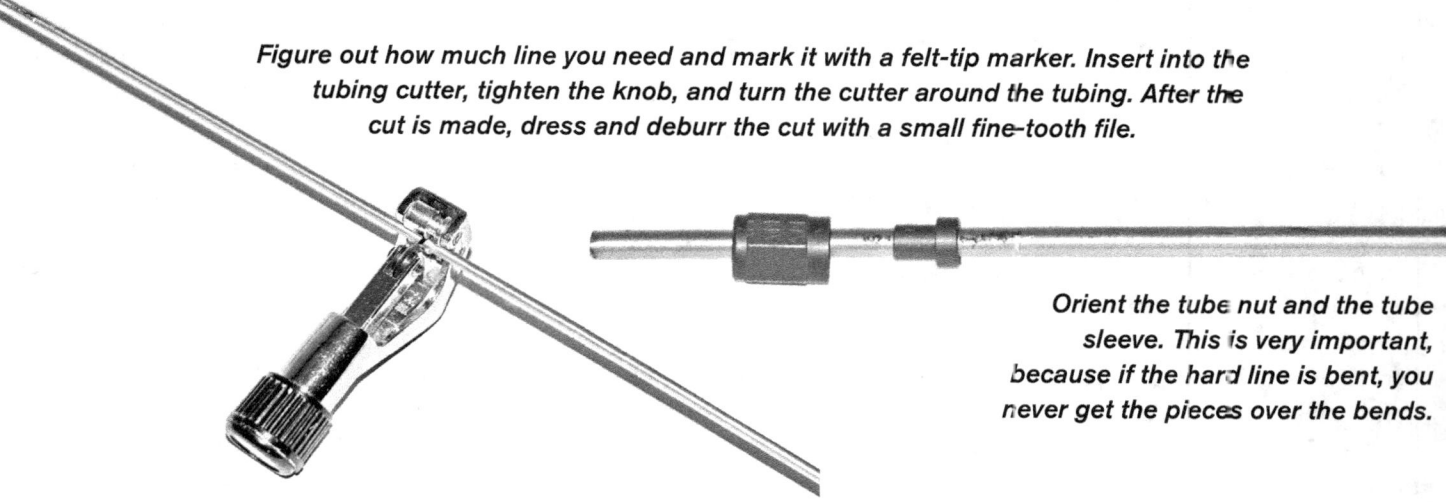

Figure out how much line you need and mark it with a felt-tip marker. Insert into the tubing cutter, tighten the knob, and turn the cutter around the tubing. After the cut is made, dress and deburr the cut with a small fine-tooth file.

Orient the tube nut and the tube sleeve. This is very important, because if the hard line is bent, you never get the pieces over the bends.

BRAKES

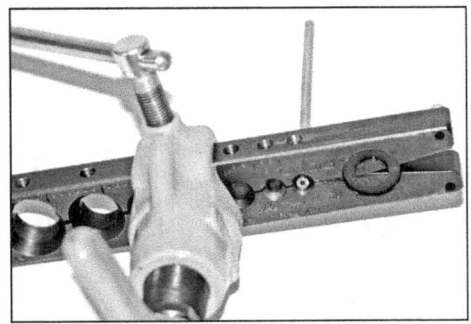

Place the tubing inside the flaring tool in the opening marked "3/16-inch." Roughly .100 inch of tubing must overhang from the flush surface of the tool.

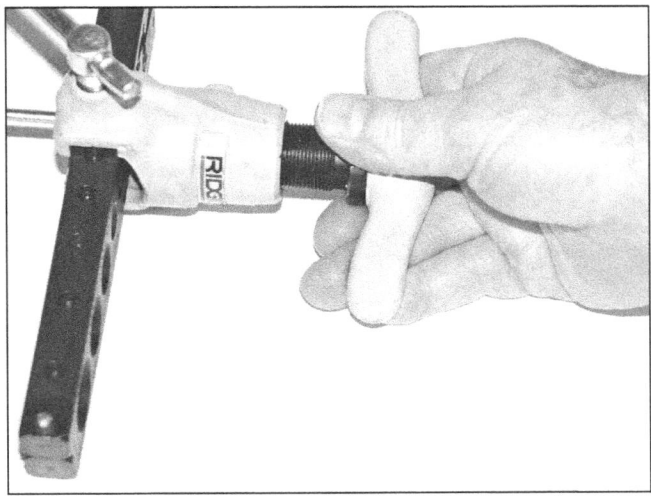

With the tubing locked into the tool (see the text for details), turn the large top handle until the internal cam releases.

Here's the finished flare. It's a good idea to lightly dress the flare with a small fine-tooth file. The idea here is to deburr it.

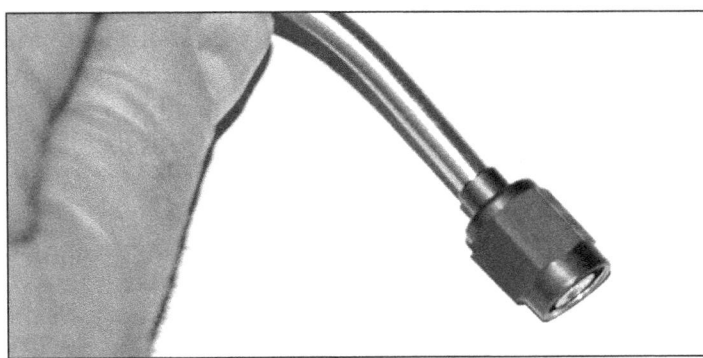

This is the finished flare with the tube nut and sleeve installed. It's ready to accept a male AN fitting (which in turn mates to a hose end).

When making a bend, examine the tubing bender closely. You find it's indexed from 0 to 180 degrees (in 45-degree increments). These numbers indicate the number of degrees for each respective bend. Making a 90-degree bend is easy. Insert the tubing between the respective dies in the tool and flip the clamp on the handle over. Simply bend the tubing with the handle so that the index marks read 90 degrees. Done.

This is a look at several completed custom bends on a Nova roll control assembly. If you take your time, you get fabulous, high-quality results; but remember that you will make mistakes. They come hand-in-hand with fabricating tubing.

CHAPTER 7

ENGINE SWAPS

The cackle of a thundering Chevy V-8 loping at idle is hard to ignore. It's addictive. Whack the gas pedal a time or two and chances are you'll be forever hooked. Chevy's V-8 engines personify Detroit-built muscle. And that's good news, because Novas from 1968 to 1974 are absolutely ripe for engine swaps. Generally, swapping an engine into a Nova is pretty simple, and the reality is, various engines can be installed without changing much. Still, though, the details make a huge difference.

A series of frame mount–engine mount combinations were used over the years, alternator locations varied with engines and model years, decidedly different transmission crossmembers were fitted, and so on. Include an LS engine in the mix and everything changes, but fortunately, the aftermarket is filled to the brim with swap hardware. In short, vintage Novas are easy enough to build in the backyard, but you have to know what fits where and how. What follows is a guide to swapping Chevy power and transmissions into your Nova. Check it out. It sure beats dragging out the torch.

Swaps such as this LS transplant into a third-gen Nova are becoming more and more common. This is a clean swap; it looks production, right down to the twin snorkel air cleaner on the EFI throttle body.

Frame Mounts

During the muscle-car era, three frame mounts were used in Nova applications: a 6-cylinder mount, a small-block mount, and a big-block mount. 1967 Camaro as well as 1968 Camaro and Nova mounts differ from 1969 mounts. Any of the engines physically fit any of the mounts, but the location and "angle" of the engine with respect to the frame is affected. Big-block frame mounts incorporate a distinct difference in height between left- and right-hand sides. The factory mounts typically place the engine farther forward in the engine compartment.

On the other hand, this doesn't mean that a fat block can't fit on small-block frame mounts. It works, but the engine sits farther to the rear of the compartment and the driver's side of the engine sits slightly lower than normal. As expected, this can create some header fit problems and makes for tight clearances between the engine and the firewall. Of course, if you want to gain some immediate engine setback (and therefore more rear-weight bias), you can use this system, or if you want to get radical, use a set of 6-cylinder frame mounts.

ENGINE SWAPS

When performing a traditional swap (for example, swapping in a big-block), the frame mounts must be exchanged. A rat motor in a Nova is moved (slightly) to the passenger's side with factory parts.

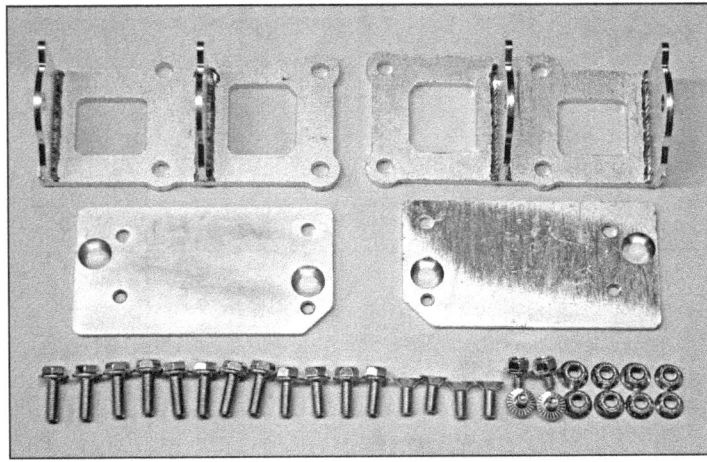

Hooker manufactures this mount package for LS swaps into Novas. The flat plates on the bottom are used to mount OEM clamshell mounts, while the top brackets bolt to the engine.

They provide even more setback. Unfortunately, with this setup the firewall often requires hammer surgery for distributor clearance. With a bunch of engine setback, the bellhousing bolts become almost impossible to reach.

Finally, I should point out that General Motors probably cataloged hundreds of frame mounts. Most of them don't exist anymore. Companies such as Classic Industries offer a good selection of quality reproduction mounts.

What about the LS engine? It's incredibly popular today, but it has a wee hitch: The mount arrangement is different than in Chevys of old. Plenty of solutions out there can get you past this, however. One that is really good is Hooker Headers' arrangement. The Hooker mounts are specifically designed for bolt-in compatibility with the Hooker transmission swap components. Essentially, it's a complete swap "system." The LS is designed to use a four-bolt motor mount. It's also situated farther back than traditional small-block or big-block mount locations (it's closer to the bellhousing on the LS). Hooker's engine mount brackets are designed to adapt the 1972–up (later model) GM clamshell engine mounts. The OEM-style clamshell mounts bolt to the subframe by way of a set of Hooker adapter plates (see the accompanying photos). Then the engine, fitted with Hooker's mounts, drops in over the top. What the Hooker system does is provide you

Frame Mount Part Numbers		
The big-block part numbers that follow are correct.		
Application Engine	Location	Part Number
1967–1968 Camaro, 1968 Nova V-8-BB	Left and Right	K702
1969–1970 Nova V-8-BB	Left and Right	K701

Chevrolet used a specific transmission crossmember for specific applications. This is a big-block, stick shift crossmember. It's positioned upside down in this photo, but you can see the offset.

Hooker Engine Swap Bracket			
Manufacturer	Engine	Location	Part Number
Hooker	LS	Left and Right	12618HKR

Motor Mount Part Numbers

Manufacturer	Engine	Location	Part Number
Classic Industries	V-8-BB	Left and Right	T82283
Lakewood Industries	V-8-BB	Left and Right	24087
Anchor	LS	Left and Right	2292

with the right geometry (driveline angles) when the engine is installed. It also ensures the headers fit correctly.

Motor Mounts

The original Chevy rubber/steel composite mounts had a bad habit of self-destructing. Factor in years of use, oil soaking, and considerable heat cycles, and the need for new mounts soon becomes apparent. Both Classic Industries and Lakewood build mounts for big-block applications. The parts from Classic Industries are reproductions. Lakewood's components are from the "muscle mount" series. They incorporate a heavy-gauge steel frame and both pieces (frame mount side and engine mount side) are vulcanized to a hard durometer rubber. They also incorporate a safety interlock design where applicable, eliminating the need for torque straps or cables.

As far as the LS swap is concerned, Hooker recommends you use an Anchor brand clamshell mount for the application.

Transmission Crossmembers

Novas were built for a wide array of buyers. Because of this, an equally wide cross section of transmissions was available. Everything from two-speed Powerglides to Muncie 4-speeds occupied the territory under the floorboards. Given this situation, many non-stock combinations are possible. Examples include Powerglides behind rat motors, Muncies behind straight-6s, and so on. In factory form the big-block either had a Turbo 400 or a Muncie.

What about an LS Swap? Hooker's mounting brackets coupled with its transmission swap crossmembers allow you to use a GM Powerglide, TH350, TH400, 700R4, 2004R, or 4L60/4L65/4L70/4L75 automatic in any 1968–1974 Nova without cutting or hammering the transmission tunnel. The use of a 6-speed manual mandates some tunnel work because the Tremacs are huge.

Transmission Mount

The actual transmission mount (known as the "mounting" in GM parts catalogs) is similar for all models.

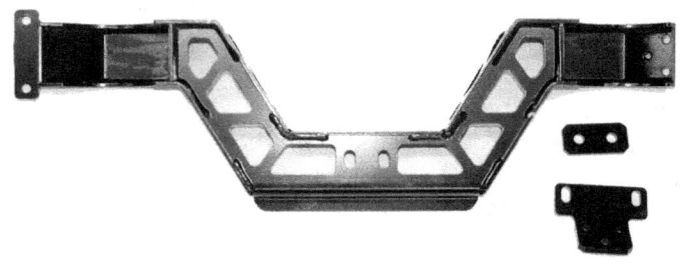

This cool girder structure is Hooker's LS swap crossmember for T56 and automatic transmissions. Hooker used high-tech FEA (Finite Element Analysis) in the design.

Transmission Crossmember Part Numbers

The following are available (I use Classic Industries part numbers here for reference).

Application	Transmission	Crossmember
1968–1974 Nova	THM400 big-block	3912573
1968–1974 Nova	4-speed manual, HD 3-speed manual big-block	HC109
1968–1974 Nova	THM400 small-block	C148561
1968–1974 Nova	4-speed manual, 3-speed manual, Powerglide, TH350	E374

Hooker Crossmembers

Application	Transmission	Part Number
1968–1974 Nova	T56 manual	12626HKR
1968–1974 Nova	4L60-4L65-4L70-4L75 automatic	12625HKR
1968–1974 Nova	4L80-4L85 automatic	12627HKR
1968–1974 Nova	Adapter – THM400 and 2004R to fit 12626HKR	12650HKR

ENGINE SWAPS

Transmission Crossmember Mount Part Numbers

Classic Industries Part Numbers

Application	Part Number
3-speed, 4-speed manual, TH 350, Powerglide	T82224
Turbo-Hydramatic 400	T82268

Hooker LS Swap Crossmember Mount

Application	Part Number
T56, 4L60 series, 4L80 series Prothane	7-1604

Aftermarket solid jobs are available, but when coupled with solid motor mounts, these parts tend to tie the powertrain together too tightly. This often results in broken mount ears on 4-speed cases or fractured cases on automatics. Stick with the rubber stuff.

Flywheels, Flexplates and Starters

LS engines use their own dedicated flywheels, flexplates, and starters. With an original small-block or big-block engine, the crankshaft flange extends .400 inch farther rearward than in an LS application. That means for LS swaps where you're using an early non-LS automatic, you need a flexplate spacer kit (Chevrolet PN 12563532K). It spaces the converter outward on the flexplate so that it can engage the crank flange. With stick shifts the LS makes use of a distinct crankshaft mounting flange, which necessitates use of an LS flywheel. If you use an LS flywheel and an early manual transmission, you'll also need a swap bellhousing (QuickTime has a wide range of swap bellhousings for LS applications).

When you get into early engines, things aren't exactly straightforward either. Two systems of balance have been used on vintage Chevy V-8s: internal balance and external

When it comes to flywheels, lots of differences are seen between various engines in the Chevrolet family. For example, some engines were externally balanced; some came with 153-tooth ring gears; some came with 168-tooth ring gears; LS engines have a different bellhousing spacing; and so on. This is a 168-tooth aluminum/steel flywheel for a conventional small- or big-block.

Flywheels and Flexplates

I use these part numbers as reference only.

Flywheels

Description	Part Number
12¾-inch nodular iron, 10.4-inch clutch, neutral balance	14085720
12¾-inch nodular iron, 10.4-inch clutch, counterweighted for 454	3963537
12¾-inch nodular iron, 10.4- and 11-inch clutch, lightweight, 1-piece seal	14088646
12¾-inch iron, 10.4-inch clutch, 1-piece seal	14088650
14-inch iron, 11- and 11.85-inch clutch, 1-piece seal	10105832
14-inch iron, 11-inch clutch, counterweighted for 400	3986394
14-inch iron, 11-inch clutch, counterweighted for 454	3993827
14-inch iron, 10.4- and 11-inch clutch, neutral balance	3991469

Flexplates

Description	Part Number
14-inch neutral balance, 168-tooth, small-block	471598
14-inch neutral balance, 168-tooth, big-block	471597
14-inch counterweighted for 400, 168-tooth	471578
14-inch counterweighted for 454, 168-tooth	14001992
12¾-inch neutral balance, 153-tooth, small-block	471529
12¾-inch, 1-piece seal	10128412
14-inch heavy-duty, 1-piece seal	10128413
14-inch, 1-piece seal	10128414

Note: Flywheels and automatic transmission flexplates are interchangeable between V-6-90 and small-block V-8 engines.

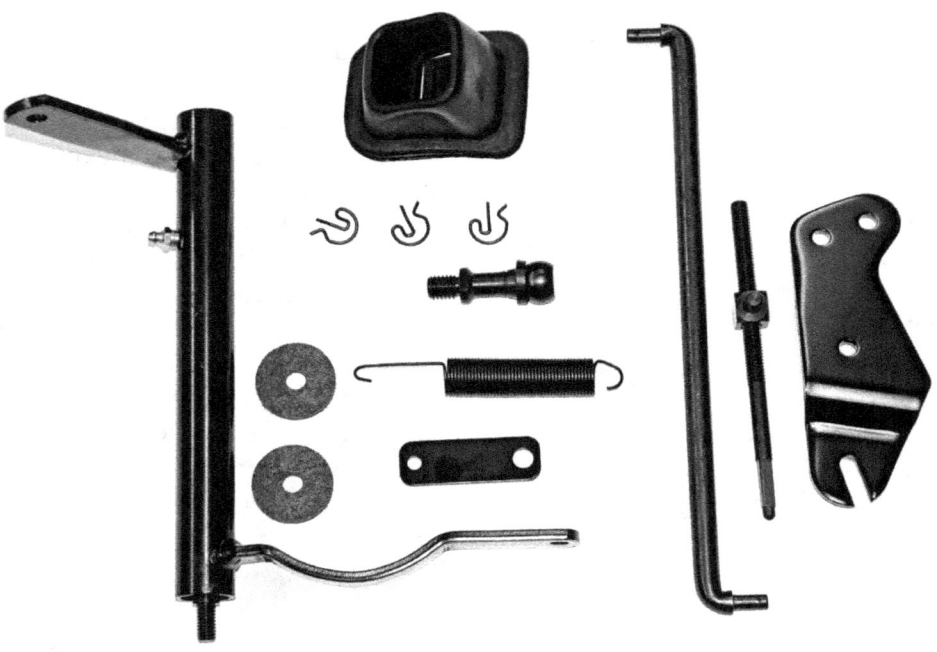

The mechanical clutch linkage systems used on Novas all pretty much look the same. This example is a big-block reproduction package from Classic Industries.

large-diameter flywheels incorporate 168 teeth on the ring gear while the 12¾-inch models have 153 teeth. The following chart shows most of the flywheel and flexplate combinations (keeping in mind that the 14-inch jobs are the most common for big-blocks).

Because two diameters of flywheels and flexplates have been used in small- and big-block applications, a couple of starter combinations are available. Large-diameter flywheels and flexplates require a starter with offset bolt holes in the nosepiece, while small-diameter models use a starter with bolt holes that are parallel. The majority of Chevrolet blocks are drilled for both types of starters.

Clutch Linkage

When it comes to clutch linkages, differences between big-block, small-block, and 6-cylinder crossshaft applications preclude interchange. The added width of the big-block causes the trouble. You need an appropriate clutch bell

balance. The 400-ci small-blocks and 454-ci big-blocks are externally balanced (or "counterweighted") and use special flywheels and harmonic dampeners. Late-model engines make use of one-piece rear main seals, whereas early engines have two-piece rear seals. One-piece rear-seal engines feature a smaller 3.00-inch crank flange bolt circle whereas earlier examples incorporate a 3.58-inch pattern. The right mix of flywheels and flexplates must be used for each family of engines.

Chevrolet offered flywheels in two sizes: 12¾ and 14 inches. The

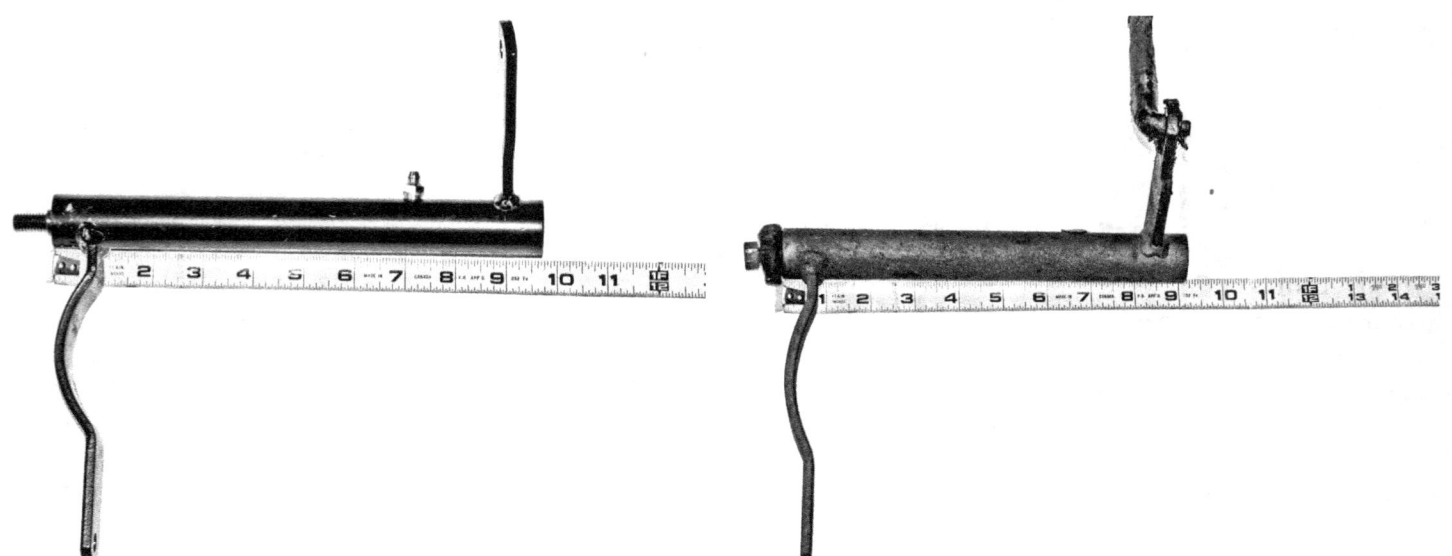

Recall when I mentioned the engine offset with a big-block? The first photo shows a clutch Z-bar (cross shaft) for a big-block application. The second photo shows a Z-bar for a small-block. Note the difference in length.

ENGINE SWAPS

Clutch Linkage Part Numbers		
Application	Description	Part Number
1968–1974 Nova	Big-block bell crank	3912602
1968–1974 Nova	Big-block clutch conversion	K510

crank. Using Classic Industries as the basis, here's the basic bell crank part number along with a part number for a complete big-block clutch conversion kit (includes everything except the pedals to install a clutch setup in a vintage Nova).

What if you want to run a stock mechanical clutch linkage with an LS engine? If the transmission is mounted in the stock location, you can use a Scoggin Dickey or Jegs adapter bracket (originally designed for the Gen V/VI factory big-blocks without a provision for the clutch ball stud). These brackets bolt to the lower two bellhousing bolts on the driver's side and place the ball stud in exactly the right position for a stock small-block Z-bar. Fair enough, but most full-length LS swap headers aren't designed to fit a mechanical clutch linkage. So, if you choose to run a clutch in an LS-swapped Nova, you're best off looking at a hydraulic setup. McLeod Racing has a setup that's almost a bolt-in for this application (PN 1434002).

Building A Bulletproof Mechanical Clutch Linkage

The standard clutch linkage setup found in a Nova consists of a fork at the bellhousing (for the release bearing) along with a couple of shafts and a bell crank (Z-bar) linkage. It was simple. It worked great. But time can take its toll. Ditto with big clutch pressures. In the 1960s and 1970s (and even later) plenty of folks regularly experienced clutch linkages that bent and buckled. The reason was massive pressure plate spring pressure. Today, clutch assemblies don't use those massive, leg-breaking pressures, but the big problem is wear. If you look closely at the clutch linkage in a well-used Nova, you'll most likely discover that the linkage rods are equally well-worn at the pin ends, and most (if not all) of the mounting holes in the Z-bar and the pedal are oval. Now what?

You can replace the parts. That's a no-brainer. Most reproduction parts houses offer a wide array of replacement hardware (and, in fact, a reproduction Z-bar is used in our example). However, if you want a slick action clutch linkage, a better option is to build a heavy-duty linkage setup incorporating rod ends and chrome-moly tubing.

Many of you are thinking, "Old news." You're right. Several magazine articles have appeared on this topic over the years, but every last one missed important details along with important pieces in the puzzle. For example, the pinholes in a typical Chevy (or other GM) measure 5/16 inch in diameter. Over time (and as pointed out above), that hole diameter becomes oval. Building a clutch linkage with 5/16-inch rod ends doesn't help much because the holes the bolts pass through (in the pedal as well as the Z-bar) are sloppy. You're pretty much forced to move up a size in rod ends. That means you should use a 3/8-inch-diameter rod end (not a 5/16-inch one). Drilling out the respective holes in a Z-bar or a clutch pedal to 3/8 inch takes out the ovaling. Furthermore, if you do your homework, you find that the tubing you need is definitely 5/8-inch OD (the same as you'd use for a 5/16-inch rod end). As an example, the folks from Mark Williams offer chrome-moly tubing in this OD with a .058-inch wall. You can use a 3/8-24 to 5/8 x .058–inch tubing adapter (weld spud) to build the linkage. This allows the use of a 3/8-inch rod end on the same-diameter tubing you'd use with smaller 5/16-inch rod ends.

Why not make it easy for yourself and build a linkage that can also be used to adjust the clutch? Use a left- and a right-hand-thread tubing adapter on each side of the respective linkage pieces instead of using all standard right-hand rod ends. With this setup, to adjust the clutch you simply back off the jam nuts on the rod ends and turn the linkage rod one way or another to lengthen or loosen the respective link. That's how race car shops such as Jerry Bickel Race Cars set up their linkage systems, and it works the same on a street-driven Nova. If the thing has all right-hand threads, you have to go through the mess of removing the bolts, holding the rod ends in place, turning the linkage in or out, buttoning it back up, and checking the gap. If you're wrong, you have to start all over again. That's way too much trouble.

So what's it like to build the linkage properly? It's not much harder than the alternative. ■

Building A Bulletproof Mechanical Clutch Linkage *CONTINUED*

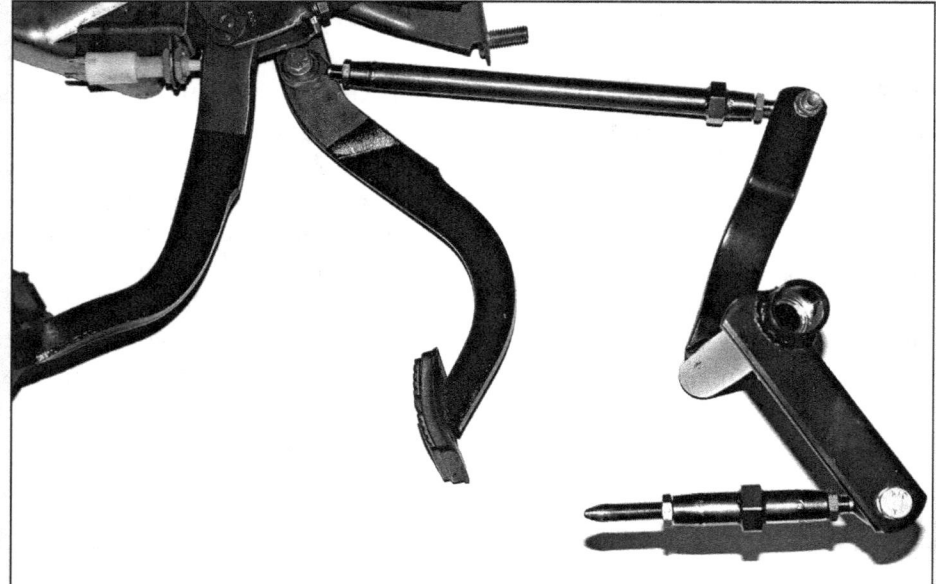

This is a modified clutch linkage for a Nova. It features spherical bearing rod ends on the upper and lower pushrods, AN hardware, and complete adjustability.

If you need proof of how the holes in a linkage oval over time, have a look at this photo. This guarantees a sloppy linkage.

The clutch pushrod setups found in a Nova have a pointed or semi-ball end at the clutch fork side. First cut the head off a 3/8-inch fine-thread bolt. You have to "turn" it by chucking the bolt into an electric drill motor. This allows you to "turn" the piece on both a stone as well as a piece of coarse sand paper. In the end this provides for a nice, clean radius.

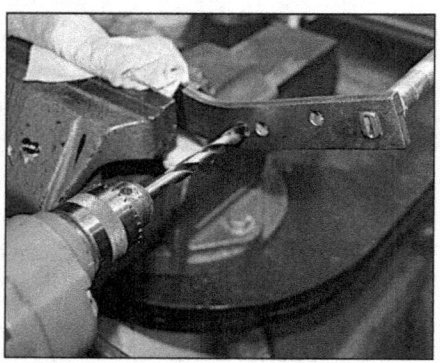

The fix for the ovaling isn't that difficult. First, drill out the hole to 3/8 inch using a sharp drill bit.

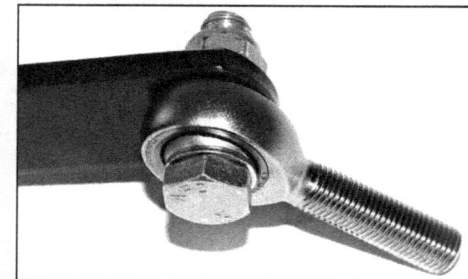

Next, drill out the pair of holes in the clutch linkage Z-bar. What you're looking at is a 3/8-inch fine-thread AN bolt that passes through a high-quality 3/8-inch rod end.

To cut a piece of 5/8-inch .058-inch-wall chrome-moly to size, you have a couple of options: Use a hacksaw butted up against a hose clamp or use a big tubing cutter. Either works.

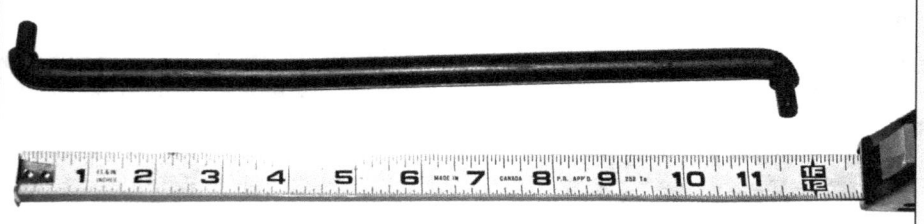

Measure each of the stock pushrods. Take the length of each tubing adapter (weld spud) into account, along with approximately one-half of the threads of a rod end for each side. FYI: Many tube adapters measure just under 7/8 inch (each) when pressed into the tube; JBRC adapters are slightly shorter.

ENGINE SWAPS

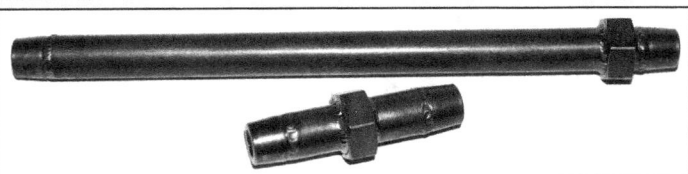

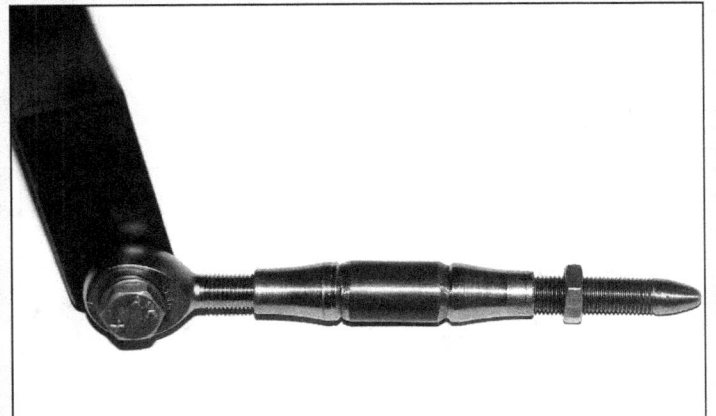

These are custom linkage rods built by Jerry Bickel Race Cars. They're the same general setup as shown in the previous photos. In addition, they are also fabricated from chrome-moly. JBRC added an adjuster nut on each of the rods. It's a great idea.

With the left- and right-hand threads on each tubing adapter, the nut allows you to turn the linkage "in" or "out" after backing off the jam nuts on the rod ends. That's a lot easier than dropping the linkage to adjust the clutch.

The ends of the tubing should be filed to remove flash, then a pair of weld spuds (tubing ends) are pressed into place. One side has left-hand threads while the other has right-hand threads. Repeat on the longer pushrod and weld the tubing adapters in place.

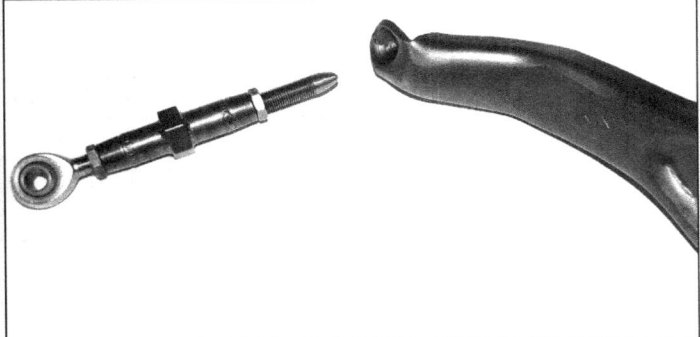

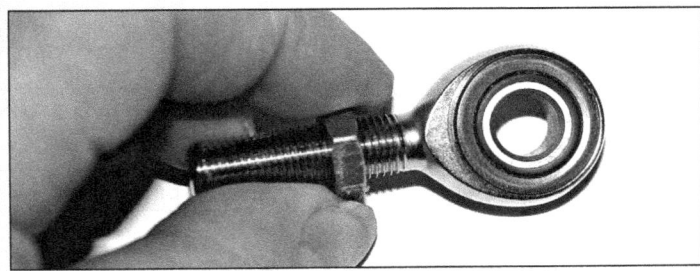

These are the high-quality 3/8-inch rod ends used in this build. You can probably get away with cheaper quality pieces, but these three-piece aircraft jobs are top of the heap.

Here's a look at the lower custom linkage next to a GM clutch fork. You can see how the modified 3/8-inch (fine RH thread) fastener works. After cutting the head off the bolt, be sure to chase the threads (with a die).

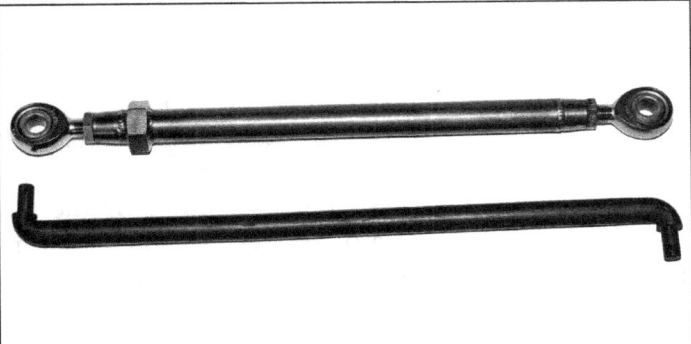

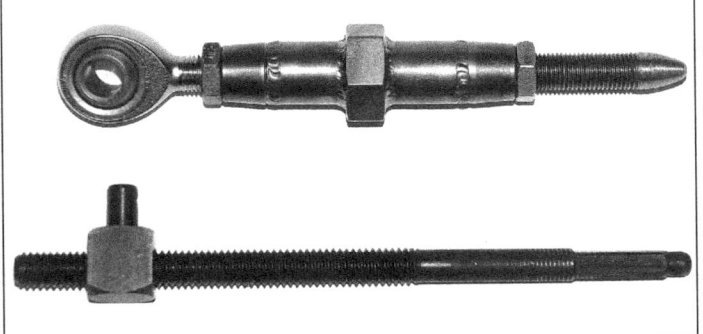

This is a direct comparison of a stock linkage (stock at the bottom in both photos) and a custom rod end setup. There's no comparison when it comes to adjustability or beef.

Building A Bulletproof Mechanical Clutch Linkage CONTINUED

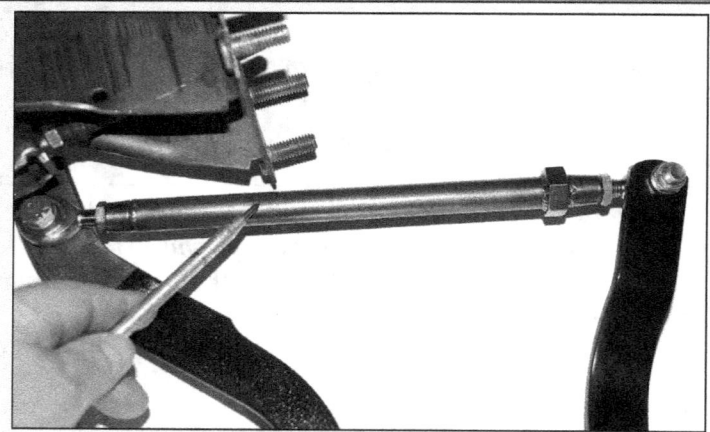
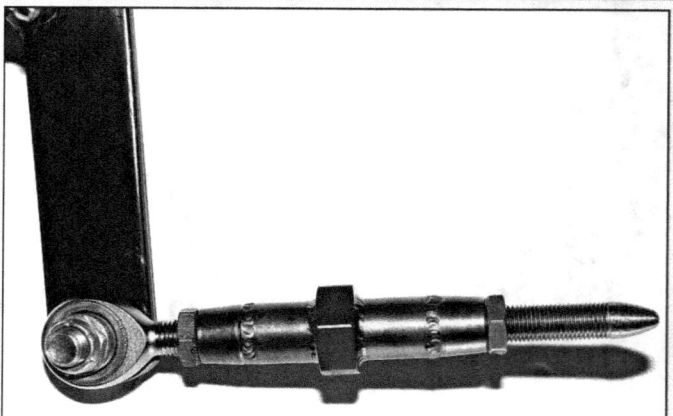

Installed in both the Z-bar and the clutch pedal, this is what each piece of linkage looks like. In the end, this setup provides you with a linkage that is smooth, easy to adjust, has no slop, and doesn't bend!

Alternators, Water Pumps and Pulleys

Vintage Chevrolet alternators are generally similar in external size and layout, but 1968-and-earlier models were mounted on the driver's side of the engine whereas 1969-and-later alternators mounted to the passenger's side. This coincides with the introduction of the "long"-style water pumps (which are slightly more than 1 inch longer than the earlier models). Because of the pump length, there is no interchange between the brackets, most pulleys, and hardware. Obviously, it's better to use the appropriate hardware for either long or short model years. The big reason is wiring. There's a hefty alternator harness lead on the driver's side for 1968-and-earlier cars whereas on later models the wiring harness is on the passenger's side.

Chevrolet's Corvette was not converted to the long water pump design in 1969; it remained as a "shorty" setup for many years. This could also be a source (particularly at resto supply houses) for complete bits and pieces, especially if you are changing over to a short configuration.

Alternator Brackets

Although alternator brackets for big-blocks look like those found on small-block cars, they're not the same. Here's a rundown on the pieces you need for a swap (Classic Industries part numbers).

Application	Description	Part Number
1968	Standard water pump	58133
1968	High-performance water pump	58133P
1969–1970	All big-block water pumps	58135
All 1969 and later	Alternator bracket kit, complete	E329
All big-block	396/375 HP deep groove alternator pulley	KW609
1969 and later	Crank pulley, without AC	KW396
1969–1970	Crank pulley, with AC	14542
1970 and later	Crank pulley, with AC	G2122
1969 and later	Water pump pulley, single groove, high performance	KW394
1970	Water pump pulley, single groove	14546

LS Drives

When it comes to accessory drive assemblies, water pumps, and associated hardware, the LS engine is a completely different animal. An LS power plant has three basic accessory drive systems: shallow, mid-length, and long. All are based off specific harmonic dampener (balancer) dimensions. The Corvette dampener arrangement is the shallowest, followed by the early Camaro/GTO systems, followed by the truck setup. With the factory Corvette drive system, the alternator is above the water pump. The factory Camaro and GTO setup mounts the power steering pump over the alternator. The factory truck mounts are bulky and take up a

ENGINE SWAPS

Holley Kits	
Holley offers so many options that I can't list them all, but here is a list of comprehensive kits.	
Description	**Part Number**
Complete drive, SD7 A/C pump, alternator, P/S pump, tensioner, belt, pulleys	20-138
Complete drive, SD508 A/C pump, alternator, P/S pump, tensioner, belt, pulleys	20-137
Complete drive, R4 A/C pump, alternator, P/S pump, tensioner, belt, pulleys	20-136
Passenger-side A/C drive, SD508 A/C pump, tensioner, pulleys	20-141
Passenger-side A/C drive, SD7 A/C pump, tensioner, pulleys	20-142
Passenger-side A/C drive, R4 A/C pump, tensioner, pulleys	20-140
Driver-side alternator and P/S pump, pulleys	20-143

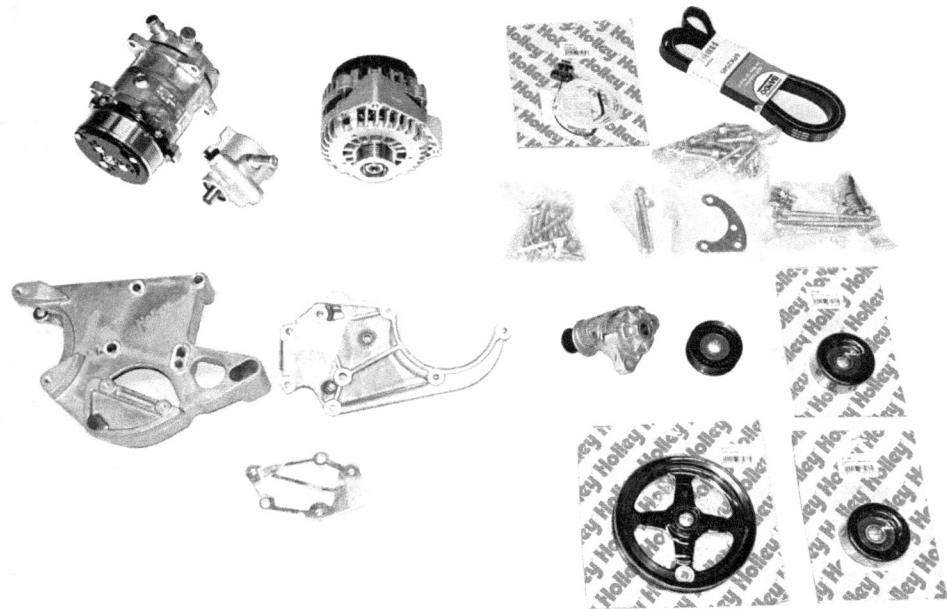

The accessory drive system you use on your Nova depends upon the engine you select. This Holley drive setup is for an LS with power steering and air conditioning.

lot of real estate under the hood. Obviously, there are a bunch of variations to the above, but the big challenge is finding the desirable drives (Corvette and to some degree Camaro-GTO). The problem is, anything that relates to a Corvette in a wrecking yard seems to double or triple the price.

Enter Holley's drive system. Holley based all of its drive packages off the short Corvette harmonic dampener (balancer) dimension. Then it uses a spacer package to make up the difference for the dampener you have on your engine. It's a simple solution that means you don't have to buy an expensive new harmonic dampener to fit the drive system.

In terms of systems, Holley offers a wide range of packages, beginning with comprehensive kits complete with an A/C pump, power steering pump, and an alternator, down to simple brackets that allow the install of an alternator only. Holley's kits are designed to accept the most common (and least costly) factory truck or early F-car alternator. Suffice it to say, it has you covered when it comes to LS drives and accessories.

Throttle Linkage

Early Novas used a mechanical throttle linkage. In other words, no cable setups but a simple lever and rod arrangement instead. While most of the Holley pieces for a big-block and

With traditional (non-LS) engines, the throttle linkage varies from engine to engine, and carburetor type to carburetor type. This is a big-block Holley carburetor throttle linkage setup from Classic Industries.

Reproduction Linkage	
The following are part numbers for a Classic Industries reproduction linkage.	
Description	**Part Number**
Big-block throttle linkage	3923549
Small-block throttle linkage	3923539

CHAPTER 7

When you install a big-block where a small-block or 6-cylinder once lived in a Nova, you should also change the heater. Big-block heaters had their cores "reversed." That meant the hoses were closer to the fender. The setup shown here is a complete big-block heater setup from Classic Industries.

If you don't need a heater, it's possible to delete it with this plate setup, again from Classic Industries. This is a reproduction C-48 Heater Delete. It certainly cleans up the firewall area.

a small-block do interchange (even though they feature different bends and have different part numbers), the other parts do not. The simple solution is to procure the right parts the first time out rather than trying to cobble up a linkage from scratch.

Heater

When the first rat motor was shoehorned into a 1967 Camaro engine bay, one of the first changes was the relocation of the heater hoses. This change applies to Novas too. In essence, a new heater core was designed: one with reversed inlet/outlet fittings. Rather than exiting near the cylinder head, the fittings were placed near the inner fender. Reproduction heater cores are readily available and by simply cutting new holes in the heater core cover, you can re-position your heater hoses.

Ignition Controls

Conventional small- and big-block Chevrolets can use any number of ignition systems. The LS engine family was born "distributorless," and while technically simpler, it does complicate things. If you have an LS swap planned, first determine if it's going to be a carbureted example or fuel injected. If injected and the power plant is close to stock, you can use an OEM production line Chevy wiring harness and Engine Control Module. Chevrolet Performance sells ECUs and harnesses, but most are very specific (and calibrated) to a given crate engine.

If your car is heavily modified, something such as a Holley (or other aftermarket) ECU is likely the best choice. If the engine is carbureted, you can use a GM Controller Kit or a similar example from MSD. Controllers for carbureted LS engines provide the ignition component. When selecting a controller of some sort for any LS swap, consider if the engine has a 24X reluctor wheel or a 58X reluctor wheel. Essentially, a reluctor wheel is what generates the firing sequence signal to the ECU. Pre-2006 LS engines have a 24X reluctor setup. The 2006 and newer LS engines have a 58X reluctor wheel.

For further insight into LS swaps, pick up a copy of SA Design's *LS Swaps: How to Swap GM LS Engines into Almost Anything*. Another good option is SA Design's *Swap LS Engines into Camaros and Firebirds: 1967–1981*. Follow the 1967–1969 Camaro recommendations. Just keep in mind, many Nova radiators are different from Camaro examples.

Headers

While it's possible to use cast-iron factory manifolds in most swaps, the difference in both performance and

Heater Core Part Numbers	
Here are the non-A/C big-block heater component part numbers from Classic Industries.	
Description	Part Number
Big-block heater core	3018864
Big-block heater core cover	AL303
Big-block heater core seal kit	K933

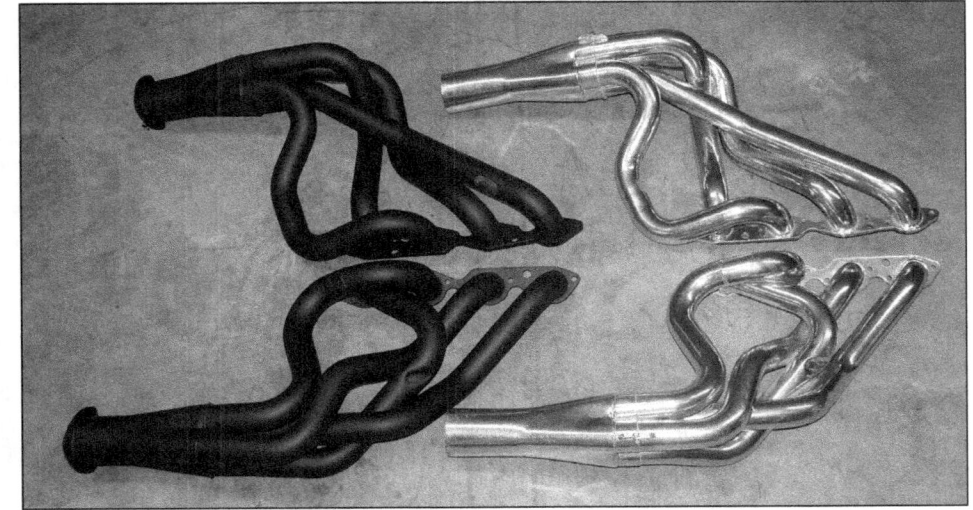

There are a lot of header configurations out there, but this is a look at some of the best. Both of these big-block header sets are from Hooker. The black ones are Super Competition street headers, and the ceramic-coated ones are Hooker Race headers.

cost when compared to headers does not justify their use. Most Chevrolet exhaust manifolds were designed for the chassis. In other words, a set of streamlined big-block Corvette manifolds don't work in your Nova engine compartment.

When it comes to headers for Novas, keep this in mind: The type of motor mount you use in the swap dictates the headers you select. In other words, if you try to fit headers to something such as a big-block positioned on small-block or 6-cylinder mounts, you're asking for trouble. Use the right mount combination and you won't have grief!

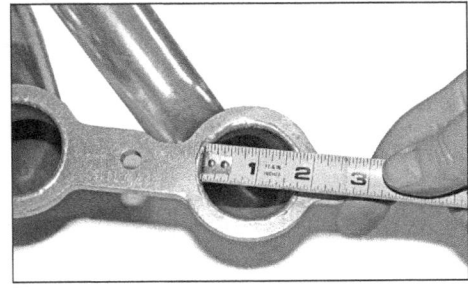

Race headers are adjustable; you can change the length of both the primary tubes and the collectors. This is Hooker Headers' complete kit for a big-block application.

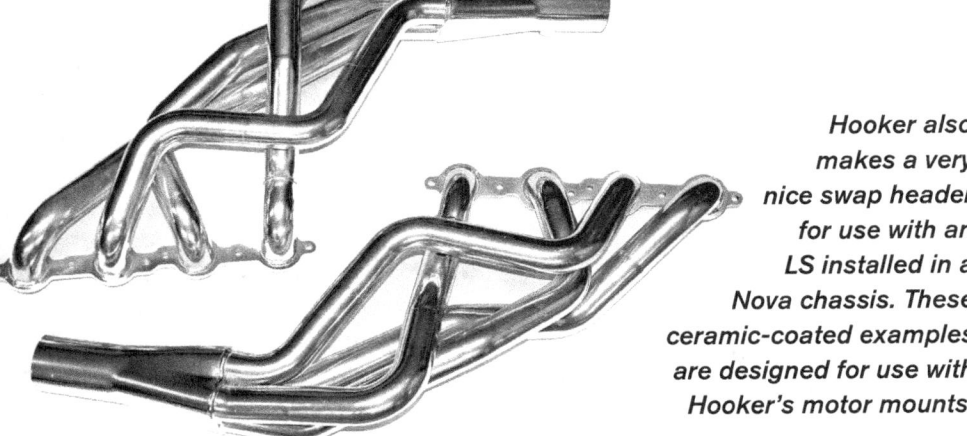

Hooker also makes a very nice swap header for use with an LS installed in a Nova chassis. These ceramic-coated examples are designed for use with Hooker's motor mounts.

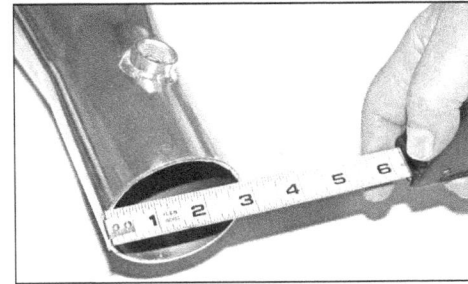

The primary tubes on the LS swap headers measure 1 7/8 inches in diameter. Meanwhile, the collector is 3 inches in diameter (second photo).

CHAPTER 7

Finally, the number of headers out there is mind boggling, too many to list all the available part numbers. Here is a look a Hooker's swap headers along with two big-block combinations. By the way, American Racing Headers (ARH) offers several clean LS swap header options. Check them out. They're all great examples. When buying LS headers, it's a good idea to be sure you have the correct engine mounts (mounts used when the header manufacturer built the headers). Otherwise fit can become an issue.

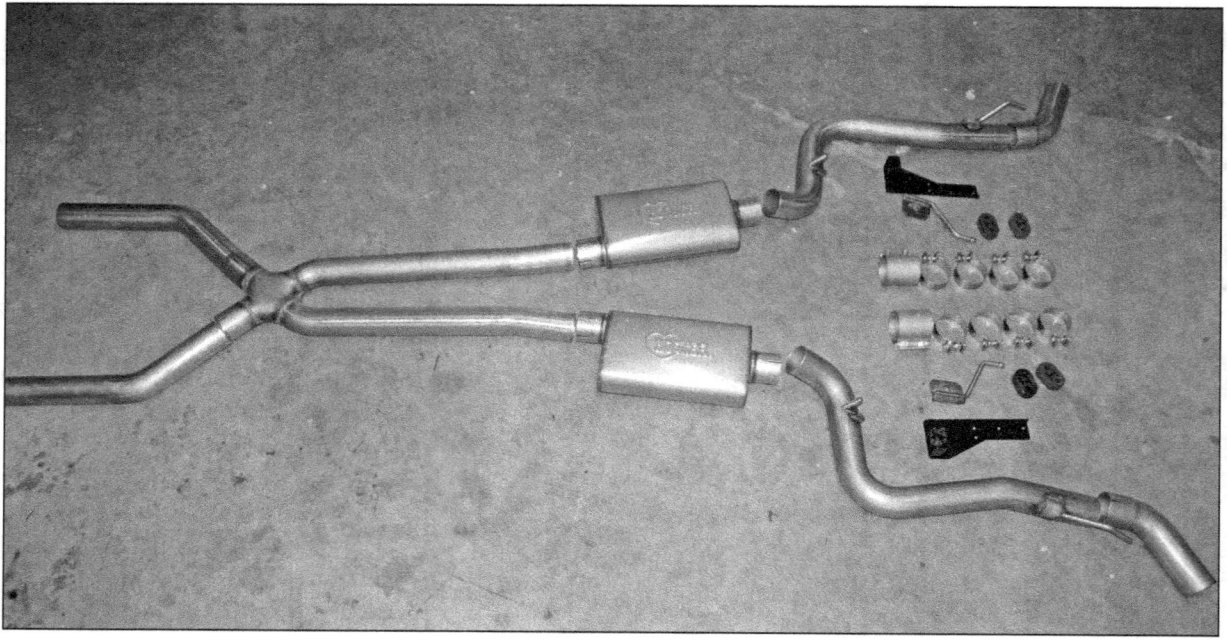

No matter what engine you choose, you need an exhaust system. When it comes to exhaust, bigger is better. This is a 3-inch Hooker setup designed to fit its LS headers.

Hooker's mufflers are big. They can be used with a healthy big-block. Note that the case measures about 14 inches in length.

Inlet and outlet on the mufflers is 3 inches in diameter. If you have a conventional small- or big-block, you can use this system with one change: The head pipes from the muffler to the header collector need to be fabricated.

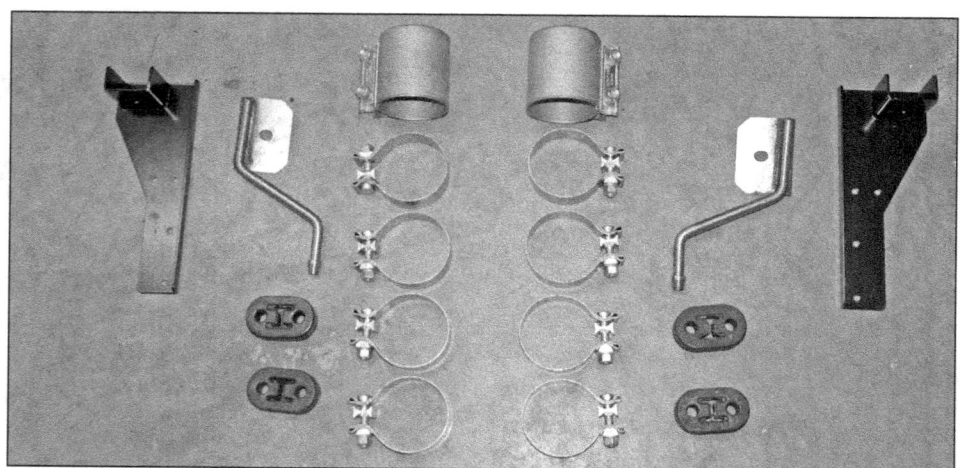

The Hooker exhaust system kit includes all the necessary hangers and mounts. It's designed so that the tailpipes exit just past the rear-wheel opening on a Nova.

CHAPTER 8

WHEELS AND TIRES

The power of a vintage, bone-stock V-8 Nova can pretty much annihilate a set of E70 x 14 Polyglass tires mounted on a set of 14 x 7–inch wheels. No secret. That's reason enough to consider adding fat tires to your Nova. In the accompanying photos, you see many wheels and tires. Not all are mounted on Novas, but that's not the point. You see, no matter what the construction methods or style, all wheels share a number of characteristics. They are, after all, automotive wheels. Before I go much further, let's look at what makes up a wheel.

Critical Parts of a Wheel

Wheel backspace is a critical dimension, particularly if you're fitting larger-than-stock wheels and tires on your Nova. This figure tells you how far the wheel is "inset," or in other terms, how much of the backside of the wheel hangs over the brake drum (or disc). The measurement is easy. Place a straight edge over the backside of the wheel lip and then measure down to the wheel-mounting surface in the wheel center. The thickness of the wheel lip affects the backspace figure. For true backspace dimensions, you should subtract the lip figure. Another term you come across is "offset." Offset is based upon backspace, but it's not quite the same. Wheel offset is the distance from the hub-mounting surface to the centerline of the wheel.

At first glance, this steel wheel–dog dish hubcap combination looks benign. Think again! That's a custom 8-inch-wide wheel stuffed into a stock, unmodified Nova wheelwell. And it's wrapped with a P275-60R15 Nitto drag radial.

Initially, everyone is swayed by the looks of the front side of a wheel. Big mistake. The business end of the wheel is the backside. It's the dimension here that determines how the wheel and tire fit your Nova.

Offset Types

There are three types of offset.

- Zero offset: The wheel hub-mounting surface is centered.
- Negative offset: The wheel's hub-mounting surface is offset toward the brake side. "Reverse" wheels are typically a negative offset (and for anyone who was involved with cars in the 1960s, who can forget "chrome reverse" wheels?). The backspace dimension on these wheels is smaller than that found on a zero-offset wheel.
- Positive offset: The wheel's hub-mounting surface is offset toward the curbside. Positive-offset wheels are used on many late-model cars such as Corvettes. Backspace dimension on these wheels is larger than that found on a zero-offset wheel. This is the type of wheel that works best on the rear of a Nova.

"Wheel face," or curbside dimension, is measured the same way as backspace. When measuring wheel face dimensions, remember that the thickness of the lip, or "wheel flange," is a factor (the same as it is when determining backspace). Take it into consideration when determining the face dimension. The face dimension plus the backspace dimension plus the thickness of the wheel mount flange (hub center) less the wheel flange (lip) dimension equal the width of the wheel. This dimension becomes critical when figuring out how much wheel and tire can fit on a given axle in a specific Nova without having the tire hang out in the breeze (a practice from the 1960s that most folks would like to forget!).

Register bore, or the wheel center bore, is the part where the hub passes through the wheel (at the mount flange). It's also where the center cap snaps in or bolts on. For some applications, this opening is machined to exactly match the hub. It is designed this way to precisely position and center the wheel while the lug nuts are torqued to spec. This centering method eliminates the chance of vibration from a wheel that isn't centered. In cases where the wheels use precision-bored registers (typically late models), the wheels are vehicle model specific. The wheel manufacturer machines the register to the precise size specified by the car manufacturer, or a series of plastic or metal "adapters" (for lack of a better word) are used to fit the wheel to the hub.

The Novas I deal with are engineered with non-hubcentric wheel register bores (the correct terminology is a "lug-centric" wheel). With some of these wheels it's a good idea to torque the lug hardware with the vehicle off the ground (for example,

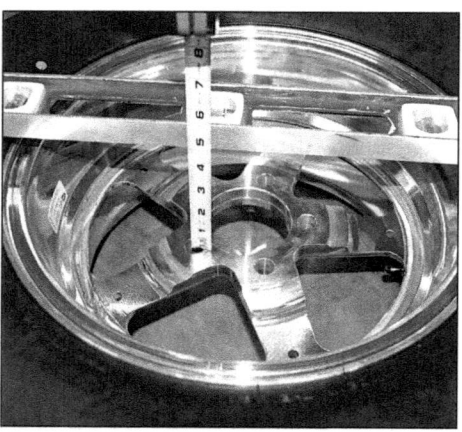

To determine backspace, measure the distance from the wheel center to the wheel bead (not the outside flange).

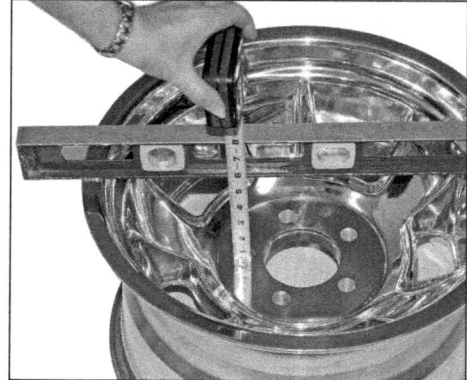

Wheel face, or curbside, dimension settings are much the same. Getting measurements is much easier without the tire mounted.

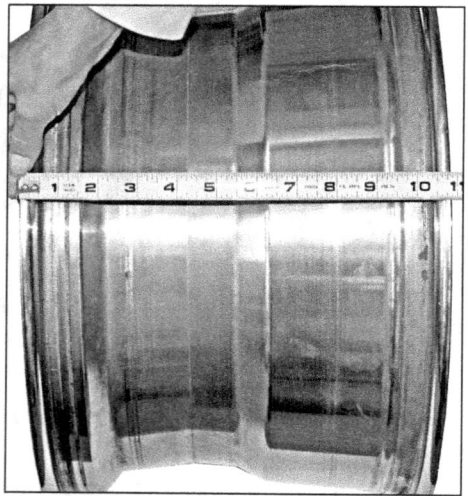

This is a 10-inch-wide wheel. What's up with the width? The rim flange is not included in the measured wheel width.

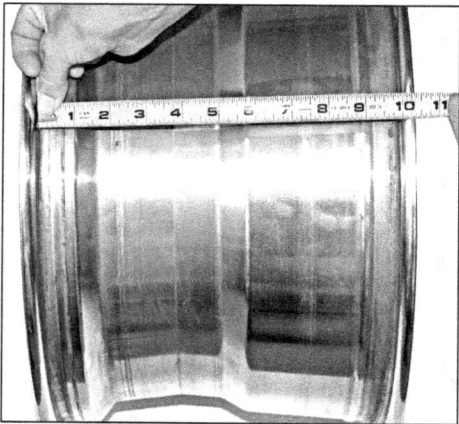

Measured from inside the wheel lip, or rim flange to rim flange, you can see that the wheel measures 10 inches. Keep this in mind when measuring any wheel, aluminum, or steel.

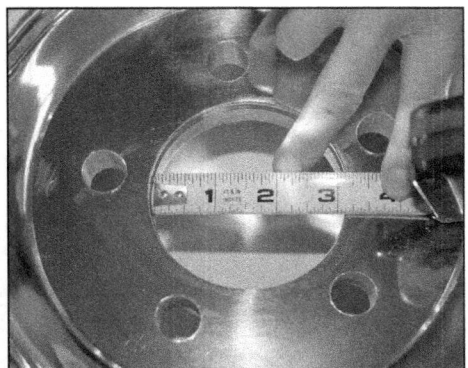

This is the wheel center bore, or "register bore," I mentioned in the text. On later-model cars, the wheel and hub register center the wheel. On a Nova, the lug nuts center the wheel.

You can determine wheel bolt's circle dimensions by measuring from one lug nut to the next in the pattern. Here, the center-to-center is approximately 2¾ inches. Consulting the chart, you can see this is a Chevy 5-on-4¾–inch pattern.

on axle stands). This practice allows the nuts or bolts to center the wheel and then be torqued into place without the car weight pushing them off center.

Virtually all third-gen Novas incorporate a five-bolt wheel pattern. Bigger usually means stronger when it comes to bolt patterns. If you don't know the bolt circle dimensions of a given wheel, try this tip from Mark Williams Enterprises: Measure between the center (B.C.) of two adjacent wheel studs.

Occasionally, you hear the term "drop center." What's that? Basically, this means the center of the wheel is built with a smaller diameter than the outside segments. This allows for easier tire installation and removal. After the tire is deflated, one of the beads can fall into the drop center. In addition, wheels are equipped with small raised "lips" or "safety beads" outboard of the drop center. The purpose of the safety beads is to keep the tire on the wheel if the car experiences a blowout or a flat.

Valve stems are more important than you might think. Two sizes of valves are commonly used today: .453 and .625 inch. Several types of high-quality valves are available from companies such as Schrader-Bridgeport including snap-in (rubber), snap-in with chrome sleeve (rubber), clamp-in nickel (metal), high-performance clamp-in chrome (metal), and high-pressure snap-in (for applications up to 100 psi). So far so good, but when shopping for valve stems be cautious. Plenty of foreign made stems are constructed from natural rubber instead of EPDM (a robust synthetic rubber used in the construction of most quality valve stems). Schrader notes that EPDM has a much broader temperature range than natural rubber and remains flexible in the coldest weather. Ozone and chemical attack can deteriorate natural rubber, but not EPDM. A concern with offshore stems is the fact that natural rubber dries out, and following a couple of years of service, they become brittle. The result? Leaks.

Torqueing lug nuts to spec is important, and even more important when you've installed fresh wheels on your Nova. The reason is, new wheels tend to move around because of thermal stresses along with compression and elongation. In case the clamping loads have changed following the initial installation, wait for the wheels to cool to ambient temperature before the re-torque (never torque a hot wheel, because the values change as the wheel temperature changes). Loosen and retighten to the torque value, in sequence on each wheel. If your Nova has stock-style wheels, you can simply use the specifications found in the shop manual. In addition, many wheel manufacturers provide their own specs for torque.

For example, a set of aftermarket cast-aluminum wheels I've used in the past mandated a maximum torque of 60 ft-lbs for 1/2-inch wheel studs and 50 ft-lbs for 7/16-inch studs; otherwise, use the figures from the following chart. In either case, the lug nuts should be torqued dry, and you should use a conventional "star" or crisscross pattern.

Five-Bolt Wheel Pattern

- 2.645 inches = 4½-inch B.C. (normal later Ford or Mopar pattern)
- 2.792 inches = 4¾-inch B.C. (normal Chevrolet or small GM passenger car pattern)
- 2.939 inches = 5-inch B.C. (normal older Olds-Pontiac or large GM passenger car)
- 3.233 inches = 5½-inch B.C. (normal early Ford or Ford truck)

Wheel Lug Torque	
Wheel Stud Size (inch)	Typical Torque (ft-lbs)
7/16	70 to 80
1/2	75 to 85

It's good practice to torque the lug nuts on your Nova and then re-torque them after they've seen miles. You might be surprised to find that aluminum wheels can move around quite a bit (lose torque) after a few miles.

Stuffing Fenders

The 1968–1972 Novas don't have a lot of room for big back tires. No secret, and in fact, tire room (or lack of it) is a concern for all Novas, no matter the model year. Certainly, you can stuff big rubber under a third-gen Nova if the wheelwells were carved out, but the truth is, it is actually possible to get some good-sized tires under the back without any real drama. You just have to determine how much "tire" can actually fit within the existing wheelwell without creating interference on the inside or the lip.

As you're well aware, wheels are available in a staggering array of dimensions. For example, you might be able to purchase a 15 x 8–inch wheel with backspaces that range from 2 inches to more than 5 inches. This means that the tire can either be tucked up inside the stock wheelwell of your car (which is good) or you must jack the Nova up and let it hang out in the draft (which is not so good).

There are likely dozens of ways to determine rear wheel dimensions. Some rely upon hit and miss tactics. The following three steps make it an easy way to figure it out using common hand tools.

Step 1

Clamp a straightedge (in this case, a carpenter's level) on the brake drum and take measurements from the brake drum mount surface to various locations on the inner wheelwell. At the same time, take measurements from the brake drum to the outer body (most likely, the wheelwell lip).

Step 2

Never clamp over the axle register in the drum; the raised lip found on the register (obviously) skews the dimensions.

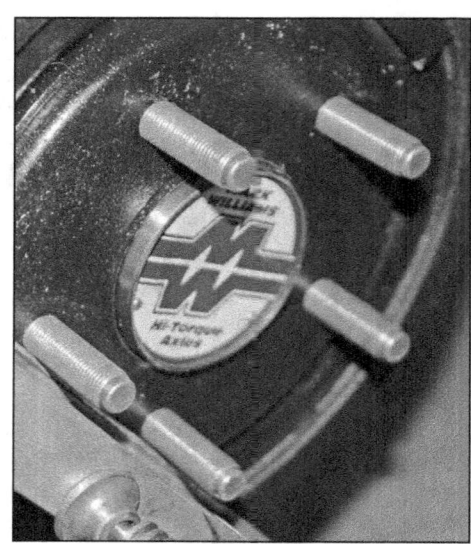

As you can see, the Chevy brake drum register bore is raised. If you clamp over it, the dimensions you come up with will be wrong.

When figuring out what kind of room you have for tires on your Nova, you need a few simple tools: A known straight edge and a big C-clamp. Here's how it hooks up.

WHEELS AND TIRES

Clamp the straight edge and measure vertically to get the distance from the inside of the straight edge to the inner wheelwell and/or shock absorber. At the same time, you can also obtain measurements from the straight edge to the wheelwell's lip area.

Repeat the process with the straight edge at 45 degrees. You should do this at 45 degrees the other way and horizontal too. That way, you can't miss any potential clearance spots.

Step 3

Repeat the process with the inside and outside measurements at horizontal, 90 degrees, and 45 degrees front and back of center. Move to the other side of the car and start all over again. Why? Simple. Most cars vary dimensionally from side to side. It could be manufacturing tolerance stack up, where the spring perches were welded to the housing, and so on. The bottom line is, you absolutely must measure both sides.

It's a whole bunch easier if you have a visual to work with when you're keeping track of the dimensions and eventually figuring out what works on your Nova. You certainly don't have to be an artist to draw up some rough sketches of the wheelwell. It's best to make drawings of both sides of the car, and have one drawing for the inside (brake drum mount surface to the inner wheelwell) and another for the outside (brake drum mount surface to the outer wheelwell lip).

As the drawings show, I took the time to add the rear shock. With a Nova, the shock absorber in the stock location is potentially the first point of interference inside the wheelwell. Measure the distance from the shock to the drum mount surface in two locations. The lower of the two aren't that significant. And the reason is, it's "low" in relation to the wheel. Where clearance gets tight is

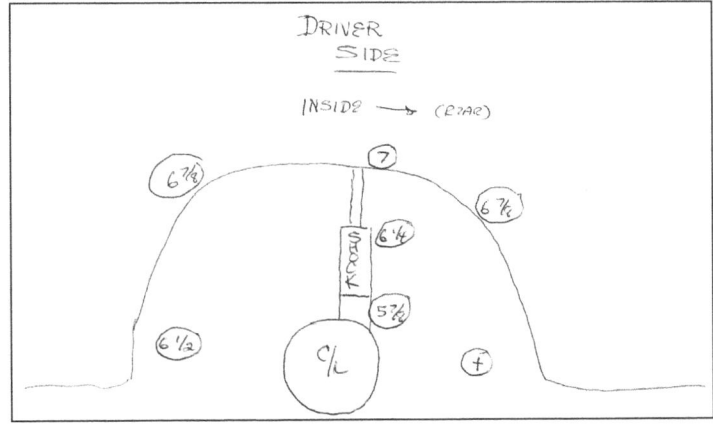

On the sample Nova, the inside clearance dimensions have been mapped out. As you can see, the illustration can be kept simple.

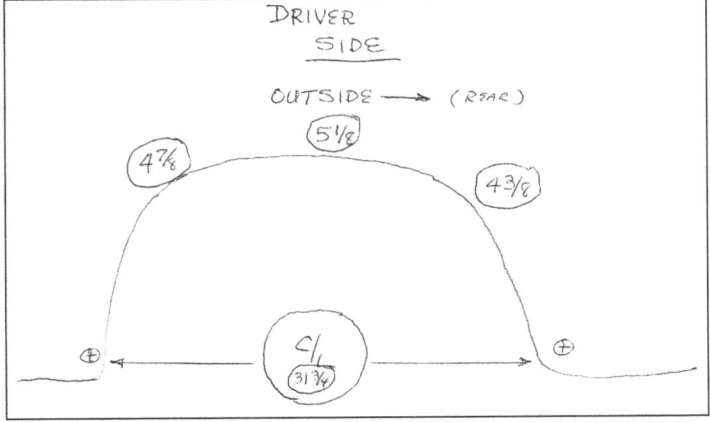

Repeat on the same side, but with outside (brake drum to wheelwell lip) dimensions.

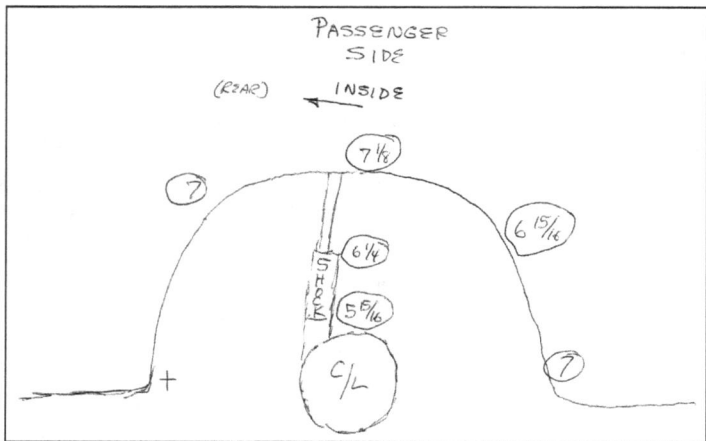

The main reason for this is that the car had a very well constructed rear end with precisely located spring perches.

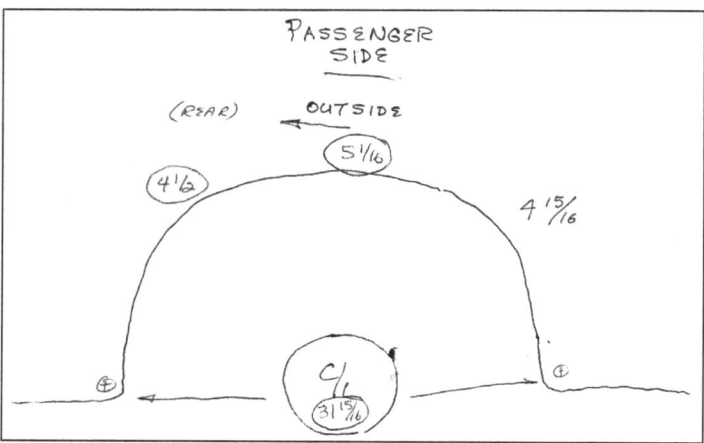

The same applies to the outside dimensions. They differ from the driver's to the passenger's side of the car. This is the why you absolutely must measure both sides of the car before you buy wheels and tires.

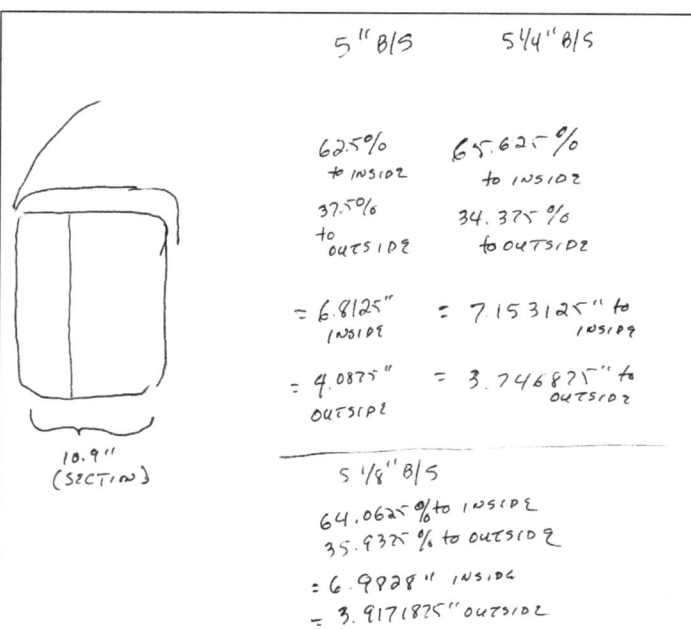

Once you have the dimensions, you can calculate the actual tire fit, based upon the section width of a given tire. The text offers more details.

When you go over to the other side of the car, you find that the dimensions differ. That's because no two Novas are the same. No two rear-end assemblies are the same either. This example is rather close, but the

where the tire bulge comes into play. I also took the time to measure the distance between the leading and trailing edges of the wheelwells. On some cars, if the tire diameter is too large, that marks the first point of interference. On this Nova, the distance is rather large; the shock body isn't huge and, as a result, it's of no consequence for a street/strip tire.

Recall that tire bulge mentioned previously? It's a critical component of measuring for wheels and tires. Each manufacturer prints a maximum tire cross section measurement for every tire sold. For example, something such as a Nitto P275-60R-15

If you need to measure tire bulge (section width), the best way is to drape a carpenter's square over the tire and nail down the section width exactly.

WHEELS AND TIRES

drag radial has a cross section dimension of 11.10 inches when mounted on a recommended 15 x 8–inch wheel. Using a 5-inch backspace wheel as an example, that means 62.5 percent of the tire is on the backside. It's simple math: 5 inches (backspace) divided by 8 inches (wheel width) times 100 works out to 62.5 percent. Take 62.5 percent of the 11.10-inch cross section, and you come up with 6.9375 inches of tire bulge on the inside when mounted on a 5-inch backspace 8-inch-wide wheel. That leaves 37.5 percent of the total on the outside, which works out to 4.1625 inches. You can then use these dimensions to figure out where the tire may or may not contact the wheelwell in your car.

For this combination, the car could use a 5-inch backspace and a 5-1/8-inch backspace wheel. Ultimately, the 5-inch backspace wheel option was selected. If there is a point of interference, the first point of contact is here.

If it does interfere the solution is to swap out this Grade-8 bolt on the lower shock mount for a shock stud. The shock stud can be bent a few degrees, and that effectively rotates the shock away from the wheel. You can't go too far because cars such as a Nova use a double bolt tie bar for the upper shock mount, which can lead to shock bind.

As you can see, stuffing your back fenders with big rubber isn't that difficult a job. Just be sure to measure twice before you order the wheels and tires.

Wheel Studs

Wheel studs and lug nuts are pieces of hardware many people simply take for granted. If a wheel doesn't fall off when you're on the loud pedal, you've found bliss. Unfortunately, these pieces regularly fall into the "who cares" domain of the car. Why worry about parts if they work? Safety is primary among the many reasons to give these components extra thought. Not only are these parts much more important than you might think, picking the proper rear wheel studs, nuts, and washers might not be as easy as you think either.

Bigger is better. The stock GM wheel stud size of 7/16 inch (or equivalent metric size) is simply inadequate on the drive axle for any vehicle destined for competition (even mild competition) or other high-performance use, and that includes Novas. All high-horsepower applications with aftermarket axles should have their drive axle studs set up with a minimum 1/2-inch fasteners. For example, axle builder

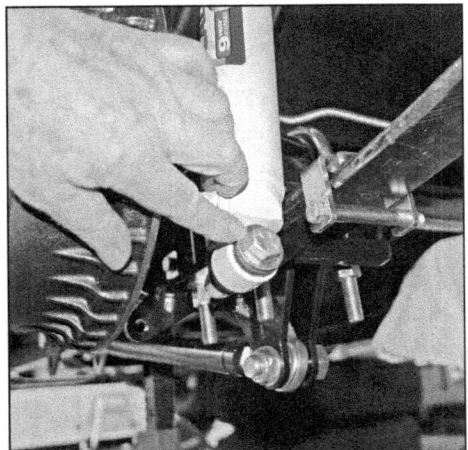

If the shock presents itself as a point of interference (not common, but can occur with a large body shock absorber), swap the bolt for a shock stud. You can bend a shock stud in a vise if necessary. This rotates the shock out of the way.

There's much more to wheel studs and lug nuts than first meets the eye. This is a mix of common and not-so-common components. The big bits are drive studs.

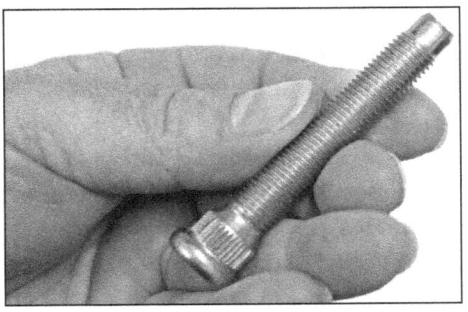

This is a Moroso wheel stud with a quick start nose. This stud has a knurled shank and presses into the axle or wheel hub. This stud measures 7/16-20 x 2⅞ inches with a knurl measurement of .560-inch.

Drag race studs are typically longer than stock, but otherwise they're similar to what a production car uses. The idea with the quick start, or "bullet" nose, is to facilitate lug nut installation. FYI: This 7/16-inch stud is destined for the front only! You should use a larger stud on the back if you have aftermarket axles.

Mark Williams sells this 1/2-20 x 3½-inch stud for use on the rear of a race car. This stud (or probably more correct, "bolt") screws in on the backside of the axle and is held in place with a lock washer. When using studs such as this, it's a good idea to use Loctite or an equivalent thread cleaner along with a "most severe service" thread locking compound (use red Loctite on the bolt/flange only, not on the actual lug segment of the stud!) The bolt head on the backside of a Mark Williams stud must be torqued to 65 ft-lbs.

extraordinaire Mark Williams does not offer axles in the 7/16-inch stud format and, as a result, supplies all axles drilled and tapped to accept 1/2-inch-or-larger studs. Proper replacement studs are fashioned from high-strength materials (often chrome-moly steel) and are threaded all the way to the head. Because of this, the stud can be fully engaged in the backside of the axle.

By the way, while it is entirely possible to have a machine shop re-drill and tap OEM axles to 1/2 inch, it's not really a great idea. You're still stuck with C-clips for axle retention, plus the original axles are now getting pretty long in the tooth. If you're using a stock (or stock-type) wheel there's a good chance you have to enlarge the wheel stud hole very slightly. A quality step drill that goes from 7/16 to 1/2 inch works perfectly for this job. Aftermarket wheels aren't much of a problem. You simply swap the supplied 7/16-inch lug nuts for 1/2-inch examples.

Keep in mind the stud is the element that transfers the load to the wheel, and the wheel and tire are what transfer the load to the pavement. Some of these loads at the axle might be much larger than you think. Just look at the basic math (and it is basic; there's nothing here that takes the tire "hook," track conditions, or overall tire dimensions into consideration).

Engine Torque x Torque Converter Multiplication x Transmission 1st Gear Ratio x Rear Axle Ratio = Load

With a typical small-block Nova hot rod, the loads can exceed 10,000 ft-lbs of torque at the axles. Arguably, there are two axles and ten studs to distribute this load over, but it's still a bunch. Because of this, really serious big-power Novas can benefit from the use of "drive studs." These are huge studs that measure up to a full 11/16-inch diameter (on the drive shoulder). Designed to fit the holes in

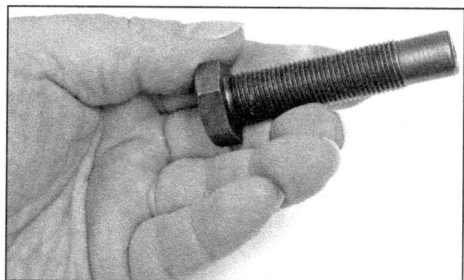

Here's another stud type you might come across. Basically, it's a Mark Williams piece that was initially designed for NASCAR competition. This stud has a "quick start" segment machined on the nose. As you've probably gathered, this allows the lug nut to be installed rapidly without cross threading. Again, this is more of a bolt than a stud, and it too is installed from the backside of the axle, using a lock washer for retention. This stud should only be used with the GN-style quick start nuts, or "acorn"-type, nuts.

aluminum race wheels (e.g., Centerline, Cragar, Weld, Bogart, etc.), the studs make use of an equally huge 5/8-18-inch axle thread (the portion of the stud that screws into the axle). Consider these components overkill if you like, but if bent or broken axle studs are plaguing your Nova, you need them.

A good example of a quality drive stud is the MW piece shown in the accompanying photos. These studs have 11/16-inch-diameter shoulders for use with racing wheels. The drive stud is threaded into a 5/8-18-inch thread in the axle flange and secured with a jam nut. Wheels are held on with an open-end flanged lug nut with an aluminum washer. The drive studs incorporate a smooth shoulder (see the photos) that physically drives the wheel. In comparison, a street lug nut for aftermarket wheels has a built-in shoulder that drives

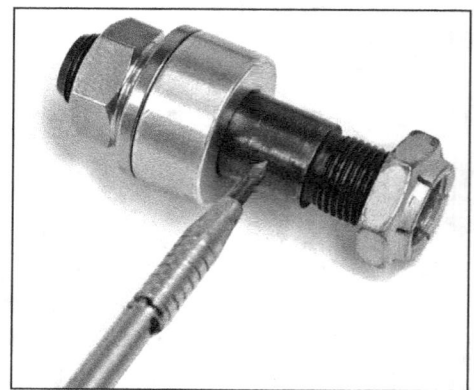

A drive stud (such as this Mark Williams version) is designed with a 5/8-18-inch thread on each end with an 11/16-inch shoulder in between. Obviously, the shorter threaded segment is installed in the axle and secured with a jam nut. Meanwhile, the shoulder (see the pointer) is the same OD as the lugnole ID in common aluminum wheels. This ensures that the stud actually does the driving of the wheel, not the lug nut.

WHEELS AND TIRES

the wheel. These street-oriented lug nuts are designed for use with small-diameter studs (1/2 inch being the largest). In simple terms, the street models use much-smaller-diameter studs and the actual lug nut serves to drive the wheel.

What gets confusing for a lot of folks (even Pro racers have been baffled by the combinations) is the number of combinations of stud lengths and washer thickness available. Mark Williams offers several washer sizes and stud lengths (the drive shoulder length of the stud differs). The reason for the multitude of combinations is the range of wheel center thickness on the market, coupled with the actual thickness of the brake drum or disc brake hat and wheel spacer (if one is used). According to Williams, the most important factor when choosing the proper stud is that the driving portion of the stud is fully engaged into the wheel. The smooth "drive" segment dimension of the stud needs to be slightly greater than the combined thickness of the brake adapter/drum and the thickness of the wheel. Meanwhile, the washer thickness should be greater than the shoulder extending past the wheel. When ordering a set of drive studs, you must specify the wheel center and brake hat (or brake drum) thickness.

As you can see, lug nuts and wheel studs are components that should not be taken lightly. More than one car has been mortally wounded simply because the owner turned into Scrooge on elementary hardware such as this. In the photos that follow, you find a selection of stud and nut combinations along with information on how to determine the right wheel stud/lug nut mix for your Nova.

Drag Radials

When it comes to tires for your Nova, you have all sorts of options. Much has been written about the various types of tires available, and I won't go there. What I will do is look at something you don't read that much about, and that's a drag radial.

This big-boy P325 drag radial doesn't fit under a Nova, but it gives you a good point of reference when it comes to tread layout. Some examples (certain M/T and Hoosier drag radials) have even less tread. They're pretty much slicks with a couple of grooves in them.

In conjunction with the drive studs, Mark Williams also manufactures a series of lug nuts, including the standard flanged model on the left and a series of reduced hex nuts. These nuts have a hex head size of 7/8 inch and are designed for use with special Mark Williams washers.

Getting a third-gen Nova to hook has its challenges, primarily due to the limited amount of wheelwell room. Two keys to making them "work" are the rear suspension components coupled with the back tires. Drag radials are a great choice out back.

CHAPTER 8

Drag radials might look tame at first glance, but plenty of cars have seen almost insane levels of performance with seemingly little street-legal tires. Some 6-second (quarter-mile) cars use drag radials.

Two things to note here, other than the size: The tire meets DOT standards and it's directional. Note the arrow pointing out the direction of rotation.

The sidewall information lays out the tire construction. These MandH tires are built with two plies of polyester, two plies of aramid, and 1 ply of nylon. In case you're wondering, aramid is a synthetic fiber that is used in things such as body armor. It also sees use in everything from bicycle tires to aerospace components. Note the maximum load (per tire) on the sidewall.

In truth, these are fair weather sticky tires that are perfect for big-power cars with limited wheelwell room (which includes many Novas out there). They wear quickly, but ask yourself just how many miles you put on your car in a given year.

It's no secret that plenty of street cars (Novas included) out there today are capable of running 8-second quarter mile ETs. Some have even dipped into the 6-second zone on relatively small DOT legal rubber.

What really brought this incredible small tire performance into focus is simple. The rules for many categories of street car drag racing mandate a tire that has Department of Transportation (DOT) approval. Many of the more popular categories mandate radial tires. DOT drag radials were born to meet both needs. The DOT requirement places a considerable burden on the tire manufacturer. The company must develop a tire that can effectively cope with an almost obscene amount of horsepower, but at the same time, it must pass a rigid set of requirements laid out by the DOT. Keep in mind that these specialized DOT-approved tires aren't for everyone. They wear quickly. They're not that happy in the rain. Nevertheless, they do hook, and that's what this is all about.

Given the mix of mandates (DOT and great hook), the "street" tires used in street car drag racing might at first glance look like slicks with a couple of grooves sliced in them, but they have a number of subtle and not-so-subtle differences. Weight of the car is a huge issue. One has to remember that a typical fastest street Nova is quite portly in comparison to a dragstrip-only car.

It's not uncommon for an "Outlaw" P275-60 drag radial racer to tip the scales at more than 3,000 pounds. That same car can have an ultimate performance well below 7-seconds in the quarter-mile. Think about that for a minute. It wasn't that long ago that high-6-second ET slips were rare in a Pro Stock racer; and those things tip the scales at 2,350 pounds and have far more substantial rubber. Building a tire to support a 3,000-pound car that runs 6-second laps is impressive, but it's not the final word in design.

It should be no surprise to anyone that drag slicks for unlimited applications are regularly constructed as light as possible. Lower wheel and tire mass almost always equates to lower ETs. But when a tire is forced to pass a DOT requirement, peeling out pounds isn't so easy. A DOT tire must have a load range (and it must have that load range cast into the side of the tire).

WHEELS AND TIRES

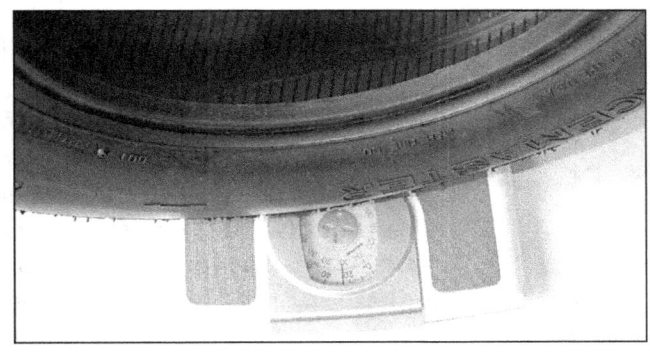

Grizzled old drag racers are the first to tell you that performance improves as tire weight decreases. Test a light tire against a heavy one and you most likely find that the Nova is quicker with the lighter tire.

Using a MandH Racemaster P325-50R15 as an example, the overall tire weight is about 25 pounds (at least on a bathroom scale). I've observed another similarly sized drag radial that tipped the scales at 29 pounds, while another one weighed a whopping 37 pounds (that's definitely big-boned). In comparison, a similarly sized conventional drag slick tips the scales at approximately 23 pounds.

Where does the weight loss come from? MandH was careful in the design of its tire. That's why the weight of its drag radial isn't over the top; however, it notes that a bit more belt material is required in the drag radial tire. This makes for a more rigid sidewall and, of course, a heavier tire. To some extent, the tire manufacturer is forced to build a more robust tire if it must conform to heavier cars and DOT requirements.

Sizing

What size ranges of drag radials are available? You might be surprised at the choices, but again, for a Nova with a stock wheelwell, the biggest you can possibly fit is a P275-60R15. When you think about sizing, it's important to keep this in mind: Don't directly compare tires based upon the size shown on the sidewall. Compare them by dimensions.

Tubes or Tubeless?

Some DOT street car "drag tires" are designed as tube-type tires (primarily bias ply jobs). There are a number of reasons for this, but safety is a primary concern. In addition, a tube helps to maintain air pressure. It's not uncommon for a tubeless bias ply fastest street car tire to deflate quickly (that even includes several of the more streetable types with a full complement of tread). That isn't the case with a drag radial. They're definitely tubeless. Besides, adding a tube effectively increases the weight of the tire.

Compounds

When it comes to sticky tires that comply with DOT specifications, compounding is a huge issue addressed by tire manufacturers. The various companies who have entered the street car drag racing arena have gone down a couple of different

P275-60R15 Tire Dimensions			
	MandH	M/T	Nitto
Tread Width	9.5 inches	9.3 inches	n/a
Section Width	10.9 inches	11.1 inches	11.10 inches
Diameter	28.0 inches	28.2 inches	27.76 inches
Circumference	88.0 inches	88.6 inches	87.21 inches
Measured Rim Size	8.0 inches	8.0 inches	8.0 inches

Without a mini-tub (and moved spring), this tire will not fit into your Nova. But you can fit a P275-60R15 in the wheelwell, as indicated earlier.

The way the tire is constructed (belt layout, belt materials) determines how much the tire weighs and how it works. Factor in the compound (which is equally important) and you can appreciate why certain tires "work" better than others. On a related note, modern drag radials work well tubeless. That might not be the case with sticky bias plies (some can leak).

avenues in response. For example, MandH Racemaster has developed an entire new line of compounds just for its newest "HB" series of street car drag race tires.

M/T incorporates its relatively soft "R2" compound in the tire, which provides for superior traction on the strip. Meanwhile, the radial construction provides for excellent ride control on the street. To make the tires "work," they use a special proprietary sidewall construction. M/T uses a combination polyester and steel belt construction, which it claims adds to the tire life. Tread patterns are directional with low voids. That provides the maximum amount of rubber on the road, but at the same time, still meets DOT requirements.

Air Pressure

How much air pressure is required for these tires? According to MandH Racemaster, proper air pressure is critical in its DOT drag radial tire, especially from a performance perspective. The folks from MandH note that recommending air pressure isn't easy, since many variables are involved; for example, the weight distribution of the car, transmission type, chassis set up, wheel size, and other factors. The truth is, in drag racing, many racers feel that "less is better" with regard to air pressure. This is not always the case. While there are exceptions to every rule, higher pressures (than you might expect) generally work best with drag radial tires. Not only do the higher pressures lead to quicker times, but they also contribute to a safer, more stable ride at the finish stripe.

MandH notes that the actual optimum air pressure may vary significantly, depending, of course, on the variables noted above.

Tire pressure is critical. There's good advice on the topic in the text, but the quick story is, start at about 75 percent of the maximum pressure and test lower. Every car might require a different tire psi.

M/T states that no tire in this series (DOT drag radial) should be operated below 11 psi. For tire sizes of P275 and smaller, it suggests that you set pressures between 12 and 16 psi at the strip. Larger tires (P295 and bigger) should have pressures set between 11 and 14 psi.

For use on the street, Mickey Thompson of Mickey Thompson Tires suggests you check the sidewall for maximum pressure and start at approximately 75 percent of that figure. As an example, the P275-60R15 Nittos shown in the accompanying photos have a maximum pressure of 44 pounds. 75 percent of that figure is 33 pounds.

Burnout

The type of burnout you perform is related to the tire compound. For a car equipped with HB11 compound tires, MandH offers this advice: "A hard burnout is not necessary. For the first pass of the day, make a light to moderate burnout. After that, a light burnout should suffice. Continue the burnout until the engine starts to pull down. A dry hop after the burnout isn't recommended. For a stick-shift car, perform a light burnout, haze the tires, and stage immediately. Generally speaking, drag radials work better with a light burnout rather than a hard burnout. Drag radial tires may require a fairly hard burnout on the first and second pass to break them in."

Mickey Thompson advises the tread compound used in the ET Street Radials is designed to heat quickly and does not require a heavy burnout. (A dry hop is where you dump the clutch or hit the gas with the converter stalled after the initial water box burnout.)

When it comes to tire life, these new-generation fast street car tires are similar to slicks. Drag slick life can vary from car to car. Inconsistent 60-foot and 330-foot times are often caused by tread wear or carcass breakdown. Take that as an indicator to change tires. While slicks have wear holes on the tread face, street car tires don't. When the grooves in a street car drag tire vanish, it's time to buy new rubber (common sense, obviously). Keep in mind that a hard-hooking Nova can cause the tire carcass material to break down. Inspect your tires carefully after 30 passes and even more often if the car is really quick.

Dragstrip Tire Pressure	
The recommended baseline pressures for dragstrip use are as follows.	
Tire Size	Air Pressure
Under 30 inches in diameter	12 to 16 psi and up
Over 30 inches in diameter	11 to 14 psi and up

CHAPTER 9

FUEL SYSTEM

The fuel system in your Nova is comprised of several key components: the gas tank (or fuel cell), the fuel pickup, a mechanical or electric fuel pump, a fuel filter, fuel line and/or hose, and sometimes a fuel pressure regulator. The performance of the engine and the entire car dictate whether you need to upgrade to something such as an electric pump with a fuel pressure regulator. Of course, if your Nova has an EFI setup, you definitely need an electric system of some sort. I discuss the fuel requirements later, but where do you really begin? The best place to start is at the source: gas tank or fuel cell.

Gas Tanks and Fuel Cells

There's no question that today's crop of "fast" street cars (Novas included) have stretched the performance envelope. It wasn't that long ago that an 11- or 12-second "lap" easily got the job done. Not so today.

As you might have guessed, it takes more than pure horsepower to run super quick ET numbers. Virtually every inch of the car has to be poked and prodded to wring out the last drop of performance. What does this have to do with you, the little-guy owner of a street-driven Nova that might be raced on occasion? More than you might imagine.

Today, NHRA Pro Stock cars are fuel injected. Prior to 2016, a legal NHRA Pro Stock car had two carburetors with a total of four needle and seat assemblies and four (or as many as eight) fuel lines leading to the fuel bowl. Your Nova likely has one carburetor and, at the most, only a pair of needle and seat assemblies

This is likely the best-quality stock replacement gas tank you'll find for a Nova. A company named Spectra Premium manufactures it. That fuel sending unit is definitely not stock, however.

Fuel cells come in all different shapes, capacities, and styles. Small drag race cells such as this don't get you very far on the street.

Building an AN Hose Fuel Line

Assembling AN hose for fuel line is straightforward, but get it wrong and you have a leaking fitting. Get it right and you have a good-looking and equally functional component. In between, you can mar the fittings, leave unsightly (and potentially faulty) gaps, and generally make a mess of the fittings and your fingers (cut braided hose is sharp).

The market offers several types of quality hose ends in tapered and cutter styles. The cutter style (such as the Earl's Swivel Seal fitting shown in the accompanying photos) is assembled in a slightly different manner than the tapered style. The cutter-style hose end is considered by many in the racing biz to be more secure than the tapered style. Both work well, but misconceptions about assembling cutter-style hose ends sometimes discourage their use. After those are out of the way, cutter hose ends become almost as easy to assemble as the tapered style. By the way, the process shown in the accompanying photos works for both styles of hose ends.

If you lock the hose with the socket (tube nut) end in a vise and try to assemble it, you'll encounter grief. Instead, lock the cutter end of the fitting into the vise and as you push the hose on, engage the threads. This way, there's far less chance of the hose backing out. Another bonus seems to be less chance of getting a wayward rubber "flapper" (loose piece of hose) in the line.

Another issue is tools. You should use a proper set of AN fitting vise jaws (Earl's Performance has a nice one, PN 1004ERL). This tool locks the fitting in place without damage, allowing you to properly engage the fitting threads. Another must-have tool is the Koul Tool. This is a unique tool that's easy to use; just insert the socket into the tool, twist in the hose, and socket assembly is complete in less than 10 seconds. If you'd like to eliminate the hard struggle of assembling hose ends, these kits get the job done.

The final issue is getting a clean cut on the hose before you attempt to assemble it. Years ago, it was common practice to tightly wrap the hose with duct (racer) tape, clamp it in a vise, and cut it with a fine-tooth blade hacksaw. It works, but you still end up with frayed edges. Instead, try using an angle grinder fitted with a cut-off wheel. It's way faster, it's way cleaner (fewer stray stainless braids), and it makes for a nice, straight cut. If you do have a crooked cut or if you encounter some wayward braids, don't bother trying to trim them with hand tools. Instead, simply dress the hose end(s) on a bench grinder. Easy, and painless too.

So how does all this stuff go together? Check out the following:

Earl's hose end, at the top, is engineered with a "cutter" and the other without. On the outside, both types of hose end look pretty much the same. Take them apart, though, and you can easily spot the differences.

An Earl's Swivel Seal hose end built with a cutter is designed to physically slice into the inner hose liner. This makes for a more secure engagement into the hose. They're more difficult to work with, however, and anytime you have to remove the fitting, the hose must be shortened because the cutter requires fresh hose to slice in securely.

In comparison is a hose end with a taper. Up close, you can see that in this sort of configuration, the hose slides over the nipple and is held in place by the compression of the threads. These hose ends are not as strong a connection (ultimately) as a cutter.

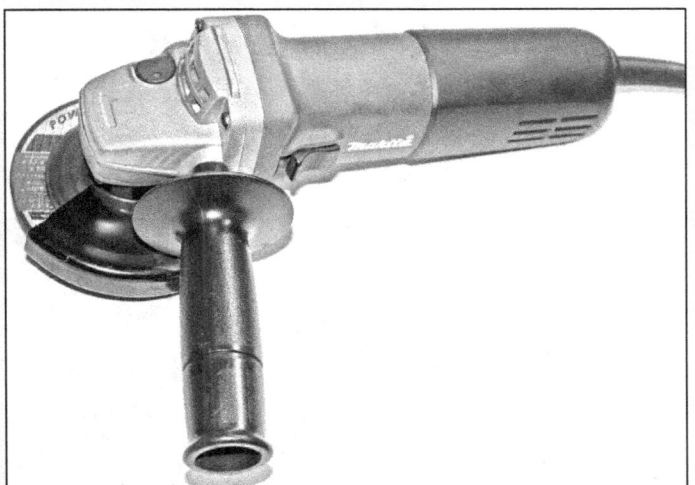

This is the best tool for cleanly cutting AN hose. It's a simple 4½-inch angle grinder fitted with a cut-off wheel. It slices through hose like a hot knife through butter.

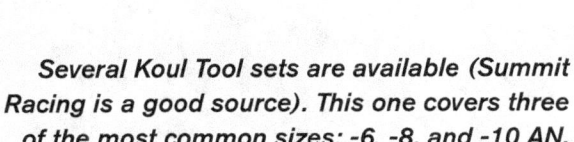

Several Koul Tool sets are available (Summit Racing is a good source). This one covers three of the most common sizes: -6, -8, and -10 AN.

Before you cut the hose, wrap it tightly with duct tape and clamp it in your vise.

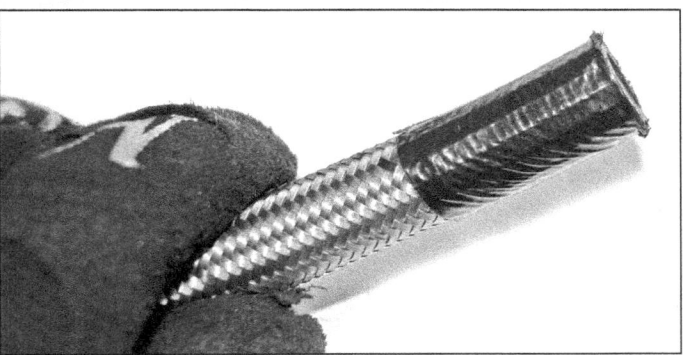

This is typical of the type of cut you get with a cut-off wheel. If there are any extra stainless strands, simply dress the hose on a bench grinder.

Building an AN Hose Fuel Line CONTINUED

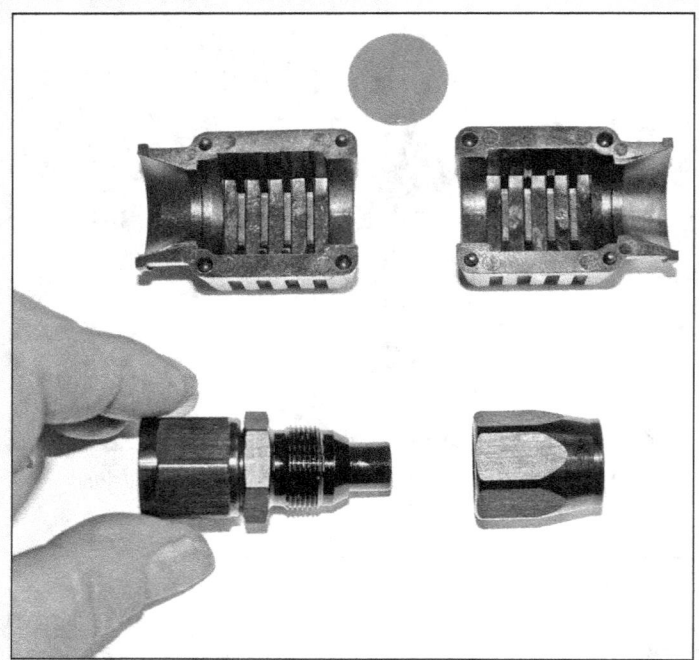

To use the Koul Tool, disassemble the hose end. See the red circle? That's a spacer that might be needed for hose ends with short sockets. It's not required for the Earl's hose ends.

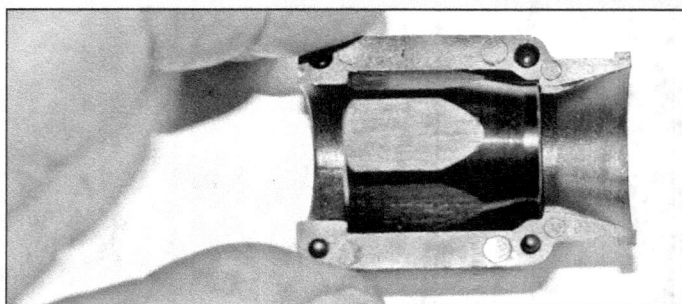

The Earl's socket fits inside the plastic Koul Tool as shown.

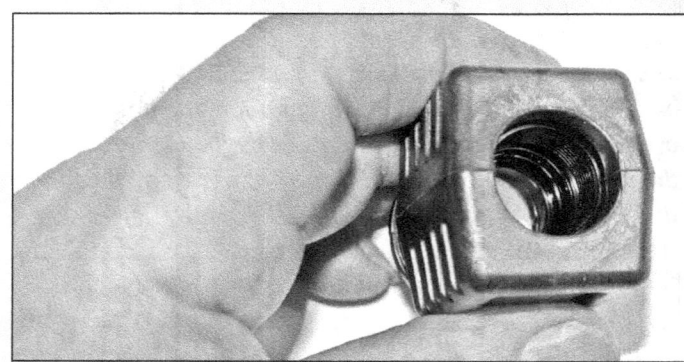

Close the Koul Tool. Add a small amount of grease to the taper in the tool (where the hose enters the tool).

Here the Koul Tool is clamped into the Earl's aluminum vise jaw set. At this point, you simply twist the hose into the hose end socket. It goes easier than you think, plus there's no chance of stabbing yourself.

Mark the end of the hose (behind the socket) and then simply add a wrap of duct tape to this spot. The idea here is to watch for hose back out.

Push the hose into the socket until it reaches the threads.

FUEL SYSTEM

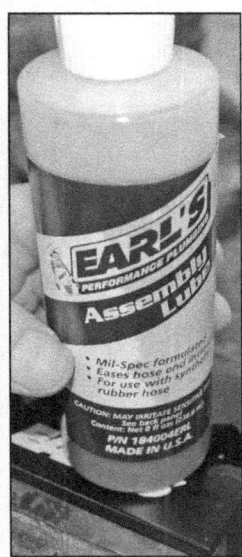

Lightly lube the ID of the hose and the threads on both the socket and the cutter. Earl's Assembly Lube (PN 184004ERL) is engineered for this job and it works better than any other lube. Period.

Clamp the cutter portion of the hose end into the vise jaws. Oil the threads and the cutter with Earl's Assembly Lube. Now you can easily push the hose and the socket onto the cutter and simultaneously engage the threads.

Using an appropriately sized open-end wrench (these Mac Tools' "knuckle savers" fit tightly), complete the tightening process. Believe it or not, a tight fitting open-end wrench is the best tool for the job. Be careful not to damage either the nipple end or the socket when tightening.

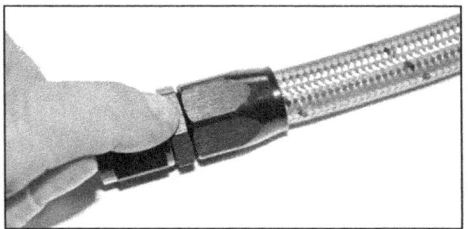

Tighten the nipple end into the socket until there is a gap of approximately .031 inch between the socket and the shoulder of the nipple. A good rule of thumb (pun intended) is your thumbnail; it's close to .031 inch. Double-check the mark for push-out. If the hose has backed out by more than 1/16 inch, go back to square one and start all over again. This often means you must re-cut the hose (back to clean, undamaged "rubber"). Also, carefully clean the hose end so that the threads aren't filled with rubber.

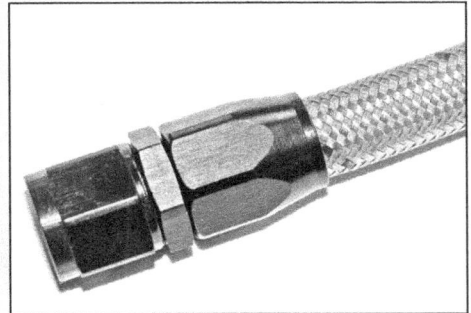

Clean the hose and hose end (good old-fashioned solvent works). Wipe clean.

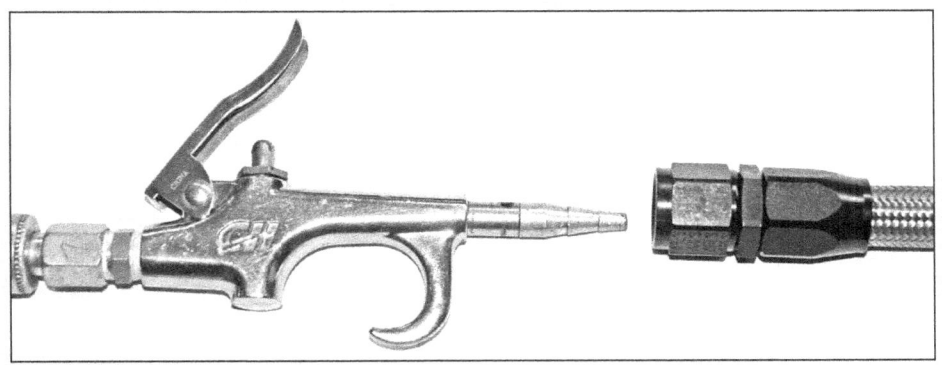

Blow out the hose assembly. A couple of blasts of high-pressure air clean it out perfectly.

CHEVY NOVA 1968–1974: HOW TO BUILD AND MODIFY

Building an AN Hose Fuel Line CONTINUED

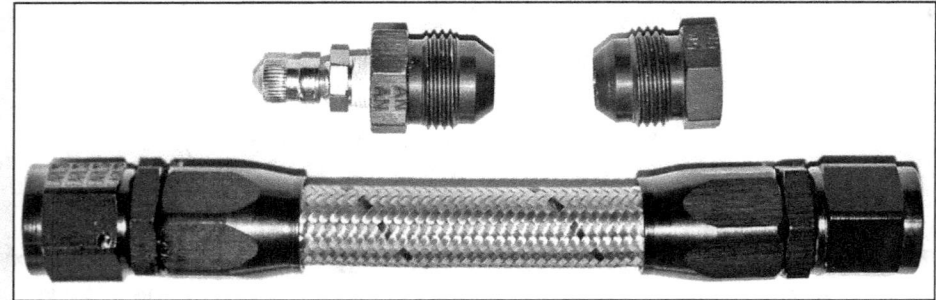

Before use, the hose should be tested. These special test fittings from Earl's Performance (PN D016ERL) are designed for the job.

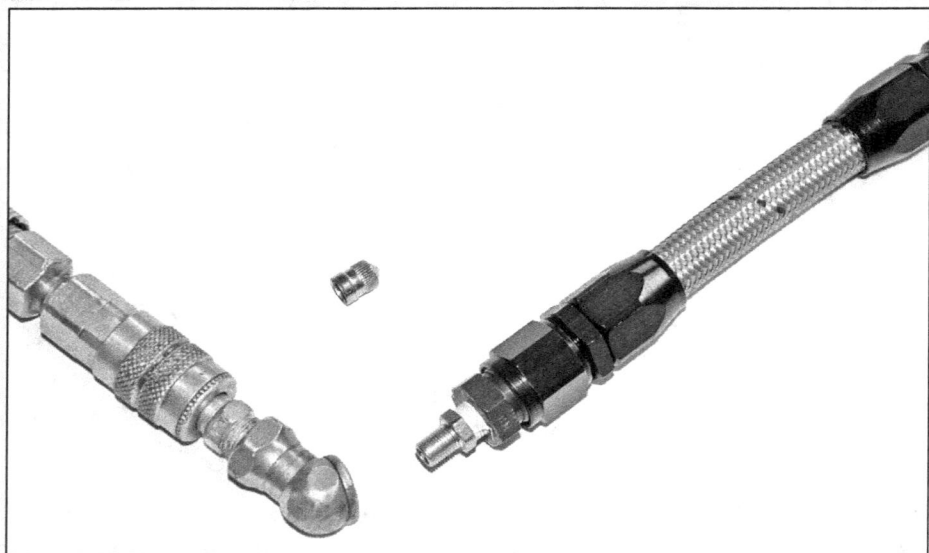

Using an aluminum hose end wrench, assemble the test fittings into your hose. Tighten so that the adapters seat. Be sure to double-check the Shrader valve to ensure it's tight. Air it up. It's a good idea to test the hose at twice the maximum operating pressure. Simply air it up with an air compressor, and then check the pressure with a common tire gauge.

Place the hose under water and check for leaks. No bubbles. No leaks. The hose assembly passed.

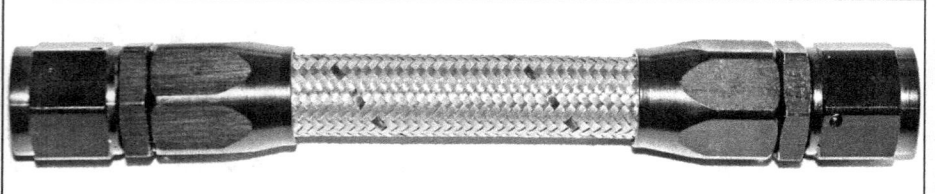

This is the finished top-of-the-line Earl's hose package.

(along with a maximum of two fuel lines leading to the respective bowls). Plenty of Novas have only one needle and seat assembly coupled with a single (small) OEM fuel bowl (for example, the stock setup with a Rochester QJ). Yesterday's Pro Stock car had a bit of fuel capacity "reserve" in the fuel bowls and fuel lines.

On the track, a "little-guy" Nova just might have a harder initial launch than some Pro Stock cars (if only for a millisecond). Because of this, it can run out of fuel quicker. How can that be? It's simple torque multiplication math. If you have an engine with 500 ft-lbs of torque multiplied by a torque converter (assume a torque multiplication factor of 2), which in turn operates through a 2.52:1 low-gear transmission multiplied by a 5.14:1 gear set, the axles see a torque output of approximately 12,950 ft-lbs. The math also shows a Pro Stock car might only have 10,000 ft-lbs of starting line torque production. What this means is the fuel cell or tank in a relatively low-horsepower car is more important than you might think.

Should you use a tank or a cell? Not all fuel cells are the same. A dedicated drag race car can get away with a 3- or 5-gallon fuel cell. With a true street-driven Nova, 3 or even 5 gallons of gas don't go far. Race cars mandate big amounts of fuel in a short period of time. Street cars and dual-duty street/strip cars demand this on occasion too, but they also have to deliver fuel over the long haul. There are quite a few similarities, but plenty of differences.

What constitutes a fuel cell? It must accomplish at least two chores: provide a margin of safety and improve performance. Unfortunately, not all fuel cells are created equal. Some inferior fuel "cells" are nothing more than plastic gas tanks. A proper fuel cell maintains integrity even when involved in a heavy crash. That's a strong statement, but what it really means is the cell doesn't leak. Fuel does not spill out of the assembly, and it resists punctures. To resist punctures, manufacturers of plastic-bodied fuel cells incorporate a type of "deformable plastic" for the outer body. That material is most often a special cross-linked polyethylene.

Cross-linking is a process that is used to strengthen plastics. Plastics such as polyethylene contain molecules that are narrow and long. They tend to be weak. To strengthen these molecules during the manufacturing process (using a system called "rotational molding"), a series of vertical supports, or braces, are added to the molecules. These vertical supports are called "cross links." A fuel cell container that has been produced with the cross-linked construction resists bursting or rupture upon impact.

Many fuel cells contain an internal foam bladder. The purpose is to prevent fuel from sloshing within the cell and, simultaneously, minimize the possibility of a fuel explosion due to impact in a crash. Some of those foam bladders can be eaten by today's pump gas. If you're using a fuel cell on the street, you should contact the manufacturer to determine if it is safe to use the cell with pump gas (if the gasoline is laced with alcohol, be double careful).

What about a gas tank for your Nova? Of the many sources, Spectra Premium builds the best. Its line of high-quality tanks is manufactured in Canada, and they're absolutely dead ringers for an OEM Nova tank. That includes everything from the construction to the materials to the appearance. They're often private labeled, but you can usually find them from better retailers throughout North America.

What about EFI applications? There are plenty of ways to sort through the EFI puzzle. One item you absolutely need is an electric fuel pump out back along with a fuel pressure regulator at the front of the car. Some form of return line system goes back to the tank. Because of this, the tank or the cell must either be able to accept an in-tank pump or it must have the capability of accepting plumbing for an external pump. It also must have a provision for a return line.

Back to the tanks and cells: Believe it or not, the proper venting of a fuel cell or fuel tank is critical. Unlike gas tanks, fuel cells don't incorporate conventional "vented" gas caps. Instead, a cell features some form of vent system. Why is this so important? A fuel cell (or any gas tank) must breathe in *and* out.

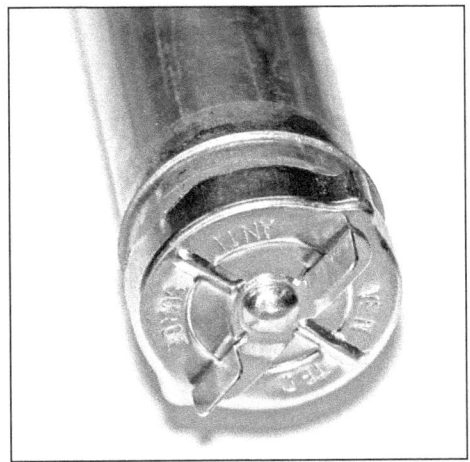

Venting a gas tank or a fuel cell is very important (a vented Nova gas cap is shown here). As the fuel pump draws the fuel out of the tank, it also displaces air. Without proper venting the tank can actually collapse.

As a fuel pump draws the gasoline, it naturally draws in air that is inside the cell. If the fuel cell or tank is completely sealed, the walls eventually collapse from the pulling action of the pump. With the advent of the colossal fuel pumps, an ordinary vent line simply isn't sufficient. The pulling action of the large electric pumps (they can actually draw a vacuum) can outstrip the capacity of a lone 3/8-inch vent line. In answer to this problem, today's race-only fuel cells incorporate a large number-8 AN (1/2 inch) vent system. Street systems usually carry a number-6 AN vent arrangement. Some fuel cells also include a special "roll-over" valve in the vent line. In most cases, these rollover valves are based upon a check-ball. In operation, a moveable ball closes the vent line if the tank is turned upside down. This prevents fuel from escaping through the vent should the car overturn.

Something a true street-driven car needs that isn't seen on pro/street or other race cars is a fuel (level) gauge. They incorporate specialized senders designed to work with the safety foam used in a modern fuel cell.

A typical "professional class" fuel cell has 12-AN pickups. Street car cells or tanks can get by with 8-AN pickups. Mounted low on the cell (in the sump area), the pickup is situated in a location that virtually force-feeds the pump. For a Nova tank, you can either modify it to accept a special AN pickup (which requires welding) or you can use one of the neat fuel pickups shown here.

High-Flow Pickups for Stock Nova Tanks

Getting the fuel from the Nova gas tank to the carb is rather important. If you don't have sufficient fuel, the ET slip will certainly reflect it. A big part of the puzzle for any Nova is to supply a sufficient volume of gasoline. You might think this is all very simple. The reality is, it's not, especially if you want to get it done with a lone stock-style mechanical fuel pump. Ponder this: You're kicking back a milkshake. Instead of using that big fat straw the shake normally comes with, substitute it for the itsy-bitsy straw you'd normally use with a soda pop. You soon discover that sucking that mouthful of shake isn't exactly easy. Replace that soda pop straw with a big milk shake straw and it's pretty comfortable. The same applies to a fuel system. That's why L78 Novas were factory-fitted with a 3/8-inch line instead of a more common 5/16-inch line.

A big restriction in a production line fuel delivery system is the fuel tank pickup/sending unit combination. If you're building a high-flow system you have two choices: Try to find a 3/8-inch replacement pickup and sending unit or replace the factory sender/pickup with a custom billet job from RobbMc Performance Products. The RobbMc setup is based upon a huge 1/2-inch-diameter pickup and it does away with the troublesome sock filter. The dilemma with the sock is that it can become plugged and you won't know it. The custom pickup requires an external fuel filter but otherwise bolts into place as stock. It's a slick piece, and

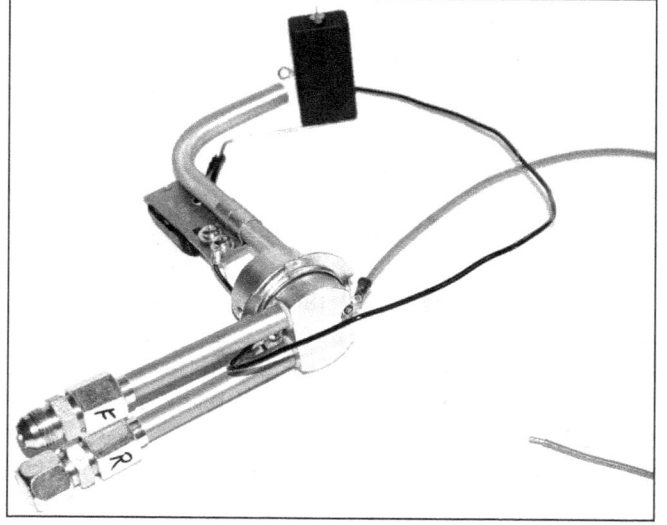

One of the slickest fuel pickup assemblies/gas tank senders available today is this billet piece manufactured by RobbMC. This Nova example has AN fittings for the supply and return lines.

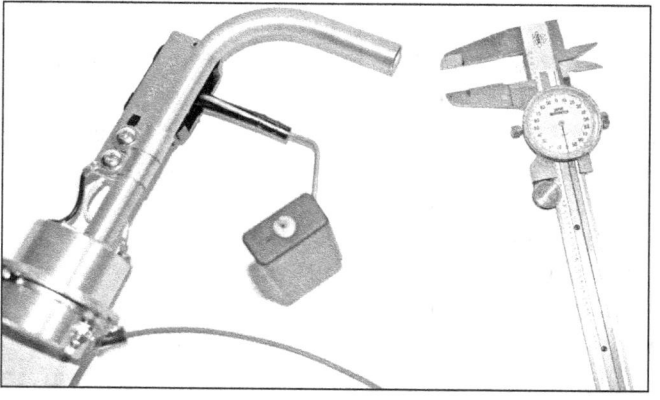

The RobbMC -8 AN pickup for a Nova measures 1/2 inch in diameter. Note there is no problematic sock filter. This means an inline filter of some sort is mandatory.

FUEL SYSTEM

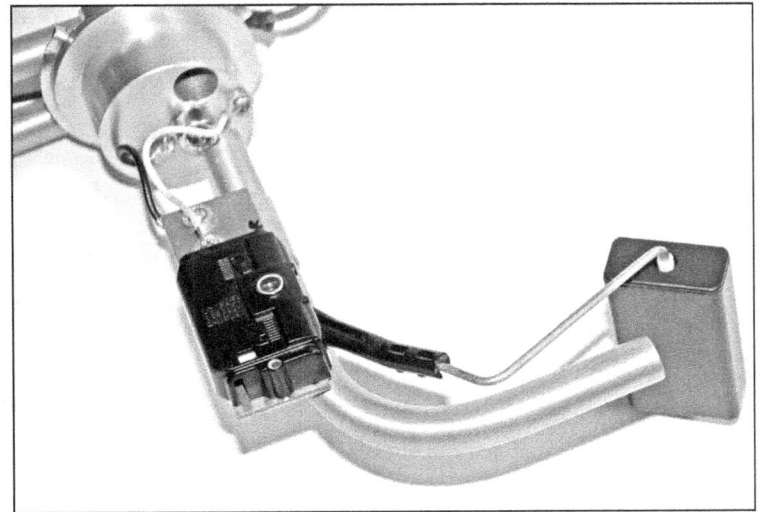

The float assembly is engineered to work with the stock Nova gas gauge. You have to splice into one OEM sender electrical wire, but that's the extent of the mods. Otherwise, it's a bolt-in.

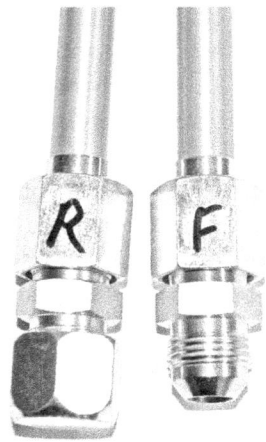

This is a good look at the AN lines supplied with the sender. For this Nova application, there's no need for a return, so it's capped off. The fittings are -8 AN.

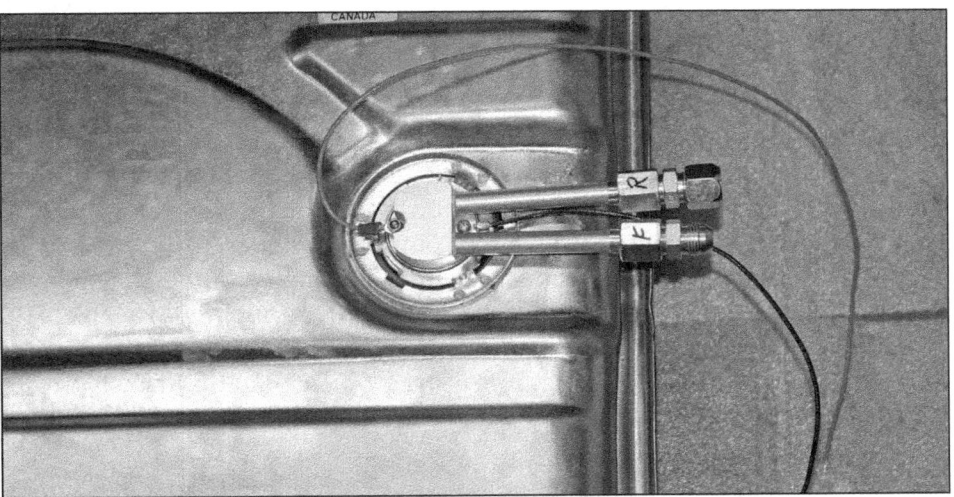

The pickup mounts easily in a stock replacement Nova tank. The lesson here is, for most high-performance applications, a large-diameter -8 or 1/2-inch feed line keeps most big-horsepower street-driven Novas happy.

if you're searching for maximum fuel flow from a stock gas tank this is the place to begin.

RobbMc has several versions for a Nova. You can order it with a conventional 1/2-inch tube outlet/return or you can specify -8 AN or even -10 AN outlet and return lines. The setup shown in the accompanying photos is designed for a Nova and comes equipped with -8 AN male fittings on both the feed and return lines. If you don't need the return, simply cap it. It's extremely well built.

These trick senders/fuel pickups end fuel starvation right at the source. They're not even that expensive. The RobbMc piece shown here costs $149 plus an additional $20 for the -8 AN package.

Mechanical Fuel Pumps

Chevy mechanical fuel pumps are driven off the camshaft by way of a pushrod. That is probably not news. With a mechanical fuel pump, as engine speed increases, so does the speed of the fuel pump. It's a good setup for a street/strip Nova.

But how much fuel do you need? According to Holley Engineering "Typically, at wide open throttle, full power, an engine requires .5 pound of fuel per horsepower every hour. A gallon of gasoline weighs approximately 6 pounds. Therefore, an engine rated at 350 hp requires about 175 pounds (29 gallons) of fuel every hour."

350 hp x .5 lbs = 175 lbs of fuel
175 lbs ÷ 6 lbs = 29 gallons per hour

"The relationship of pressure to volume is inversely proportional," states Holley. "That is, as pressure increases, volume decreases, everything else being equal. A certain amount of fuel pressure is always required to maintain engine performance by assuring that fuel is available on demand. Also, other factors and conditions must be taken into account, such as acceleration G-forces and friction within the fuel system itself. At the same time, an adequate fuel volume is needed to ensure that the proper amount of fuel can always flow to the engine, especially during peak demand situations. A basic understanding of this critical pressure/volume relationship is needed when designing the proper fuel supply system for your vehicle."

Some of today's mechanical pumps are perfect for high-flow applications. Plenty are not. Some good examples include Holley's High Output pumps (with or without external fuel pressure regulator), along with Holley's HP series pump. The basic High Output pump has a gallon per hour (GPH) rating of 110. The High Output pump with the external regulator has a rating of 130. The HP pump carries a rating of a whopping 170 gph, while the billet models flow 170 and 200 gph respectively.

Holley 170 GPH

This pump has a flow rating of 170 gph at 8 psi. It incorporates a cast body with a lower housing that can be rotated. This allows for any number of plumbing situations. The inlet and outlet ports are machined for -8 AN fittings (O-ring configuration). The pump features heavy-duty construction and is designed for continuous high-RPM operation. Internally, the high-flow valving has been redesigned to ensure adequate fuel delivery. Because of the 8-psi setting, a fuel pressure regulator is required. This pump is for gasoline-fueled applications only.

Holley 170 GPH (Billet)

This is one of Holley's HP billet-aluminum body mechanical fuel pumps. It too has a free flow rating of 170 gallons per hour. This pump features a pre-set idle psi rating of 7.5, which means it can operate without an additional external fuel pressure regulator. The inlet and outlet are both pre-plumbed with -8 AN male fittings. Like the pump above, the lower body of the pump can be rotated for various plumbing situations. The pump is designed for gasoline only. Holley offers rebuild (service) components for these pumps so that you can rebuild them at home, if necessary.

Holley 200 GPH

This is a black-anodized billet-aluminum body Ultra HP job with a flow rating of a whopping 200 gallons per hour. The body is machined from 6061-T6 aluminum and is hard coat–anodized for corrosion protection. The inlet and outlet ports are machined for 1/2-inch pipe thread, but fittings are not included. Like the other pumps, the base can be rotated, but there's a difference here: The lower base (inlet) can be rotated independent of the upper base (outlet). Basically, the lower pump body is a two-piece affair, which (obviously) adds to the versatility. The pump is designed for use with gasoline (although a similar alky job with a 225-gph rating [!] is available). This gasoline fuel pump is designed for use with an auxiliary fuel pressure regulator.

All sorts of mechanical fuel pumps are available. This cast (tumbled finish) Holley pump delivers 170 gph at 8 psi. You need an auxiliary fuel pressure regulator for this pump.

Here's another Holley mechanical fuel pump for a big-block, manufactured from billet aluminum. This pump also delivers 170 gph, but it's pre-set at 7.5 psi, so no regulator is needed.

Need a monster mechanical pump? Holley offers billet-body mechanical pumps that can produce a whopping 200 gallons per hour. An auxiliary fuel pressure regulator is mandatory with this big boy.

FUEL SYSTEM

The Ultra HP pumps are also fully serviceable. In fact, Holley has a maintenance schedule for Ultra HP fuel pumps such as this. The diaphragm assembly should be replaced every 750 to 1,000 hours. During the rebuild, the gaskets should be replaced (kit number 12-757). The fuel pump lever arm should be examined for excess wear, and replaced as necessary. Finally, when the pump is apart, Holley recommends you inspect the valve body for damage to the rubber diaphragms, and replace as necessary.

Electric Fuel Pumps

When it comes to delivering fuel, consider what's hot on the quarter-mile–only cars. "Big" is pretty much the operative word when it comes to drag race pumps. Big works perfectly. When a drag race system must operate perfectly for a few minutes at a time, a street system has to function flawlessly any time, every time, and it has to work over the long haul. If you have a Nova that does double duty (street and strip), fuel injected or carbureted, you face a fuel delivery conundrum. If you have a big-cubic-inch engine between the fenders, or if you have a power-adder or two (blower, turbo, nitrous, or even a combination of the three), fuel delivery becomes critical. Here's the hitch: Those honking fuel pumps that feed an all-out race car don't particularly like to run for extended periods of time. They were not designed for that purpose. They consume plenty of electricity (amps), and before long heat becomes an issue. There are some solutions, but before I get to them, ponder the following.

There are essentially two very different types of fuel delivery systems in use today: one for carbureted vehicles (low pressure) and one for fuel-injected vehicles (high pressure). Carbureted cars were almost always originally fitted with a mechanical pump. Late models with EFI have an electric system. EFI cars can use an internal or an external pump. The most common you find today is an internal pump, which is basically an electric pump submerged inside the fuel tank. Some systems and many high-volume aftermarket electric fuel pumps for late-model fuel-injected vehicles are externally mounted (with fuel pickup lines mounted to the tank).

There are all sorts of pumps out there. The following are several electric pump examples that work for most high-performance Nova applications.

Holley 97 GPH

This is one of the original Holley electric pumps that have been available for decades (although it has had periodic updates). At one time, it was the standard of all fuel pumps for carbureted applications (it doesn't have the pressure necessary to operate an electronic fuel injection system). The pump operates by way of a rotor vane assembly (at the base), and it's easily serviced. It is rather tolerant of fuel contamination (something to consider with a street-driven car), but it is not compatible with alcohol or methanol fuels. The pump produces 97 gallons per hour (free flow) and 71 gallons per hour when regulated to 4 psi. The pump is fitted with an external pressure relief valve that can be set for a maximum of 7 psi. The pump draws 2 amps of current and weighs 2.88 pounds.

Holley 140 GPH

Holley's pump with the black logo is an upgraded version of the 97-gph pump. The lower casting has been modified for enhanced flow. This pump has a free-flow rating of 140 gallons per hour, while the flow at 9 psi is still 120 gallons per hour. The pump has a maximum pressure

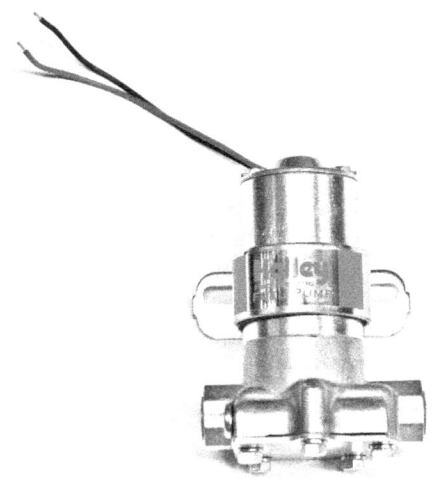

Holley's 97-gph "Red" electric fuel pump has been available for decades. Tens of thousands have likely been sold, and it's always been regarded as a reliable workhorse.

Holley's "Black" electric fuel pump is a step up from the red model. It produces a higher line pressure (140 gph) and, as mentioned in the text, it mandates an external fuel pressure regulator.

rating of 14 psi (set by way of the external pressure relief valve). This fuel pump does not have the pressure capability to operate an EFI system. This example is safe for use with gasoline, alcohol, or methanol. An external regulator is required. Holley recommends PN 12-704 for gasoline and PN 12-707 for alcohol/methanol. The pump draws 4 amps of current and weighs 3 pounds.

Holley 150 GPH

The 150-gph pump is a newer design with a gerotor setup instead of a vane- (blade-) style impeller. This configuration has less noise than vane impeller pumps. It has a free-flow rating of 150 gph, and at 7 psi it still flows 140 gph. The pump is compatible with gasoline along with E85 as well as other alcohol and methanol fuels. It is designed for use in carbureted applications only (there isn't sufficient pressure for fuel injection). The pump is internally regulated to 16 psi and it includes an adjustable fuel pressure regulator (4½ to 9 psi),

PN 12-803. At maximum pressure (16 psi), the pump draws 10 amps of current. The pump is slightly larger in size than the vane-style jobs (it measures 6.25 inches tall). It has 3/8-inch NPT inlet and outlet ports (the same as the previous two pumps).

Holley 160 GPH

A big step up in streetable fuel electric pumps is the Dominator "shotgun-style" dual pump setup from Holley. This pump is a twin design that allows you to use one pump for cruising and both pumps when you get on the power. You can also use the second stage of the pump when you activate the nitrous switch or, in the case of a blown or turbo engine, when it begins to build boost. The pump's layout (staging the second pump) eliminates unnecessary recirculating and heating of extra fuel. This pump is also engineered so that it can be fully submersed within a fuel tank. In terms of size, the pump is 7.66 inches long by 5 inches wide by 2.5 inches tall. It weighs 5.1 pounds and draws 28 amps of current at maximum performance. At a "mere" 43 psi and 13.5 volts DC the current draw is 17.2 amps. The pump has a free-flow rating of 160 gallons per hour. It can be used for either carbureted or EFI applications (the regulator choice dictates the application). Inlet and outlet ports are -10 AN

(huge!). Holley has other examples that work with E85, methanol, alcohol, or diesel (!).

Fuel Pressure Regulators

Before fuel enters the fuel line or fuel rail(s) in your Nova, and ultimately, before it reaches the fuel bowls or the fuel injectors, some sort of device is often necessary to harness the flow and pressure of the fuel. That job belongs to a fuel pressure regulator. For EFI applications, a regulator is mandatory. For carbureted applications with fuel pump pressures higher than approximately 7.5 psi, a regulator is required too. For these carbureted applications, too much fuel pressure for a given needle and seat assembly can overload the needle and seat and may cause flooding or drivability problems. In the case of Holley examples, each fuel pressure regulator is fully adjustable, so regulating the fuel pressure to your engine requirements is a simple task. These regulators are pre-set at the factory, typically, so there is no guesswork when first installing the regulator.

On the EFI front, some companies build fixed regulators (most common in OEM applications), but others (particularly aftermarket vendors) offer adjustable regulators. What's the advantage? An adjustable regulator allows an engine tuner to

Moving to the HP 150 electric fuel pump from Holley is a big step up. Instead of a vane (which is standard in the smaller pumps), this one makes use of a more efficient gerotor.

This is a very good fuel delivery concept for an ultimate Nova. Basically, Holley siamesed a pair of pumps in one body to create the shotgun-style Dominator pump. Each side of the pump can be separately switched, which means you can add the second stage when necessary.

FUEL SYSTEM

test varying levels of fuel pressure to find the exact level the engine is most "happy" with. You want a regulator that doesn't "creep." Creeping means the regulator has difficulty maintaining a set level of pressure. Most high-quality (more costly) regulators meet these criteria.

Some high-flow EFI systems also bypass the fuel. What that means is they take in more fuel than is necessary and return the balance to the gas tank. This is done to eliminate fuel aeration and efficiently pump fuel, not a frothy mix of air and fuel. When equipped with a bypass system, a valve of sorts controls the amount of fuel that actually bypasses and is returned to the fuel tank. The following are some good examples of readily available regulators.

Holley 12-803

This is the standard fuel pressure regulator that has been used for what seems like forever. At one time, they were painted blue (and that was the identifier for most speed shops). Today, they're shiny with a tumbled exterior. This regular has a .220-inch restriction and 3/8-inch NPT ports: one inlet and two outlets (non-return style). The range of adjustment is between 4.5 to 9 psi.

Holley 12-704

Holley's 12-704 fuel pressure regulator looks a lot like the standard 12-803 model until you place them side by side. The 12-704 is much larger, as are the inlet and dual outlet ports. For this regulator, use the large 1/2-inch NPTs. This regulator also has a much larger restriction size (.437 inch). It is not a bypass (return-style) regulator; however, it's suitable for use with gasoline or alcohol fuels. The range of adjustment is from 4.5 to 9 psi.

Holley 12-843

Next up is a huge-by-large billet-aluminum regulator. This is a non-return regulator with a range of 4.5 to 9 psi. It's obviously for carbureted applications. The big billet reg-

A newer regulator from Holley is this PN 12-843 model. It's manufactured from billet aluminum and fitted with a massive -10 AN inlet and a pair of -8 AN outlet ports.

ulator features a huge -10 AN inlet port along with a pair of -8 AN outlet ports. Both ports mandate an O-ring for sealing. This big, high-volume regulator can be used with electric or mechanical fuel pumps.

Holley 12-848

The last regulator in our selection is a billet bypass unit that is designed for use in electronic

With many pumps (electric or mechanical), there may be a need to regulate the pressure. This is the standard of fuel pressure regulators (Holley PN 12-803). Holley has produced this for what seems like forever and it has been used in myriad applications.

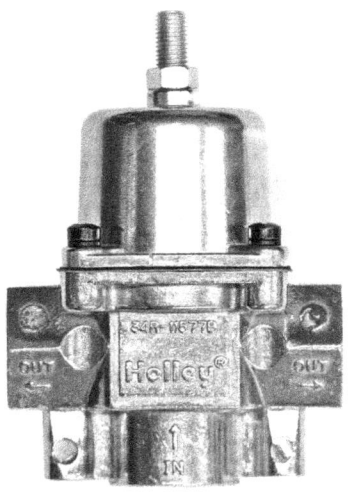

Next up is Holley's PN 12-704 pressure regulator. This piece is much larger than the PN 12-803, and it's fitted with larger inlet and outlet ports (1/2 versus 3/8 inch).

If you run EFI on your Nova and you have a high-horsepower combination, consider this regulator. It's billet aluminum with a bypass circuit. It also has a vacuum reference port (brass fitting on the right of the body).

fuel injection applications. The billet-aluminum regulator has a range of 40 to 70 psi and is equipped with a -10 AN O-ring inlet; a -10 AN O-ring outlet, and an -8 AN O-ring return port (that should be plumbed back to the fuel tank). Near the top of the regulator is a vacuum reference port. This port can be connected to full manifold vacuum to slightly decrease fuel pressure at idle and cruise. Holley notes this is a requirement on forced induction engines, so that the differential fuel pressure stays constant under boost.

Fuel Filters

Fuel is filthy. That's no secret, and pump gas is regularly worse than race gas. That's why a fuel filter is especially important. It's a good idea to use a high-capacity in-line filter, or even a pair of them, one before the pump (pre-filter) and one after. Of course, there are a lot of fuel filters available today. You can even track down ones that are pure vintage in the looks department. Unfortunately, from a flow perspective, some of those vintage fuel filters don't do so well. A good option is Holley's latest line of billet in-line filters. They're huge-capacity jobs machined for -8 AN–and–larger fittings. Holley's filter easily disassembles, allowing you to access the internal wire mesh filter. Typically, these filters have a GPH flow rating of 260 or so gallons per hour. Obviously, for the majority of situations, these filters do not act as a restriction in the system.

Where do you locate the filter? The arguments regarding filter location will probably never end (before the fuel pump or after the fuel pump), but in the interest of saving any electric pump from carnage, the best location is *before* the fuel enters the pump. Unfortunately, this sometimes places the filter in an awkward location, and in some cases, the large aftermarket filters are difficult to mount and even more difficult to service in a street-vehicle application.

So, what can you do about the problem? That's where the Holley filters come into the equation. They're big in capacity, but in terms of size, they're quite compact. The body diameter is 2 inches while the

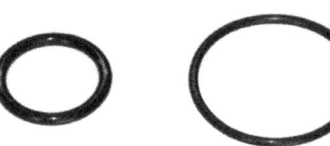
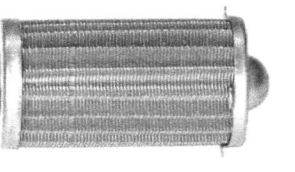

The Holley filter is easily serviced too. If you remove the end cap, this is what you'll see inside. The wire mesh filter can be cleaned, which means replacement isn't necessary.

These two billet clamps are available from Holley. They're designed specifically for Hooker's big in-line filter. Obviously, this addresses the question about how you mount a round filter on a Nova.

Forget plastic fuel filters. They're restrictive and dangerous. Use something such as this in-line filter. Holley manufactures it, and it's available in several formats (varying micron capacities).

If you look under a third-gen Nova, you'll find a good spot to mount a filter on the passenger's side, just below the door. This location keeps the filter out of the way and it's protected somewhat by the rocker panel (and, of course, the frame connector if you have them).

FUEL SYSTEM

When planning fuel line routing it's best to start at the tank. Here's a Nova with a stock tank fitted with a RobbMC pickup/sending unit. The feed line is open and the return is capped for this application.

This is a good look at routing fuel line. The -8 AN hose is held in place by way of Adel (aircraft) cushioned clamps. Careful routing keeps the hose away form any suspension components, and it's well above the scrub line.

length is 5½ inches overall. Other readily available aluminum body assemblies do a decent job of filtration on stock combinations, but many are just too small and cannot handle the volume of fuel required for a healthy engine. They can therefore constitute a restriction in the fuel delivery system, even if they aren't plugged.

What about the disposable plastic filters? When you look at them from a performance perspective, they're a waste of time and dollars. To make matters worse, they can be dangerous. Cheap plastic filters constitute a rather large fuel system restriction; they plug easily; and on almost all examples the inlet/outlet port is too small for high-performance use.

Dirt is the real enemy of any fuel delivery system. It can spell immediate grief and possible engine damage. In the accompanying photos (and captions) are several filter options, along with a mounting solution that's perfect for third-gen Novas.

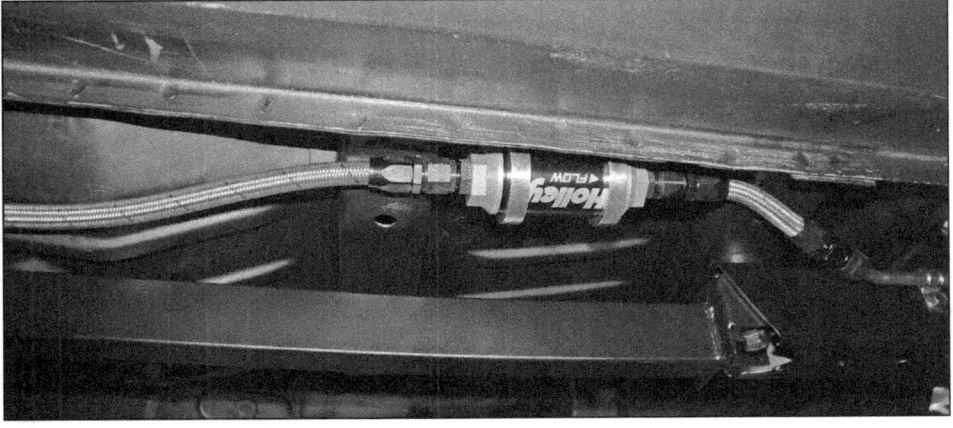

The line runs from the tank to the filter as shown here, and then forward in the car. This is a nice, clean arrangement and it keeps the fuel line tucked away from possible damage.

CHAPTER 10

RADIATORS AND ELECTRIC FANS

Most folks leave the cooling system to the end of their projects. I'm probably just as guilty (after all, it's near the end of this book), but that certainly doesn't mean that the cooling system isn't important. Far from it. Without it, you won't be driving far. In this chapter, I dig deep into radiators, cooling fans, and accessories. There's a lot more to keeping your Nova cool than first meets the eye.

Radiator

When the dog days of August roll around, you'll be quick to think of the radiator in the nose of your Nova. If you've added horsepower over the winter, there's added pressure, because more horsepower equals more heat. And with that comes the need for cooling system attention. One trip to a local car show in the heat of the summer with an inadequate cooling system will make you wish you had paid more attention to that heat producer under the hood.

Fair enough. Everyone knows that a high-performance engine produces heat, and a bunch of it. Roughly one-half of the total heat energy produced by the engine is transferred back to the cooling system. In a conventional liquid cooled application (your typical Chevy), the heat energy moves into the radiator and is then "radiated" back into the atmosphere. Taking this one step further, the liquid cooling system in your Nova operates very simply. As the coolant (to keep things simple, let's use plain water as an example) temperature approaches 212 degrees F, air pressure begins to build. Since the radiator is closed (with a cap), pressure builds from within without any opportunity to escape. This air pressure actually expands, which in turn allows the water to reach a temperature higher than 212 degrees F before boiling. As the air pressure increases, so does the boiling point of the water. Basically, this is an efficient system that works well in passenger car applications, but if the coolant temperature continues to increase (without leveling

There's a lot of choice out there for Nova radiators. Here's a great example built by Ron Davis Racing Radiators. During the radiator build, CNC-cutting results in precision to .005-inch, which in turn results in a perfect fit and a high degree of repeatability. Davis is one of the few, if not the only, aluminum radiator manufacturer that can manufacture to the high tolerance needed in military and aerospace applications.

off), the internal pressure will be too great for the radiator cap to handle. What happens next is predictable. Your Nova boils over.

The radiator in such a system is a huge tank that allows large amounts of hot coolant to contact an equally large amount of cool (it is hoped) air. The coolant is first forced into the radiator side tank (upper tank if you're thinking of the old-fashioned non–cross flow system). From this point, the coolant makes its way through rows of very small copper or aluminum tubes, finally returning to the adjoining side tank where it is returned to the engine. While the coolant marches through the tiny tubes, it is cooled by air flowing over and alongside the tubes. The primary purpose of the "fins" contained within the core (and surrounding the little tubes) is to direct airflow into the proper area of the radiator; however, there are secondary reasons for the fins, as you soon see. (The most common core construction is the tube-fin or the ribbon-cellular design.)

Fin count plays an important role in cooling. As a rule, a radiator has between 8 and 14 fins per inch. When the fin count number is increased, the radiator can "radiate" more heat to both the surface airflow and the surrounding air. Unfortunately, as fin count increases, so does the opportunity for plugging, especially by bugs, dirt, and other foreign road junk.

Copper or Aluminum?

When it comes to radiator construction material, what's the better choice for your Nova, copper or aluminum? That's a good question. Most recently Detroit has embraced aluminum as the radiator material of choice. The reason for this, aside from considerable vehicle mass reduction

Cores for a Davis radiator are of proprietary design. They're Nocolok furnace brazed and, whereas most companies offer one fin count, Ron Davis Racing Radiators sizes the fin count and thickness to the application. Davis incorporates quality Spal fans in the package. Note the way the fans are completely sealed to the rad by way of the aluminum shroud.

This is likely the best OEM-style radiator available for a 1968–1972 Nova. It's an exact reproduction of the stock copper-brass "gooseneck" radiators fitted to COPO Camaros and a select few 396 Novas. Classic Industries offers these radiators as special orders.

(aluminum radiators, on average, can be as much as 1/3 lighter than an equivalent copper-brass radiator), is cooling capability.

Certainly, the choice of copper is a good one for radiators. It has better heat dissipating properties than aluminum. But there's a caveat: Tubes are the primary source of cooling in any radiator. Heat dissipates from the coolant through the tube walls. This heat is then transferred to the fins that are in contact with the tubes. In turn, this provides a secondary source of cooling. As air passes through the fins, the heat is carried away. Radiator manufacturers know that wider tubes are more efficient because there is more tube-to-fin contact (in a typical modern aluminum radiator, the tube-to fin contact surface area is increased by 20 percent over an identically sized copper/brass unit). This isn't possible with a copper-brass design because of tube wall thickness limitations. Today's radiator technology, which uses wider tubes inside aluminum rads coupled with multi-louvered fins, has allowed the aluminum radiator to cool efficiently. Just as important, aluminum rads are now as strong as, if not stronger, than their older copper-brass relatives.

The truth is, today, an aluminum radiator in your Nova cools better. Tests from various sources document a 28-percent increase in performance over a brass-copper equivalent, provided both radiators are identical in size. The reality is, the use of aluminum in radiator construction can lower engine temperature by 30 degrees. Any vehicle, including your Nova, benefits from an aluminum radiator.

But what if you want something really close to stock, something built in the traditional copper-brass format? Today, original Harrison radiators are next to impossible to find. Moreover, to score something such as a super-rare new or mint gooseneck heavy-duty radiator, well, you should invest in lottery tickets. Those old gooseneck radiators were the very best pieces available for a Nova (they also showed up on 427-powered COPO Camaros). In the 1960s and early 1970s, if you had to pick a go-to radiator for a stubborn cooling problem, that's the piece you'd select. Unfortunately, originals aren't available, but the good news is you can buy a perfect made-in-the-USA reproduction from the folks at Classic Industries; for example, the copper-brass gooseneck radiator in the accompanying photos. It's a dead-ringer for the original. You note that this radiator comes unpainted. Following manufacture (soldering) the radiator sees rapid surface rusting. It's not a big issue though;

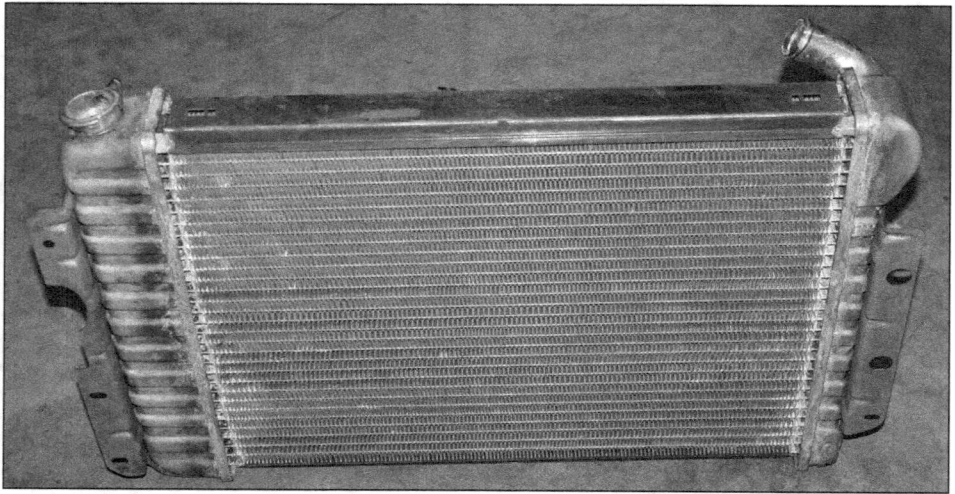

Classic Industries' gooseneck repro comes unpainted. What you see is flash rust that occurs almost immediately following construction. When you receive it, the core should be masked off and the tanks media blasted. Then you can paint the entire works with quality radiator paint.

All stock Nova radiators have this mounting format (a pair of flanges on each side of the radiator). Some of the mounting hole locations on various stock radiators are different. Depending upon the radiator you select, the core support might have to be modified. It's not a big deal, however. In most cases, you just drill a couple of holes. Some examples might also need a weld nut added.

RADIATORS AND ELECTRIC FANS

It's a small thing, but some of Classic Industries' exact reproduction radiators even have the old GM "Harrison" stamped into the tanks.

Here's a good example of a lower radiator hose for a Nova. Several very good reproductions of factory formed hose are available today. Because of this, it makes no sense to use universal fit (ribbed) hose.

The same applies to upper radiator hoses. Classic Industries and others offer a wide choice of hose. Keep in mind that the layout of the radiator determines the radiator hose configuration. As an example, a gooseneck radiator mandates a different hose than a conventional neck radiator.

Classic Industries simply recommends you glass bead the tanks and then paint the assembly with radiator paint.

The tanks and mounting brackets are exact copies of the original. This is a four-core HD radiator for a Camaro or Nova. In the photos, you can see the Harrison logo is accurately reproduced on the side tank. Another of the photos shows the gooseneck inlet at the top of the radiator (and yes, very late big-block Novas circa 1969 could in fact have a gooseneck radiator, just like a COPO Camaro).

Outlet Shapes and Sizes

Believe it or not, the shape and form of the radiator outlets might have a profound effect upon cooling. I don't have concrete proof of this, but I've witnessed one particular car (a high-horsepower 427 big-block) that went through multiple radiators in an effort to resolve a cooling issue. One was constructed by Ron Davis while others came from other manufacturers. The only (visible) external difference was the shape of the outlets. The Davis-built radiator had formed outlets with soft bends. The other had fabricated outlets with sharp bends (virtually a series of 45-degree joints). The car consistently boiled over with the sharp-bend-equipped radiator. With no other changes (aside from the radiator swap), the operating temperature was entirely satisfactory with the formed outlet radiator. The theory was that the sharp outlet corners restricted coolant flow.

A formed radiator hose (the type Chevrolet uses on its vehicles) usually delivers superior performance to one of the universal "fits-all" ribbed hoses available at the local discount auto parts stores. The belief is there is considerable laminar flow in the hose, and the ribs of the universal radiator hose disturb this flow. What is the solution? Simple. Watch out for cheap universal hoses, and be careful when selecting a radiator; smooth outlet bends are likely much more efficient than sharp, angular turns.

See the wire on the inside of the lower hose? The purpose is to keep the hose from collapsing. The wire support is found on most quality hoses.

Cooling Fans and Shrouds

In the hypothetical world, a fan wouldn't be required if a Nova was constantly driven at high speeds (definitely an enticing concept, but not exactly practical). Airflow from the vehicle's velocity would provide

CHAPTER 10

There are plenty of ways to cool a Nova, and of course a fan is mandatory. One outstanding option is this dual electric Spal fan setup from Ron Davis Racing Radiators. The fans are obviously set up in puller fashion. Note how the fans are tightly sealed to the radiator.

sufficient airflow over the radiator surface, with the result being proper cooling. After all, that's pretty much how World War II aircraft with liquid-cooled engines worked (good examples being the P51 Mustang, Spitfire, Warhawk, and so on). While this would be an ideal situation, it's seldom possible. Or realistic. Because of this, a fan of some sort becomes a necessary evil.

Given the fact that a fan is pretty much an essential commodity, it's probably a good idea to install one that works. The market offers several good-quality fans, ranging from OEM, factory-produced models to stainless-steel flex versions. Electric fans are common on late-model Chevys and are used with regularity on many modified Novas. The typical "standard" fan assembly is fixed. It rotates constantly with the water pump shaft. A thermostatic fan is just that: a fan that slows down when cooling requirements have diminished. This type of fan has seldom been used in North American passenger car applications of any sort (cost, size, and complexities being factors).

Flexible fans reduce their pitch as engine RPM increases (or, more correctly, as pulley speed increases). Fluid coupling fans (sometimes referred to as "viscous clutch fans") speed up or slow down, again, depending upon engine or pulley speed. Viscous, or "clutch," fans were regular fixtures on high-performance Chevys for years. But on factory big-block Novas, they weren't installed. Why not? There isn't sufficient room. All big-block Novas instead made use of fixed fans. Electric fans are simply remote units that depend upon the vehicle's electrical system for operation. Depending upon the application, electric fans can be manually switched or can operate via an integral thermostatic coupling. Of course, late-model cars all came factory-equipped with electric fans.

Certain types of fans require more horsepower for operation than others. Leading the pack in terms of least power absorption is the electric fan. They rely upon battery power to operate, but keep in mind that the battery will be drained when the unit is in operation. That means the charging system must keep up (basically, the engine must power the alternator demands instead of turning the fan, and it still must power the water pump

There's nothing wrong with a conventional fan, provided you include a tight-fitting shroud on the Nova. This is a reproduction fan for a 396 Nova.

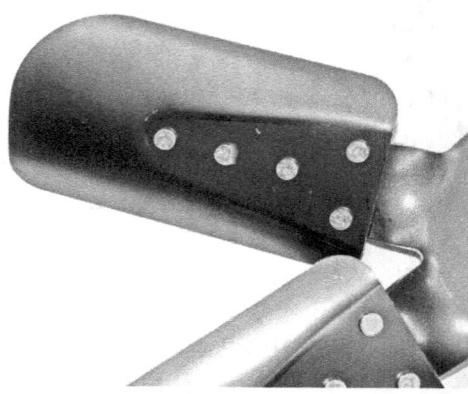

When looking at OEM-style fans, keep a close eye on the blades, and the rivets in particular. If a blade decides to depart, it can make a huge mess of your car.

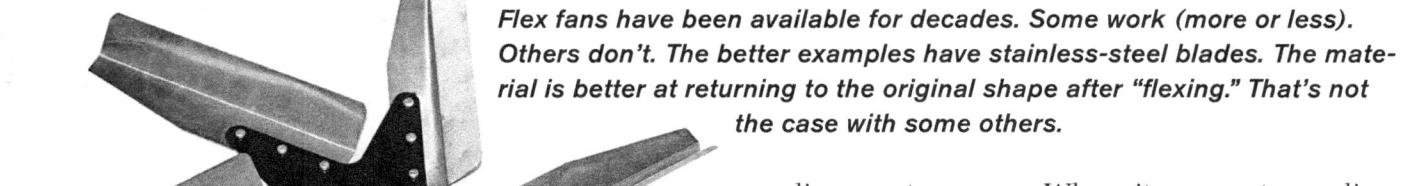

Flex fans have been available for decades. Some work (more or less). Others don't. The better examples have stainless-steel blades. The material is better at returning to the original shape after "flexing." That's not the case with some others.

and other accessories). In terms of conventional fans, both the flex fan and the "clutch fan" offer considerable advantages as far as horsepower losses are concerned. Obviously, a flex fan is far less complicated than its clutch fan stable mate, but it too has some drawbacks. Plenty of flex fan designs simply take a "set" at a given position following sustained use. The result, of course, is too little fan action and, ultimately, reduced cooling. Depending upon the Nova, one of the safest fan bets is the original equipment–style clutch or fluid coupling system. When the "clutch" mechanism is in competent operating condition, the fan works flawlessly, de-clutching as the engine speed or pulley speed increases. (Keep in mind that you don't have room for a clutch fan on a big-block Nova.) The outcome is more available horsepower when you need it.

When dealing with conventional fans, one area that you should think about is a phenomenon called "blade stall." In this condition, the fan attached to your Nova engine can in fact be turned too fast, like an aircraft propeller. A massive amount of turbulence is created, which effectively decreases airflow through the radiator. Obviously, overheating is the consequence, but fixing the problem might be more difficult. The only real solution is to reduce the speed of the fan, which can be handled easily with different-diameter pulleys.

When it comes to cooling you absolutely must figure out a way to bring the air to the cooler. The goal is to provide a constant supply of air through the radiator so that the coolant is reduced in temperature. Increasing airflow through the radiator improves cooling. A shroud that facilitates airflow is, therefore, almost mandatory on high-performance applications. Unfortunately, they are often missing on older Novas. Keep in mind, shrouds were often manufactured from plastic, so the condition typically degrades dramatically over the years. If you don't have a shroud or if it fits poorly, get the right one (that's a big hint if you end up sitting behind Old Faithful on a regular basis).

How does the shroud work? Basically, the shroud surrounds or partially surrounds the fan. It butts up tightly to the face of the radiator, effectively sealing the cavity. This isolates the pocket of air behind the radiator, allowing the fan to efficiently draw the required air through

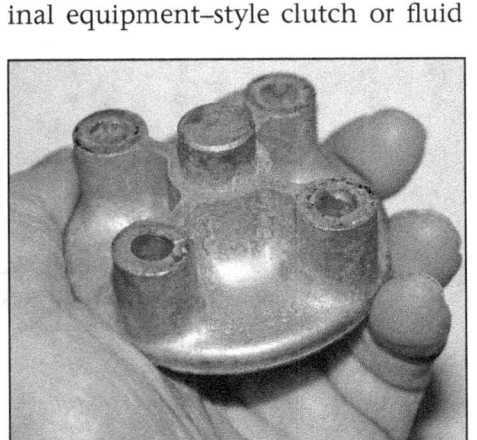

A factory fan spacer is pretty much mandatory on many Novas. It positions the fan as closely as possible to the radiator. That definitely helps with cooling.

A tight-fitting OEM-style shroud such as this is a big key to keeping your Nova cool. Typically, the fan blade tips are very close to the edge of the shroud. This directs all incoming air through the radiator. This example is from Classic Industries.

 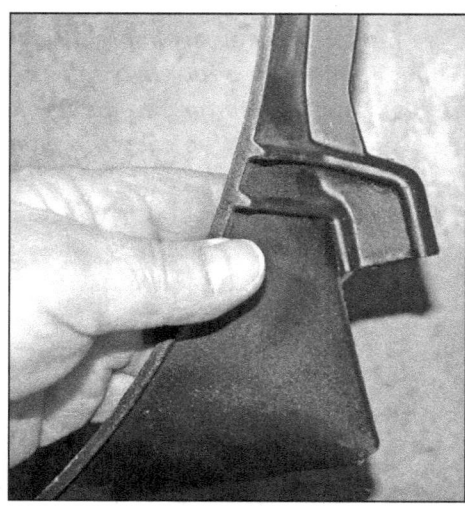 

Good reproduction fan shrouds have tabs molded in on each side. They are designed to accept a set of clips that affix the shroud to the radiator (just as Chevrolet did in the 1960s and 1970s).

Upstairs the shrouds typically mount to a bracket that is affixed to the radiator support. The top bracket keeps the shroud in place while the side tabs (with clips) keep the shroud tight against the radiator.

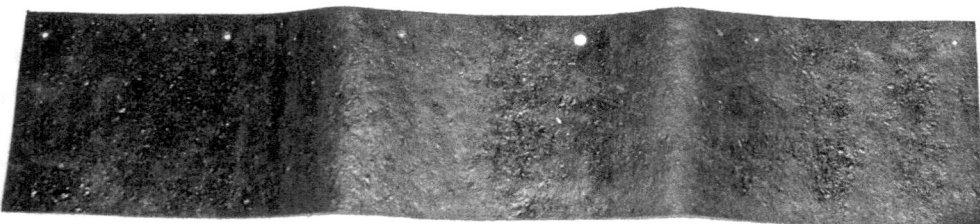

On factory big-block Novas, this rubber "flap" was fitted to the top of the radiator support. The idea here was to seal up the works so that air was forced through the radiator. If you have a big-block car and you're using a stock shroud, be sure to use this piece.

You can make use of an electric fan in any number of ways, such as using a single fan as a pusher, mounted in front of the radiator. This format works only if it's used in conjunction with a regular engine-driven fan.

Another option is to fit a pair of puller fans to the backside of the radiator. With this arrangement, be sure the plastic shroud fits tightly.

the radiator. If the shroud is not present, it creates a considerable amount of "dead" space behind the radiator that in turn destroys the effectiveness of the fan assembly. The bottom line is simple: If you don't run a proper shroud, you're asking for overheating grief. Classic Industries has a complete selection of quality reproduction shrouds for all Nova applications. They work.

You basically have two options in electric fans: a pusher fan or a puller fan. Chevrolet has used both configurations in modern passenger cars and light trucks, although puller fans are the most common. Sometimes electric fans are used in conjunction with an engine-driven clutch fan (typically, an electric pusher fan mounted ahead of the rad). This arrangement is particularly useful if heavy cooling tasks are mandated by the application (a good example is a pickup truck with a factory towing package). This might be a good choice for a Nova that's either blessed with a cooling challenge or sees double-duty as a weekend racer.

Companies such as Ron Davis Racing Products and DeWitts Radiators have spent considerable time researching cooling fans with these criteria. Davis offers a trio of fans: 12-, 14-, and 16-inch diameters.

All the above have a low-amp draw, but Davis points out that one of the other secrets to properly cooling a high-performance car is to effectively

Even though the fans overlap the sides of this radiator, the tight-fitting aluminum shroud directs all of the air through the radiator. As you can see, everything on the radiator backside is covered. This setup is from Ron Davis Racing Radiators. Not only is it good-looking, it flat works!

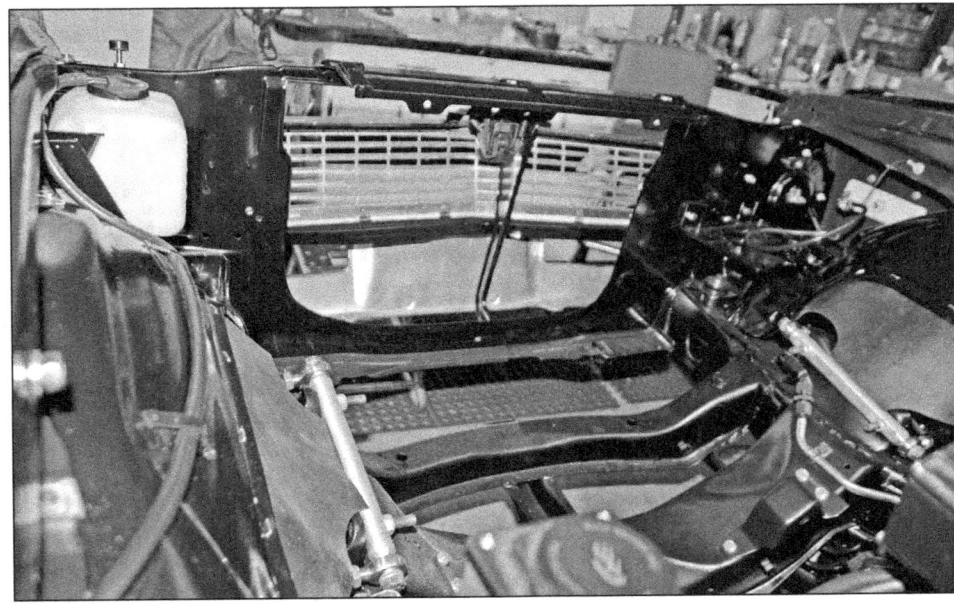

On this Nova, the radiator support was opened up to allow more air to flow through the radiator. Stock small-block Nova supports have an embossed outline of a big-block opening. You can simply trim it back to copy the opening for a big-block radiator.

Davis Fans			
Part Number	Diameter (inches)	RPM	CFM
EF 120	12	2,300	1,576
EF 140	14	2,400	1,828
EF 160	16	2,400	2,197

seal the radiator to the fan. Typically, this is accomplished by way of an integral shroud surrounding the electric fan. The shroud simply allows the largest volume of air to be pulled through the radiator (usually in a pull through application). If you take the time to effective seal any gaps between the fan shroud and the radiator, cooling can improve. It's not that difficult to accomplish.

The best fan for your Nova depends upon the application and the space you have to work with. If you have the room, a Detroit-style engine-driven clutch fan with a full shroud is most certainly a good bet. Another really good arrangement is a dual electric puller system, complete with an integral shroud (as shown in the accompanying photos). The worst possible arrangement is an inexpensive discount store flex fan without a shroud, or a single pusher electric without a shroud (with these setups, you're asking for trouble). All other combinations fall somewhere in between.

When all is said and done, keep in mind one major point: There is virtually no way to "over cool" your Nova. And the more power your engine produces, the more cooling capacity you need.

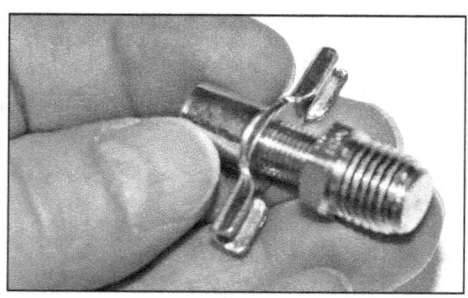

It doesn't help you cool your Nova, but this new radiator drain petcock makes servicing the cooling system a bunch easier. This is a nice reproduction from Classic Industries.

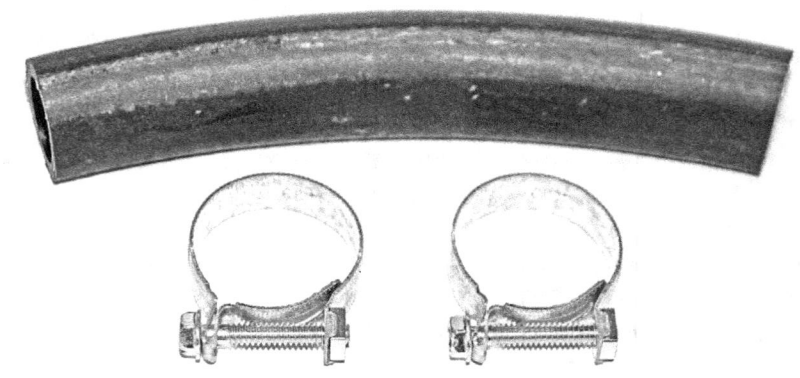

Something else you shouldn't leave to chance is the water pump bypass hose. If you run a thermostat (and you should), don't leave the bypass hose off the water pump.

Remember those OEM radiator mounting points I examined at the beginning of the chapter? Here's the hardware used to mount the radiator. The pair of well nuts goes to one side and the pointed fender bolts are used on the other side. Again, reproductions such as these are readily available.

The most universal of thermostats is a 180-degree job. They work well on modified Novas because they keep the coolant in the radiator until 180 degrees. This allows time for the fans (and the radiator) to do their job, which is to reduce the coolant temperature before it goes into the engine.

These three radiator caps are all for a Nova. Each has a 15-pound rating. The one on the left is a reproduction, at top right is an original, and the one on the lower right is a replacement cap. For a modified Nova, the replacement RC26 on the lower right works perfectly.

SOURCE GUIDE

Aeroquip Performance
Eaton Corporation
Hydraulics Group USA
14615 Lone Oak Rd.
Eden Prairie, MN 55344
952-937-9800
aeroquipperformance.com

ARP
1863 Eastman Ave.
Ventura, CA 93003
800-826-3045
arp-bolts.com

Aurora Bearing Company
901 Aucutt Rd.
Montgomery, IL 60538
630-859-2030
aurorabearing.com

Baer Brakes
2222 W. Peoria Ave.
Phoenix, AZ 85029
602-233-1411
baer.com

Belltech
300 W. Pontiac Way
Clovis, CA 93612
800-445-3767
belltech.com

Calvert Racing Suspensions
4530 Runway Dr.
Lancaster, CA 93536
661-728-9600
calvertracing.com

Chevrolet Performance
Parts available at your Chevrolet dealer
chevrolet.com/performance/overview.html

Classic Industries
18460 Gothard St.
Huntington Beach, CA 92647
800-854-1280
classicindustries.com

Competition Engineering
Moroso Performance Products
80 Carter Dr.
Guilford, CT 06437
203-453-6571
competitionengineering.com

Detroit Locker (Eaton)
Contact your Eaton Dealer

Detroit Speed
185 McKenzie Rd.
Mooresville, NC 28115
704-662-3272
detroitspeed.com

DeWitts
1275 Grand Oaks Dr.
Howell, MI 48843
517-548-0600
dewitts.com

Earl's Performance
1801 Russellville Rd.
P.O. Box 10360
Bowling Green, KY 42101
270-782-2900
holley.com

DTS Custom Service
4052 S. State Rd. (M-66)
Ionia, MI 48846
877-874-7327
dtscustom.com

Hollander
2955 Xenium Ln. N., Ste. 10
Plymouth, MN 55441
800-825-0644
hollandersolutions.com

Holley Performance Products
1801 Russellville Rd.
P.O. Box 10360
Bowling Green, KY 42101-7360
270-782-2900
holley.com

Hotchkis Sport Suspension
8633 Sorensen Ave.
Santa Fe Springs, CA 90670
877-466-7655
hotchkis.net

Hurst Performance
100 Stony Point Rd., Ste. 125
Santa Rosa, CA 95401
707-544-4761
hurst-shifters.com

Jerry Bickel Race Cars
141 Raceway Park Dr.
Moscow Mills, MO 63362
636-356-4727
jerrybickel.com

SOURCE GUIDE

Lakewood
1801 Russellville Rd.
P.O. Box 10360
Bowling Green, KY 42101
270-782-2900
holley.com

Lamb Components
1259 W. 9th St.
Upland, CA 91786
909-985-1901
lambcomponents.com

Mark Williams Enterprises
765 S. Pierce Ave.
Louisville, CO 80027
866-508-6394
markwilliams.com

Mickey Thompson Tires
4600 Prosper Dr.
Stow, OH 44224
800-222-9092
mickeythompsontires.com

MandH Racemaster
800-299-8000
mhracemaster.com

MSD
1490 Henry Brennan Dr.
El Paso, TX 79936
915-857-5200
msdperformance.com

Nitto Tire U.S.A.
P.O. Box 6064
Cypress, CA 90630
nittotire.com

RobbMc Performance Products
1717 La Mirada St.
Carson City, NV 89703
775-885-7411
robbmcperformance.com

Ron Davis Racing Products
7334 N. 108th Ave.
Glendale, AZ 85307
800-842-5001
rondavisradiators.com

Russell Performance
2700 California St.
Torrance, CA 90503
800-416-8628
edelbrock.com

Spectra Premium
1421 Ampere
Boucherville, QC Canada J4B 5Z5
450-641-3090
spectrapremium.com

Strange Engineering
8300 N. Austin Ave.
Morton Grove, IL 60053
847-663-1701
strangeengineering.net

TRZ Motorsports
1651 Kelley Ave.
Kissimmee, FL 34744
407-933-7385
trzmotorsports.com